PLOT 34

WITHDRAWN

MARK KEENAN

PLOT 34
BLOOD, SWEAT AND ALLOTMENTEERS

BRANDON

A Brandon Original Paperback

First published in 2010 by Brandon
an imprint of Mount Eagle Publications
Dingle, Co. Kerry, Ireland, and
Unit 3, Olympia Trading Estate, Coburg Road, London N22 6TZ, England

2 4 6 8 10 9 7 5 3 1

ISBN 9780863224058

Cover design: Design Suite
Typesetting by Red Barn Publishing, Skeagh, Skibbereen

www.brandonbooks.com

Contents

In loving memory of Rita Keenan

Special thanks and a great big kisss for Lisa (I always agreed you'd never be a Her Indoors) for her patience, support, love and more patience besides. To Oisín (my ever inquisitive Head of Secret Tunnels) and Evie (my Waterer of Everything) for the inspiration and joy they have always brought me. To my parents Michael and Geraldine for their valued opinions and their support over the years and to my siblings Niall, Dermot, Ronan, Patricia and extended family for all their help and input. Thanks, Steve, for belief in the book. Finally, to my grandparents for all they taught me without either of us realising.

Chapter One

Welcome to Plot 34

Ankle-deep in mucky water on the side of an exposed and sodden slope, I'm leaning hard into the wind, teeth gritted, and trying to stay on my feet while trudging a spade into sludge. It's one of March's madder days and gales are tearing through the valley. A few minutes ago, it started snowing. Sideways. Down the hill is the scruffiest, most addled flock of sheep I've ever laid eyes on and in these gales, early lambs are being batted about like scuzzy sports socks in a tumble dryer. Further down, beyond the baby blizzard, is the city, where sensible people are on a day like this.

Welcome to Plot 34, my new allotment. Only today, my first in the field, it's more Gulag 34. And amid the climatic onslaught, forlorn figures flail at the ground with their implements, all surrounded by a maze of grim, wired-up fence posts. All that's lacking is some sombre balalaika music and a camp flunkie to whack us at every breather.

Despite my Russian flapped hat, I still feel cuffed about the ears with each one of those icy blasts. So why am I here when I could be relaxed at home this Sunday, on the sofa, cup of tea in hand and watching the Discovery Channel?

Because for me, it's the beginning of a quest of sorts. I've decided to try to grow my own food, or at least as much of it as I can over the next season, and hopefully the season after that and the one after that. Food growing is a skill our grandparents learned from when they were knee-high. Not so long ago, almost everyone knew how to cultivate their own food for the table in times when it was an obviously vital skill for life itself. Even in living memory, city families relied on their food-growing skills in gardens and allotments for much of their home diet. We in the Western world seem to have largely lost that widespread skill within a couple of generations, and perhaps with preposterous consequences.

Today we rely unquestioningly on 'the system' to supply us not only with jobs, healthcare, transport, education and banking, but also with food. We have lost touch with our relationship to our food to the degree that we no longer understand the growing of it. We don't question how 'the system' has procured it, and we don't ask what has been done to it before it ends up on our tables. Where our forefathers were independent-minded animals, each relatively able to supply their own food from even the smallest patches of ground, ours has become the 'battery chicken' generation, kept and fed entirely by a system of our own creation.

That great system of unfettered Western capitalism, to which we have all so long subscribed, has started to show its cracks. The same system which has brought so many wealth benefits has simultaneously been busy destroying the world around us, and this destruction has reached such a pitch and pace that, through global warming and pollution, it even begins to threaten our very existence. The system we have created is an oil-reliant one in which the fossil fuel provides almost all of the transport which brings us, among other things, our food. Peak oil is now threatening. New mega economies like China and India are clamouring to join that same consumer-driven surge.

In taking on an allotment, I wanted to detach somewhat from that system—to do something small yet significant for myself. I wanted to learn something new and important. Over time I had begun to think about what we have been eating, particularly given the fall in the quality of food on the shop shelves. I had come to detest the idea that I couldn't provide for myself at perhaps the most basic human level of all—knowing how to grow food, and with it, some personal understanding of those vital plants which produce the food we take for granted. Without them, we wouldn't be here at all. To me, as a human being, not being able to grow my own food is a bit like never learning to tie my shoe-laces or how to dress myself.

The recent international global banking collapse and subsequent financial crisis is probably the single biggest global cock-up of our generation. But it does show us what can happen when the cracks open in the system we have created and what happens when we trust the uncontrollable consumer machine to run our lives on our behalf.

Sometimes the cracks open unexpectedly to create economic collapse, famines and wars. Today we are in the aftermath of another Great Depression. Sometimes when the cracks open it's far worse. We saw it in the former Yugoslavia when a 'civilised' society rapidly degenerated into war and genocide. We saw it in the cosmopolitan city of New Orleans when, after the floods of Hurricane Katrina, ordinary citizens and family men were transformed into desperate looters reduced to stealing food to feed their families. We saw how the capital of the Western world itself ground to a complete halt when the great north-eastern blackout of 2003 struck New York and all at once killed its technology, transport, phones, computers, domestic heating and lighting. The fridges conked out and stored foods, from the salads in domestic fridges, to the meat piled in commercial warehouses, began to perish.

Some time ago, a spokesman for a food security study group in the UK quite seriously asserted: "We're only nine meals from anarchy—and food is the basic prerequisite."

Our acceptance of our system has also caused us to accept without question processes which are in some cases unnatural and in others, daft beyond belief. Consider for example travelling back in time a hundred years and explaining the concept of a gym or fitness club to an average person. "You pay a lot of money each year to go indoors, to run on a machine belt, under fluorescent lighting to lose weight and stay healthy." Just like hamsters on wheels or chickens in a battery.

What would our forebears make of our modern lifestyles? Progress has unquestionably improved our lot in most ways through developments in science, health and technology. The internet is the communications miracle of the modern generation. But that doesn't take away our right to question processes within our modern lifestyle which don't seem to make sense at all, until, like the banking crisis, we find out the hard way. We know now that we shouldn't have let bankers build an international pyramid of credit based on worthless products. It seems all so obvious now, but few questioned the logic when this was happening.

Have we ever, as a species, spent so much time indoors? Has there ever been a time when we've eaten so much unnatural crud which has been degenerated and debased by countless processes designed, not to provide maximum nutrition and flavour as we might reasonably expect, but to produce the most product for the least effort and cost? Has our once crafty species ever been so out of touch with the essential natural skills that are still, despite our progress, prerequisites for our health and survival? Not office jobs, not banks, not fashion, not corporations, not marketing, not America, not production lines, not computers but nature itself. In a very short time, we in the Western world have become completely detached from the way the planet really works as opposed to the myriad ways we try to force it to work.

Somewhere in the last few generations our children stopped learning how to grow food, how to catch a fish, how to identify edible plants and fruits in the wild—since the beginning of time the most important skills of all.

Through our domestic gardening hobbies a lot of us might think we've kept an ear to the ground. I've always enjoyed my garden and for years I was complimented on my annual floral display. But some time ago I began to realise that my planting had also become processed and system reliant. I didn't grow anything from seed. I realised that despite years of stocking my herbaceous borders, I genuinely knew very little about the plants and how they behaved and reacted to their environment. Like every other system-fed suburbanite, my gardening had also become processed and fed to me. Like most other 'gardeners' around me, I would make a trip to the garden centre once or twice a year and drop a load of money on overpriced ready-grown flowering plants, mass produced in a factory hothouse. I would take these home, dig holes in the relevant spots and plant them all in with colour co-ordination; small ones to the front, big ones to the back. Some would live, some would die. In truth it had nothing to do with me. I ended up with a nice display of osteospermum, dahlias and campanulas but it wasn't proper gardening. It was join-the-dots gardening. I was told I had green fingers and I believed it.

It was only after I started growing my own food that I came to realise my past garden displays didn't depend on what I wanted to put into them, or what I wanted them to look like; that even this was determined by what the system wanted.

My choice was always limited to whatever plants the garden centre stocked at any given time. The system dictated what flowers I put in my garden and made me pay through the nose for that privilege. I gardened the way I had chosen my food for consumption—by filling the trolley with whatever the system served up to me on any given day.

I do owe the commercial garden centre one very big favour, however, in the form of a single plant that I bought on impulse one year in a retail barn—the plant that ultimately inspired me to start growing my own. During my usual annual jaunt around the centre I came across a juvenile Gardener's Delight, a variety of cherry tomato which stood about 6in high in its square plastic pot. Like any good consumer, my choice was made by impulse, spurred on by an attractive label showing clusters of bright, red-berry fruits.

It was also cheap—about three quid I think—so I stuck it on my trolley and took it home with the rest of the flowers I'd purchased. I stuck the plant in a sunny corner, and then I forgot about it until it had grown so tall that it had started to flop about. I staked it for support and eventually it flowered with a sprinkle of small yellow blooms. Tiny, pea-sized green fruits started to develop in the centre of those flowers. On a particularly fine summer's day I noticed that one of those fruits had ripened to a beautiful deep red. I picked it, wiped it off, and popped it into my mouth.

That was my eureka moment. That fruit burst between my teeth and its flavour exploded in my mouth. It resonated, and zinged and pinged on my tongue. It tasted like nothing I'd ever eaten. And I didn't even like tomatoes back then.

Then the questions started. First of all, why did this little tomato taste so incredibly different to any other tomato that I'd eaten? Even those tomatoes bought in those specialist greengrocer shops—the ones with the reputations for good fresh produce—didn't taste like this. The shop-bought tomatoes tasted completely flat in comparison. If you'd asked me back then to describe the taste of a tomato, I would have said something like:

"watery and neutral". But my little Gardener's Delight cherry tomato was rich, zesty and thoroughly vibrant.

And if you'd asked me to describe the texture of a tomato, I would have said: "It's a rounded, slightly squidgy fruit, with fleshy insides." In contrast my tomato was firm and tight, its insides tautly blistering with pockets of zappy juices.

So when is a tomato not a tomato?

It took some reading and research on the subject before I got my answer: my homegrown version tasted as a tomato is supposed to taste. It's as simple as that. My cherry tomato was as nature intended it to be, with all its components intact and alive. It was a tomato before the system had started messing with it.

Now I had a big problem on my hands. If, all my life, I'd been eating tomatoes which had somehow been changed into something altogether less inviting, did that also mean that other 'fresh' foods were similarly denigrated, flattened and neutralised? Did other fruits and vegetables taste the way nature intended, or have we managed to corrupt them too?

I learned that the changes in my shop-bought tomatoes had been brought about by the industrialised and consumer-driven processes. Firstly through processes which suit the producer and vendor and secondly through processes designed to please the consumer. Tomatoes are forced, fed artificially, and sprayed with chemicals to keep pests away. Even their genes and strains are tampered with as growers select those designed, not to enhance taste and nutrition, but to increase yields and profits, to be more pest resistant, to last longer in transport and on supermarket shelves and to fit standardised shapes, colours and sheens which supermarkets and customers now insist upon. All at the expense of taste, texture and nutritional value.

Finally, fruit begins to die as soon as it is cut from its parent plant. My shop-bought tomato may have already travelled hundreds or even thousands of miles. My homegrown tomato could be eaten as soon as it came from the vine. In short, it was more alive.

Armed with this knowledge, the following growing season I decided to make a point of finding out whether other homegrown foods could also prove so different. That spring I bought some packets of seeds for carrots, lettuce, broccoli and courgettes as well as sets for onions. I dug up a patch of lawn in the back garden and planted these. I grew the tomatoes in containers on the patio.

Perhaps because life can be so cosseted, my little private backyard experiment somehow seemed terribly exciting to me. A bit of an adventure. By autumn, the results were mixed. The broccoli had to be pulled out because it shot up and completely overshadowed the carrots and onions. This was to be my first lesson in correct crop situation—not to crowd smaller crops with larger ones. The carrots, when they were harvested, were stubby and small because I later learned that I hadn't tilled the ground to a suitably fine and well-drained consistency.

But like that first tomato, the carrots, courgettes and onions I did get to eat from those efforts also tasted supreme and so completely different. The carrots were 'carrotier', the onions were 'onionier'. They were crisper, sweeter and more pronounced in their flavours.

The older generation who remember growing their own food will say: "Well of course—you're stating the bleeding obvious here!" But back in their day, shop-bought food was of far better quality and more comparable to homegrown. Over thirty years, that gap of difference has been significantly widened without anyone seeming to notice. Meantime I could forgive anyone under the age of forty for thinking that all of this sounds more than a little bit made up. Those who have never grown their own food or tasted homegrown produce, remain (as I did) blissfully oblivious to its magical qualities.

Food provides the most basic building blocks on which our bodies, and minds, are constructed. And most people believe that while processed products in tins and jars can be messed with, fresh food surely cannot. Surely a carrot is a carrot is a carrot? Surely they can fool us with badly made washing machines, mobile phones which haven't been deglitched, and nonsense financial products, but that orange tubular root I see before me surely still is a carrot?

Through my own research I have learned that the shop-bought carrot you eat today is not at all the same as the one your grandfather bought. Increased mechanisation and processing coupled with the drive for profits at all costs means that the old adage, "they don't make them like they used to" also applies to the fresh food we eat.

Learning this just made me want to grow more food—in fact as much as I possibly could. I wanted to taste everything for the first time, just as nature intended it to be. But there were obvious limitations to what I, as an individual, might be able to do. As an urbanite, I don't own land, so where would I get the ground on which to conduct my experiment? I'm a busy city-dweller with a job, two children and the usual commitments and restraints on my time. I needed to find out just how much food my lifestyle and my small suburban garden would allow me to grow. And I didn't want to lose all of my garden to food growing either. Like anyone, I wanted private outdoor space for my children to play safely and for summer barbecues with extended family and friends when the weather permitted. So I put my name down for an allotment.

In Dublin, where I live—as in many other European cities—the local authorities are the custodians and providers of allotments. And like most cities, there are always years-long waiting lists. As it turned out, I was extremely lucky in my timing. The councils in Dublin had just closed a number of older city complexes for development. They were obliged to rehouse the allotment holders elsewhere and did so by opening new and considerably larger sites right about the time I was putting my name down.

A few months later I got my letter confirming the success of my application. Mine would be located at Bohernabreena, a hillside rural location about five miles from our home.

Bohernabreena brought back memories for me because, when I was a boy, my grandfather would take me shooting for rabbits, foxes and pheasants here. Both he and my grandmother are buried in the new Bohernabreena cemetery alongside numerous other family relations and friends.

From the graveyard, heading uphill on the winding road, you pass St Anne's Church, an old Victorian country church with its own, much older, tiny graveyard attached. It's located at an ancient site believed to go back to Druidic times. The area includes a smattering of prehistoric passage graves, and Bohernabreena translates roughly as 'Road to Hospitality'—from *bothar* (road) and *brugh* (hostel).

The site of the allotments was once the Friarstown House estate, but it had subsequently become the site of one of Dublin city's biggest open refuse landfills. I remembered a day in the past when myself and my granddad cleared a hill to find ourselves looking down on its vast sea of smelly refuse, noisily patrolled by squalling and squealing masses of seagulls.

Now the dump had been filled in and the ground immediately uphill from it, once part of the refuse delivery complex, had been ploughed and fenced off for our new allotments. The first day I visited it, the place was beautiful. Here we were raised high above the city, flanked by the Glenasmole valley on one side, with farmland surrounding us and the bell of the old country church sounding the hour below us. Inside the complex, council workmen were busy ploughing land and hammering in fence posts.

I signed my lease and sent it back with the 48 quid rent money, and the key to the gates arrived by post. I was now officially an allotment holder!

And so, on that first truly awful Sunday I arrived with Lisa, spade in hand at the top of the hill, where my plot was located. Our plot had its number '34' stencilled in white paint on the entrance fence post. It ran about 6m wide and 20m long and roughly covered the ground space of the combined upstairs and downstairs floors of an average semi-detached house. At the back of my plot was the complex's 8ft boundary fence of chicken wire, handy for the raspberries I planned to grow.

Lisa was keen and wanted to help with the allotment project. This was good because she could drive and I couldn't. Having spent all of my life within a short bus hop of my workplace and my family and friends, I've never needed a car. Only one bus travelled up to Bohernabreena, and only a few times a day. So I had to rely on Lisa's canary yellow Honda Civic and her sustained enthusiasm to get us up there, at least until I would take the plunge and learn to drive.

For that reason, I also planned to open up small plots in my back garden which I could keep a closer eye on, on those days we couldn't travel. I was even going to make use of the little greenhouses that are our inside windowsills at home. My goal was to grow as much food as I possibly could and use all my available space to achieve that.

That was 2006 and the 'grow your own' zeitgeist hadn't yet taken off. Even so, it still surprised me how many people regarded us as being eccentric in our plans. Food growing, we discovered, was perceived to be the realm of dizzy, earth-wor-shipping hippies or crusty, flat-capped granddads who brewed up tea in jerry-built sheds as they pored over secret fertiliser recipes for turbocharged marrows.

I certainly wasn't planning to become a self-sufficient good lifer—because I don't believe that's possible for a modern city-dweller. But what I was curious to find out was exactly how much food one or two people could produce while still holding demanding jobs, looking after a family and taking time to stay in touch with friends and relations.

I wanted to see how much better our diets would become, whether we would be healthier, whether our meals would be more enjoyable, and whether I could develop any real under-standing and respect for the processes by which we produce our food. And then I wanted to see if we would save any worthwhile amount of money by growing and eating our own produce. Given the work and time it was obviously going to take, would it all be worth it?

Then there was my health. As someone who once upon a time used to go to the gym, swim and play football regularly, I wondered if hard agrarian work would get me fit again. Once upon a time I paid 400 quid a year to sit down indoors doing exercises that pretty much imitate the sort of digging and lifting you do on an allotment. Maybe I could do with that sort of exer-cise again?

I was thirty-seven starting this quest, my hair was fast deplet-ing and I sat at a desk in an office all day. And for someone lat-terly riled up about the quality of food, I didn't eat particularly well—I was prone to the odd kebab or pot noodle and I loved takeaways. I also smoked more than twenty a day.

And maybe growing my own food on a rural hillside would reacquaint me with some of those sights and sounds of nature I had lost touch with since my childhood days climbing trees and exploring woodlands.

I've never been on a round-the-world trip, I've never jumped out of a plane and I've never owned a motorbike. I'm the polar opposite of an adrenaline junkie. While an allotment might not be quite the same thing as disappearing up the Amazon in your own handmade canoe, it was a challenge of a different kind. And perhaps it was a more fundamentally important one. The food I was hoping to grow was what we ate at home—lots of onions, tomatoes, peas, corn, cabbage and spuds. And maybe some more besides.

I'm not a diehard greenie. Despite my fears for the world, I also know that growing food isn't going to save me if the lights ever do go out on civilisation—I'd certainly lose the harvest to wild roaming packs of feral accountants. But I do want my kids to know where their food comes from and to have some respect for it. My son Oisín was five when we got our allotment. Like many his age, he doesn't like his vegetables, preferring instead anything which comes in a bread-crumbed nugget. It would also be nice to have him help me, as my brother and I helped my dad or my granddad in the garden when we were his age. Good for some old-fashioned character-building.

When I asked him what role he might perform at the allotment, he came up with a rather ambitious plan, complete with a drawing of how it might pan out. With a view to the rainy weather, he opined that he could use his sandcastle shovel, a sturdy Swedish-made affair with a wooden handle, to excavate a secret tunnel from the allotment back to the house, a distance of only five miles. This tunnel, known only to us, would save us getting wet on the journey there and back. He made good on his promise by devoting at least two days to what would become a fairly decent hole—that I would end up stumbling in many times over—and canvassed me for the position of Plot 34's Head of Secret Tunnels (HST). In view of his excellently drawn plan, his enthusiasm, and the lack of competing candidates for said position, I readily agreed. Anything to get him up here would be encouraged.

Since I took the allotment, myself and Her Outdoors (she has always said she never wants to be the traditional Her Indoors) have been blessed with a baby girl, Evie Margaret, later to be known as Plot 34's WOE, or Waterer of Everything, thanks to her subsequent fondness for roaming around with the watering can, sprinkling on everything from seedlings to her dad's socks. Her birth at the end of our first year with the allotment would impact on our time and our ability to keep it in order.

I began reading books on the life and requirements of food plants. I read the backs of seed packets, and I began to learn by trial and error. My ace card in my allotment education was the great and wise Dr Interweb, the all-knowing sage of Googleland who could find the answer to almost every problem and query I would have. I also pledged to get to know some of the older guys on our complex, the ones who know what they're doing without even thinking about it.

So if you've ever considered growing your own food, then I might be of some assistance. In this book you'll get a diary of my progress through the first two years and an index at the back to show you what I've learned about each food plant. But this isn't an instruction manual—there are enough of them out there already. It's about relating the experience of what happens when a newbie is thrown into the deep end of growing food for the first time. Hopefully, through my trials and triumphs, you'll understand what the experience is about and what to expect if you decide to give it a go.

I work in a leading Sunday newspaper, *The Sunday Times*, where I edit the Home section. So to make matters even more difficult for myself, I successfully pitched the idea of a weekly allotment diary column to my initially dubious editor. The 'Plot 34' column is running into its fourth year as I write this. Not only has it become the basis of this book, but it also made me take stock of what I was doing as I went along, and gave me the incentive to keep at it when it proved difficult. There could be no slinking off when 350,000 Sunday readers require a further instalment.

Allotment Diary, Year One

March to Easter

On our first day we felt jubilant turning the first sod as the blizzard began. We made our first acquaintance. Forty-something and wiry, our comrade-in-farms peered up from under his Benny cap (hats are an allotmenteer's signature it seems) and eagerly shook hands. He pointed down with satisfaction at the straggly leaves poking from the muck and nodded grimly: "Rhubarb". We nodded back with respect. "Rhubarb," we intoned. Slowly, the information trading began.

It soon became clear that each of us hoped the other possessed the sort of experience that brings top tips, miracle fertiliser formulas, and growing secrets. We were both disappointed: he hadn't had an allotment before. Three plots over, a plummy sort—ironed slacks tucked into spotless wellies—eased himself out of his car and stood, hands on hips, grimacing into the gale. We shook our heads. Not him, either.

So it was back to work. The council was two months late giving us the keys and we had lost digging time. Squall or none the 15 fruit trees we'd brought were going into the ground, come hell or high water. We had both.

Despite the council ploughing up the whole complex earlier in the year, the weeds were everywhere and we would have to dig through a thick, green thatch and prise them all out. The taps still weren't connected and if they didn't get a move on, there would be no point because most plants have to be in by April. But council officials probably don't realise that.

Some of the books I've referred to have recommended scale sketching your plot on grid paper, which helps me map out what goes where on my new allotment. I've made a list of what I want to grow and have tried to draw out the beds as they'd measure out. I was also taking into account the maximum height of crops so I wouldn't overshadow any of the smaller ones. Broccoli and peas are quite tall, for example, whereas carrot foliage lies closer to the ground. I sketched in the onions, carrots, cabbages, broccoli, rhubarb, fruit trees, peas, sprouts.

By night I was sitting on the settee with a brand new box of colouring pencils, a ruler and an ink pen laid out on the coffee table, sketching out the dimensions of our allotment, about 20ft by 60ft. I'm annoyed because the council told me I'd get one twice that size. When Her Outdoors joined me I was diligently colouring the carrots in orange, their tops in dark green. "No it's not totally necessary," I agreed, "but it makes it look more authentic."

We decided the first plants to go in would be our new fruit bushes, most obtained at a local discount supermarket at a quid a piece and sitting in pots outside for the last few weeks while we awaited our keys. About a dozen go in two neat lines, blackcurrants to the left as you look in, gooseberries to the right and raspberries and tayberries at the back. I paid a hefty 15 quid for a single blueberry bush, but given that the berries cost a fiver for a cigarette-box-sized punnet, I'm reckoning it will pay for itself in its first year. My books tell me to dig a deep hole, throw in some manure, mix it with the soil, stick in your bush, fill in the soil and tramp it down firmly all round. We haven't filled the soil to the top of the hole which leaves little hollow craters around each bush. These will make watering easier.

By now, we've also dug our first proper bed! It's for the onions, of which we've planted 200. We bought sets, or juvenile one-year-old bulbs, from Tesco at about four quid all in. Myself and Her Outdoors dug out two square plots with our spades and then busted the sods with a fork, knocking out the weeds. Then we got down on our hands and knees and went through the whole lot again, teasing out smaller roots and picking out the stones. The digging and preparation of beds is the first shock you get upon taking on a big vegetable garden because it takes about ten times longer than you'd expect it to.

The weed roots all need to come out or they'll regenerate into lots of little weeds. The stones obstruct growth, so we collected them and used them to make a neat little path to let us walk between the two plots. This did provide us with good grip in muddy conditions but also turned out to be a haven for weeds which were almost impossible to extract later on from between packed rocks. As we progressed we realised that for every two things you do right when you're starting an allotment, you do one completely wrong.

Knowing they like good drainage, we dug neat little ridges and furrows for the onions so they'd be raised above the water level. We arranged sticks and string with bits of plastic bag tied on to keep the birds from pulling up the sets—something magpies in particular seem to be fond of doing, perhaps in an attempt to unearth grubs and worms beneath them. If they pull out the bulb, we simply pop it back in again until it roots.

Next up for the following weekend was the carrot bed. We read that carrots need ultra-fine, well-drained soil so they don't rot or get misshapen. This took considerably more work than the onions. It took most of a day for both of us working together to prepare this one bed, but it should be more than worth it because carrot seeds are incredible value for money with 344 in our packet of Nantes variety carrots for just a few quid. Now all we have to do is keep the carrot fly (the main pest) off.

On the other hand, the biggest rip-off I've ever been taken in by is a packet of strawberry seeds which came with just nine in the packet. An internet search shows me a single strawberry has around 200 seeds on its surface, so this gives the seed supplier about 40 quid per berry. Only three of the blighters germinated and because they're so feeble, all have been placed in a warm, covered indoor space: the bin.

At home in late March our time was spent planting up seeds in compost into trays and most of those have sprouted as we near the end of the month. We've probably spent 20 or 30 quid on seeds already.

Almost all of the seedlings are being germinated and kept indoors to protect them from the elements and from outdoor pests. For many allotment plants, northern European weather can damage them until at least April so they need to be started indoors. The trouble is that we never really thought about where we were going to put all our seedlings. So in the absence of a greenhouse, we've been forced to share our home with them and the buggers are simply everywhere. So if you are planning to grow food and you don't have a greenhouse, here's the sort of morning routine you can expect:

I get up and go to the hot press—also the chilli hatchery—for a towel, taking care to avoid breaking the chilli seedlings. This is where I start off the jalapeño and cayenne red chillies and the sweet bell peppers. They need a higher temperature than other seeds to germinate which is why they're in there in trays covered with Clingfilm. Most, thankfully, have by now sprouted and have been moved to the downstairs kitchen windowsill, alongside the herbs. Then I wander into the en-suite bathroom for a shower alongside a large tray containing about a hundred 1ft-tall tomato seedlings on the windowsill. The tightly packed and exuberant toddlers are the variety Gardener's Delight, and if nothing nasty happens to them between now and July, they should produce hundreds of juicy cherry tomatoes each. Not knowing any different, I planted the whole packet at once. I suppose I can give some of them away.

I wander from the shower back into the bedroom, where the Ailsa Craig tomato seedlings (for medium-sized tomatoes) hang out on the windowsill, blocking about half of the bedroom's light. Then it's downstairs to the kitchen to put the kettle on amid more window boxes—sage, thyme, mint, parsley and some of the part-grown former hot-press chilli peppers over by the kitchen sink. Near the sliding doors I've had to install a sort of wide-open bookcase for seedlings. It's packed out over four levels. This is the rack of a seed tent I've bought for about 30 quid. It's essentially four wire shelves on a rack which you cover with a plastic see-through jacket. You open it with zips on either side. The jacket will go on and it will go outside on the patio once I find a way of anchoring it down properly. Right now, minus its jacket and indoors, it's got the unruly courgettes on top, intertwined and wrestling. Then 40 individual peas are sprouting from 40 half-toilet-roll innards and yoghurt cartons (a mistake because I later learn that peas should go directly into the ground). Also the first batch of cucumbers, dwarf beans, the experimental sweetcorn, and last and certainly least, a tray of hopelessly overcrowded basil, so packed in that much of it has collapsed or else produced a strange-looking mould. Our first three lots of plants are in and we have loads of seedlings on their way to maturity. But thus far, only one thing can be relied upon—the fact that our basil is well and truly faulty!

Chapter Two

The Good Old Days

I owe my late grandfather PJ for many things, among them the ability to know my options when a bee gets stuck in my hair.

As kids we spent a lot of time over at my grandparents' house and we played football in the garden where PJ kept, among other things, hives of bees. Sometimes a stray shot would whack up one of those hives. For this reason, our wild solo runs around the garden shouting loudly and waving our arms in the air after scoring a goal often had less to do with celebratory glory than simple evasive action.

Being a curly-haired lad, I faced an additional hazard. Bees which flew into me at head height tended to get stuck in my mop and then emitted a frightening high-pitched stress buzz, sort of: "Zeeeee! Zee-eee!" as they struggled to get free.

I soon learned that when this happens, you have a number of options open to you.

(a) You can try whacking the bee hard (and also, by default, your own head) and perhaps you'll kill it, but in doing so you risk driving the needle-like stinging end of the bee, hammer on nail style, into your head. On top of this, PJ warned that the smell of a squished bee made the other bees attack; because squished bees meant the hive was being threatened and it was time for the lads (ladies actually) to get stuck in. Thus an initially successful and stingless squish could vastly increase your subsequent jeopardy.

(b) You can try to untangle the struggling apoidea yourself, but this risks the already angry and confused insect stinging either your hand or your head as you attempt to interfere.

(c) You can stand still and hope the bugger gets out by itself. But in my considerable experience with the old live-bee-in-the-hair dilemma, they usually work their way tighter into your hair before eventually stinging you anyway.

My own most commonly employed solution was to (d) run in frantic circles emitting a high-pitched wail until an adult came out, slapped me in the head and dragged me inside.

At one point PJ had about 30 hives of bees, either housed in the garden or on other sites in more rural parts of Dublin which had been loaned to him by acquaintances. He once appeared in a photograph in the *Evening Herald* newspaper. He was snapped, stood on a ladder at a busy city shopping centre in the middle of rush hour, in the act of removing a stray swarm of bees which had attached themselves to a shop sign. He bagged this and many other swarms which certainly weren't his, on account of the tip-offs he got by phone. These in turn were generated by the small ad he would run in the *Herald* through the summer swarming season. It said simply: "Swarm of bees lost—phone 973673". And it worked extremely well—except when he got called out to collect wasps.

PJ was born in 1910 in Stradbally, County Laois, into a farming family of eleven and he left home to make his fortune as a travelling salesman, latterly in garments and shoes, but initially selling habits—the lacy white bibs in which most people were buried back then. Of those days he would chirrup: "I never had a single complaint from a customer!"

Working usually alone, PJ was ultra resourceful and had a cheeky sense of humour and an appreciation for practical jokes which he inherited from his own father, a farmer. Once during a long business trip to Dublin, his father borrowed a uniform from a British soldier, had himself photographed in it, and then sent the resulting snap home to the family as a postcard purporting to be from Flanders.

PJ's travelling job took him to Dublin where he stayed in a guesthouse/hotel on Leeson Street run by my grandmother's family. This was how they met. PJ married Rita and moved permanently to the big smoke, taking with him his farming family ways and outlandish bog phrases such as "be the hokey!" I never heard him curse once.

They bought a big old red-brick Edwardian in the leafy

suburb of Rathgar. Rita, a devout, popular and ever-smiling woman, kept the house abuzz with visitors of all generations coming around for tea. As a homemaker of old, her kitchen included the sort of Victorian era implements and outsized pots and pans that went with domestic food preparation on a far larger scale than we know today. Lots of hand-cranked, windy-wheel thingies and strangely shaped bits of metal fused to painted wooden handles. Slightly genteel, she would always answer the telephone in her poshest tone, reciting the number the caller had just dialled. She rolled her butter into barrel-shaped 'pats' with wooden paddles and ran a poker school on a Sunday night which could see upwards of twelve assorted septuagenarians, usually extended relations, hustling one another for pennies on the big dining room table, which she covered in a sheet of green felt for the occasion.

We were often over there and in the summer we lived there for weeks at a time on our 'holidays'.

When PJ retired in the 1970s from his successful one-man sales career, he became busier than ever. In his urban garden he kept all sorts of birds in an aviary—chickens, ornamental pheasants, ducks, finches, doves...the list goes on. So on top of fresh honey, they had fresh eggs from chickens, ducks and even quail. In the run-up to Christmas PJ kept a gaggle of turkeys which he hatched out, and let run loose in the garden. With a dozen of them roaming in a posse and stretching to two foot tall, they'd chase and peck any small kids who annoyed them.

PJ also used the garden to grow food, particularly fruit. As children we picked pears, apples, cherries, plums, gooseberries, loganberries and redcurrants straight from the tree or the bush. He made homemade wine in vast amounts, concocted with double the sugar levels to increase its potency. This he employed to dose up the elderly matrons who came to play poker, rendering them considerably more flippant with their coppers.

And on numerous other sites borrowed from friends who were farmers, or from those homeowners he knew who had a large garden going to waste, PJ grew varied crops. I can recall afternoons spent picking at a minor plantation of blackcurrants he'd somehow organised in the grounds of a huge old house round the corner. He had another allotment in the back of a big Victorian town house known as 'Purcells', and he kept hives on a narrow stone ledge bordering a river on a friend's farm located just out of town.

PJ wasn't just an example of how far a city smallholder could go in terms of food-growing and general self-sufficiency, he was also a textbook lesson in how to acquire land to grow when you don't happen to have any. When PJ couldn't find the ground to grow or to hold his bees, he began making enquiries about those who had ground going fallow or for gardens which owners didn't want the bother of maintaining. He kept a constant country eye out for opportunity. When he struck gold, he kept the owners sweet with banter and with his produce, be it vegetables, fruit, fresh eggs, honey or whatever else he had going at the time.

He was also a man for forage and took me picking hazelnuts from the trees in country lanes. Myself and my siblings were usually recruited for missions collecting fraughans or blackberries. Anything to be got for cheap or for nothing and which could be eaten was procured. He even pulped the rosehips from his rose trees to make medicinal syrup (a rich source of vitamin C). He grew grapes in his greenhouse and once even brought on his own tobacco, which was left hanging for years unsmoked in great bunches in the rafters of the garage.

His great quest for free healthy food also extended to hunting, his big passion in life. He shot pheasants, rabbits, duck, pigeons, the occasional deer, snipe, grouse, geese and anything else that was unfortunate enough to fly, crawl, hop or scutter into his crosshairs.

It fell to my grandmother Rita to turn this vast, PJ-generated cornucopia into wholesome table food, whether it was jarring honey, turning rhubarb into tarts, making blackcurrants into jam or stewing rabbit complete with a lead shot in every bite. PJ was so careful with food that he would even eat the marrow from the inside of chicken bones.

PJ was also a staunch environmentalist, although he didn't know it—because common sense wasn't called 'environmentalism' back then. But most likely he would have had no truck with today's middle-class brand of green-mindedness with its political correctness and holier-than-thou disciples. Being from a country background, he had an ingrained appreciation for the land and for the ways of nature. He believed that hunting was the natural order of things and that if you looked after nature then it would look after you. Before recycling became *de rigueur*, PJ recycled everything. Things were always mended rather than thrown out. An old television set case was transformed into a birdhouse on one occasion. On another he attached a ladies umbrella handle to a kitchen spatula after the old wooden handle had split. I still have it at home. Egg shells were kept, dried, heated and broken up to feed back to the chickens for calcium in their diet. Compost was made. Table scraps were fed to the dogs, used newspapers were twisted into firelighters, string and twine was wrapped up and put away, every plastic bag was kept and every type of nut, bolt, nail, or hinge—no matter how rusty or damaged—was salvaged and filed in a vast multi-drawered file of orphaned ironmongery kept in the garage. He even held on to all the sample, single, left shoes remaining in storage after he retired from his shoe-selling career, and used them as fuel to keep the kitchen stove stoked up.

Much of all this rubbed off on his sons, including my dad, Michael, who brought home fish (fishing was his thing) as well as game from hunting. Dad liked to forage for wild mushrooms and grew apples and rhubarb in our garden. Thanks to PJ we city slickers had a taste of rural life and an appreciation for home-grown food. Perhaps we took it all for granted. But with the opening of more supermarkets, and the increasing level of wealth Ireland was experiencing, the need for growing food at home was fast fading.

Thus my dad's inherited horticultural gene was instead channelled into exotic cacti and rose trees—at one point his plant-grafting skills saw him produce a single rose bush which sported five different varieties of blooms. So when I was ten, I learned to graft roses.

The urban food forager also came out in my dad. He once took home a bag of crabs bought for almost nothing from a fisherman in Sandycove. The agitated crustaceans had to be batoned live into the waiting pot of boiling water with quite a few managing to drop off the hob to the floor and scuttle around the kitchen in an attempt to make a break for it.

On my mum's side of the family, Dermot, my other grandfather, was also a very enthusiastic vegetable grower. A kind, reserved and gentle man, he was an army private who moved into a career working as a maintenance man for the national lighthouse service. After a life spent abseiling between ships in stormy seas and living in lighthouses, his garage was filled with giant light bulbs and the end of his garden was a vast vegetable patch for cauliflowers, onions, carrots, potatoes and cabbage. He had a large greenhouse in which he grew tomatoes. He also got his photograph in the newspaper—in this case for an 8lb bass landed on Killiney Beach.

What all this meant was that in the 1970s and 1980s, we children grew up eating a good deal of wholesome, home-sourced food long after everyone else had begun buying all of theirs down at the supermarket. When my friends had a Granny Smith in their lunchbox, I had a gnarly eater from the tree at the end of the garden which usually came with a dead wasp somewhere inside.

Having lived through rationing and tougher times generally, my grandparents' generation had a deep ingrained respect for food and a complete disdain for waste. And long after incomes had risen and food prices fallen, their lifelong habits lingered.

Of course they weren't unusual. In their time everybody did it. In the first half of the twentieth century, allotments were widespread in urban centres here. Dublin had allotments right in its centre and a few have survived today on the banks of the Grand Canal. In my grandparents' early married years, the advertising they saw around them reflected different aspirations. Instead of the smug exec in his new car, or the happy accident victim who has benefited from the compo lawyer, the ads of their day showed a different aspiration—lots and lots of rosy-cheeked and healthy children. Sturdy, touselled-headed scallywags adorned almost every poster, be it for liver salts, soap or custard. Even Guinness touted that it was 'good for you'. Because for their generation, having healthy children was your greatest aspiration in a time when youngsters still got rickets from vitamin deficiency and TB was a rampant killer of children as was scarlet fever and many of the now relatively minor illnesses we are familiar with today.

In times when obviously malnourished children were still visible on city streets, a big part of your life insurance policy was the practice of growing good food. It also made financial sense when incomes were far smaller and food was relatively much more expensive. So everybody did it. It's the very reason why gardens in city houses built up until the 1960s always came with plenty of ground attached—100 feet until the 1900s.

The very origins of formalised city allotments in Ireland are tied in with this urban poverty and with times of particular crisis. In his university paper 'Uncovering the Plot', Michael Cullen says the first recorded local-authority-controlled Dublin allotments were launched in 1910, the year PJ was born, to help feed poorer city-dwellers in a time when Dublin's inner city was being compared with Calcutta's. About 23 were opened in Clontarf, the Coombe and on the seafront next to the Pigeon House. During the Great War, numbers predictably surged from 437 plots in 1917 to 3,000 by 1919. Subsequent efforts to expand the city then saw many of those allotments taken away for development, in a cycle of allotment creation and destruction which would repeat itself again and again right up to the present generation.

By 1926 the city's growers felt so threatened that they finally mobilised to set up the United Irish Plot Holders Union. They kicked up such a stink that their lobbying and protests for legislation to protect their right to lease land for food led to the 1926 Allotments Act. To this day the legislation enshrines in law the right of Irish city-dwellers to have a space each to rent in order to grow food.

Predictably there was another peak in allotment allocation during the Second World War, with Dublin's plots soaring to 3,500 in 1941—an all-time high. But since the 1950s with the arrival of supermarkets and relatively cheap food, interest waned and allotment numbers went into steady decline until very recently. In the 1990s and early 2000s, a property boom saw the councils once again attempting to push remaining plot holders off their patches to cash in on the new development spree. Once again Dublin's growers resisted and drew on the 1926 legislation to ensure the councils created a new round of complexes, mainly on the periphery of the city. Among them is Friarstown in Bohernabreena where Plot 34 is situated.

With the new recession and greater availability came a renewed surge in interest in allotmenteering, also led by a change in popular culture through both the environmental and foodie movements.

Throughout the world there is a history of people turning to the soil when times become fraught. In post-war Berlin, that city's citizens began growing vegetables in the ruins of the city centre to help feed themselves and many of these plots are still in place today. In Cuba when aid from the old Soviet regime collapsed in the 1990s, Havana fast became the most concentrated city of urban growers in the world and today has by far the most developed urban food system on the planet. More recently, detainees at Guantanamo Bay were caught by their jailers attempting to grow secret vegetable gardens from seeds picked from their meals.

Thankfully for me, both of my grandfathers had kept up the growing habits of a lifetime back when I traipsed around after them. Thanks to them, I was at least equipped with the memories of what could be possible when it comes to urban food growing. And while I often wished that that apple in my school lunchbox was neat and uniform like everyone else's, rather than a knobbly garden version, looking back now, I'm glad that I got them. These days I believe that the problem apples are those bred to be uniform and without blemish.

Just before I took up my allotment, the last vestiges of our family's homegrown efforts were to be found stranded at the end of my mum's suburban garden. Her generation was the first to go back to work after having children. The two-job family is another reason we've lost touch with growing food because what we've gained in our incomes, we've lost in free time, the spare hours needed to grow food, prepare it, store it and cook it properly at home.

As late as 1979 when we moved into our last family home, growing food still held some sliver of importance in our family, albeit a token one. The first plants to go into the garden were two apple trees, an 'eater' and a 'cooker'. Through the last decade most of those apples have been left to rot on the ground where they fall. Recently I picked a bag of windfalls and took them home to make into apple sauce. Far nicer than the packet.

By the time we moved to that house in the 1970s, a marked change had already taken place in how society viewed urban food growing. In the era of acrylic, nylon and plastic, people began believing that urban food growing was outmoded and even backward. Why grub in the ground for gnarly looking pest-infested vegetables, when you could drop a bag of neat clean ones into your basket down at the supermarket?

That change in perception was also reflected in the popular culture of the day.

The big sit-com of the 1970s was 'The Good Life' featuring

Richard Briars and Felicity Kendal—a couple whose attempts at urban self-sufficiency produce hilarious results. 'The Good Life' portrayed urban food-growing as an activity carried out by well-meaning but dotty people.

In the 1980s, another well-known allotmenteer of popular culture came into view. Arthur Fowler of the popular long-running British soap *EastEnders* was the harried flatcap from Albert Square, transforming the role of urban grower from a hairbrained young idealist to that of a daft, grumpy pensioner. "Arfur" was the fusty old codger whose penchant for food-growing was as outmoded as his war stories and chest-high trousers (also a staple of PJ's wardrobe).

A decade on again and popular culture's best-known urban grower was now Wallace, the gormless inventor in Nick Park's wonderful *Wallace and Gromit*, who lives in a world of cosy old nostalgic cliché in a cosy town where they drive Morris Minors, use coin-fed gas meters, wear tank tops and striped pyjamas, drink nice cups of tea and hold giant marrow growing competitions. In this world populated by eccentric characters, all of them grow their own veg with hardcore devotion.

But as the modern environmental movement began to develop, interest stirred once again in urban food-growing. It was helped along by a twin surge in our interest in food and cooking, itself reflected in the popularity of new cookery programmes brought to us by a slew of imaginative celebrity chefs.

Among them, all on his ownsome, was Hugh Fearnley Whittingstall with his fabulous 'River Cottage' series. In it, HFW showed us the setting up and running of his new life as a smallholder. His series, launched at the end of the nineties, was a slow burner which was initially brushed aside to the off prime time slots and sideline cable TV channels. HFW's fundamental message—that the best food does not come from supermarkets; that it is time to consider growing your own as an alternative; that we are wasting the resources and food opportunities we have—began to sink in.

His popularity grew and his slots moved from outside placings aimed at the corduroy-jacket brigade to mainstream positioning until he eventually topped ratings for his channel.

He was followed by cheekie chappie chef Jamie Oliver, second out of the blocks. Despite fronting up the Sainsbury's advertising campaigns, Oliver took the baton and ran with it in his excellent School Dinners campaign, which revealed to us the sort of rubbish that our generation is both marketing and feeding to its children. Non food. Numpty nuggets.

Both demonstrated a deep respect for grown food not seen for two generations. Today through most cities in Europe, would-be urban farmers are clamouring for allotments. Private farmers are renting out tiny patches on their land for as much as €400 per annum.

In the three years since I started the 'Plot 34' column with *The Sunday Times*, I have witnessed homegrown food moving from steady growth to full-blown zeitgeist alongside the new recession.

I'm glad my grandparents are buried close to our allotment complex. PJ would have enjoyed pottering around the place, poking his nose into what more than a hundred growers are busy getting up to on weekends. He'd be wandering around, secateurs in hand, cheroot cigar in his mouth, swapping fruit bush cuttings and shooting the breeze over fences. In so many ways they were all looking over my shoulder when I dug that first sod.

Allotment Diary, Year One

May to Early June

Dusk, Easter weekend on our new allotment complex. It's hot and humid. Amidst the undergrowth, standing in a hole, our hero gives the spade one last push before flinging it aside. He stops, sways wearily on his feet, and reaching up a mucky forearm to mop his brow, he turns to drag the corpse by its ankles towards the hole... Well, maybe not that last bit. But I've been digging for days like I'm on a chain gang. Across forty or so new plots are hunched dozens of half-light diggers, frantically getting stuck into the ground with the urgency of coverless infantry who've just been told to expect enemy ordnance.

Because of the council, we're all late. If we want any crops from our patches on this, our first year, we have to keep digging, and fast, because the water still hasn't been turned on. Now just a few weeks into our virgin allotments and an unseasonal heatwave has turned the ground from sludge into pig iron.

We newbies have quickly discovered that the reality of owning an allotment is hard work and time pressure, particularly at this time of the year. Most of us have full-time jobs and have only weekends or weekday evenings to get this work done. The longer daylight hours are a blessing but with rush-hour traffic, most of us won't get here before seven. From then on it's a race against sundown to get as much digging in as possible before dark.

Most seeds and plants should be in by now so a day of digging lost now could mean an entire crop bed forgone. I've got seedlings in at home, so they can be transplanted in when the ground's ready, but root crops like carrots, parsnips, swedes, peas and beans need to be planted *in situ*. I've also taken the shortcut of buying young plants from the garden centre including cabbages, calabrese and sprouts.

In the hot, fly-ridden air, with sweat streaming into my eyes and down my back, and amidst the mass clinking of metal on hard earth, I can perhaps be forgiven for feeling like an extra from *Cool Hand Luke*—"Hey boss, permission to piss, boss?" Digging is a bummer, but there's no getting away from it. And I haven't had any prolonged physical exercise like this in years. Like the exercise bike machine at the gym, it's boring and painful in a long-drawn-out sort of way and it takes an age to dig just a little ground properly.

My books and the internet tell me that the ideal time to have dug this ground was January or February before the weeds got going. Ideally you should be able to turn the sods over and leave them to dry out for a bit before coming back to break them up. This weakens or kills the weeds, making them easier to shake out. This is also the time for the allot-menteer to introduce some well-rotted manure to condition the soil and give it nutrients. I don't have that luxury right now so I'm hoping the virgin ground will have enough in it already before I need to go looking for a friendly farmer. Buying it from the garden centre really isn't an option, at five or six quid a small bag, it's just too expensive for this amount of ground.

Some of my new-found brethren have called in the heavy artillery in the form of heavy-duty rotovators which plough through the earth at pace and cut digging time down to a fraction. But my fellow manual labourers have whispered bad cess about this shortcut. Apparently the rotovators break up the roots of the weeds and spread them around, thus leading to an explosion in weeds down the line. Tee hee, I'm feeling better already. I've learned the hard way that what you need is a good spade, one that won't break or bend when you bash the ground. For some reason garden centres sell a lot of brittle, bendy versions. For breaking and teasing out sods, a good T-handle fork with four prongs would appear to be the ideal, with a T-head rake and a solid heavy trowel best for the finer work. Then you'll need gloves if, like me, you're a tender-footed and palmed office worker. Being the muscle, and more likely to blister, I've opted for tough leather gloves, while Her Outdoors prefers thick rubber ones for finer pickings and rummagings.

Apart from a few allotments that had been rotovated, all the men were digging while the women sat observing and commenting.

It's an unspoken rule that the heavy digging and sod-turning, like taking out the bins, is a man's job. As I get under way, Her Outdoors is parked in the deckchair, munching chicken wings off the barbecue, glass of vino in the other hand and issuing a commentary on other plot-holders. This was not how I'd imagined our allotmenteering partnership to be.

But her butt is parked only for a half-hour, until there were enough sods turned. Unlike some other ladies, Her Outdoors is not afraid to get stuck in—thus far at least. I've already noted with both approval and deep concern that she's a mean hand with the pitchfork. Like the Tasmanian devil of the Looney Tune cartoons, she whizzes along the busted sods, running the fork through them, shaking them out, throwing up little dust storms.

Digging removes weeds and stones, but I read that it's also a vital practice to aerate the soil, to condition it and allow it to breathe. Roots need to be able to spread unimpeded through the ground. Digging also helps water and nutrients to spread properly through the soil and makes it easier for earthworms to travel, to bring more nutrients and to aerate it further.

Having looked up digging practices online we've opted for a variant on what's called 'trench' digging. This means starting off with a spade-deep gulley or trench on one side of your intended bed and then stepping back and digging the next row of fresh sods over into the waiting trench. The new trench you have just created takes the next row of sods and so on you go. Then you go back and break up the sods and remove the roots, stones and weeds.

Because we were working on virgin ground, with about 4in of growth already on it, it took us five hours between us to get 40sq.ft done—dug, sod-bashed, shaken, sieved and levelled. That's 4ft x 2ft an hour, enough space for only twelve cabbages. More than three-quarters of that time went into getting the weeds and their roots out. But over stolen evenings and the odd weekend, we're getting there.

Soon we've dug beds for peas, onions, cabbages, broccoli and carrots. Seeds for peas and carrots, sets for onions and Lidl-bought green and black cabbage and calabrese (what most of us erroneously call broccoli). Finally the rhubarb and the Brussels sprouts. After weeks of back-breaking digging, weeding and sorting the soil, Plot 34 is finally starting to look like a proper allotment. I've also learned through these weeks that keeping an allotment makes you truly appreciate rain, especially when our plants are gasping for life in a drought. And as the country wallows in sunshine, and the water taps remain unconnected, I find that I'm the only one among my friends praying for rain. We haven't had a sustained downpour since St Patrick's Day, and a good 24-hour deluge of the sort we're more used to, would give the soil enough soaking to keep some moisture locked in.

With global warming, growing conditions here seem to be changing. In hotter weather traditional temperate vegetables such as swedes and potatoes will become tougher to grow. On the upside, it opens the door to more exotic outdoor produce such as tomatoes and squashes. At our allotment, we're trying both traditionals and exotics.

But only six weeks into our project, we're running up and down constantly to the allotment on nightly, life-saving watering trips.

Because the ground was so dry when we planted most of our crops, we opted for our own version of Mediterranean style planting. Each seedling was planted in a hollow. We lined these with manure to help retain moisture in our brick-hard clay soil. The indent around the plant means the water we pour in is captured, doesn't run off, and soaks directly to the roots.

The good news is that by now we've got a decent variety of fruit and veg growing. Over to the left are the nine blackcurrant bushes, which get half a watering can apiece. Near the top on this side are two blackberry bushes and some redcurrants. Most are doing well.

At the top, against a high fence, are two raspberry canes and two tayberries, and in the top right-hand corner is the most expensive addition to our patch, the blueberry bush, also doing well.

Close to the entrance, and less needy of a draught in the drought, are the 200 or so onion sets on the ridges of small furrows. While they like a bit of a sprinkle, I've read that too much water sends all their energy into the tops, not the bulb itself. Planted six or seven weeks ago, they've already sprouted about 8in and, unusually for sets, nearly all have come on.

Next to the onions is the pea patch. I've planted 40 or so petits pois plants, which were raised indoors at home to a height of about 4in. They are flanked by an improvised bamboo-cane support system. Like many men, I discarded the instructions before starting the job, and read later that I should have sown the peas at twice the density I've planted. So I've sown seeds—dried peas—in the gaps.

Then there's a patch for the dwarf beans, raised like the peas, in the house and transplanted into their own bed beside the peas. I've bought a job lot of thick 6ft bamboo canes and made a teepee frame over both peas and beans to give them something to climb on.

Up the other end is the calabrese, which has really shot up to about a foot high. Next are our rows of green and red cabbages. Cabbage is one of my favourite vegetables. Having been brought up on cabbage cooked the old-fashioned Irish way—boiled to a goo—I've since had an epiphany courtesy of Her Outdoors who showed me how good they taste with crunchy, semi-steamed leaves or lightly fried in butter. They also provide nutritious food for the effort and expense put in. We've got about forty planted.

Then come the brussels sprouts. Also bought as bargain

seedlings, they need plenty of room to flex their muscles as they grow quite tall and have been spaced suitably. Beside these are the carrot seeds. Thus far we haven't seen a single sprout yet and have real reasons to fear for their safety. Our research tells us that carrots are tricky on account of the fact that they're prone to the dreaded carrot fly, but also because they need a very fine soil. The roots tend to grow around obstacles like stones, thus producing misshapen multi-fingered roots. We raked our allotment patch and pain-stakingly removed a quarryload of stones, but I'm still not sure the ground is fine enough. We've also thrown a load of manure in with them to give them a start and help retain some moisture in the soil, but despite our waterings a couple of times in the week, the bed has now cracked in the heat, and the 340 or so expectant seedlings may have been baked alive.

I'm even considering covering the patch with newspaper or black plastic to keep the moisture in. I have since discov-ered that seeds of all sorts can sometimes stay below ground for longer than expected periods depending on temperature and water conditions and it's worth waiting before planting more. While I've had seed packets where half have failed to sprout, it's only in rare cases that the whole lot have been duds.

Finally, in the top right-hand corner, we've buried four rhubarb crowns in a trench filled with two bags of horse manure. Rhubarb is the allotment masochist, happy to take loads of crap. Our research says it likes moist ground and part-shade, which the scorching sun and our busy routine have denied it. It already looks as though we've lost one. In the coming weeks we'll dig more ground for the frost-fearing, sun-loving exotics, such as tomatoes, cucumbers, courgettes, dwarf beans, sweetcorn and an assortment of squash seeds we've bought, including butternut, Turk's Turban and pump-kins. We're also hoping to put in seeds for more everyday root veg such as swedes and parsnips. We'll be planting some of the above in the back garden at home, bits of which we've also dug for our food growing mission. But for now, all our energies go into watering rehab...and those of our residents still suffering from a serious drink problem.

Meantime back at the house, perhaps the most interesting looking of the seedlings we've been nurturing are the courgettes. You only get fifteen or so seeds in the packet. I'm told these guys will feed an army and that the courgette is one of the most productive plants there is.

But there's trouble with the courgettes, which I've planted individually in small plastic yoghurt cartons. They grow fast with huge bushy leaves and they sprawl all over the place. They like to tangle with each other. Worse is that in this aggressive juvenile form, they're also delicate buggers. Brush off one, and the stem snaps and they're gone. On account of this they're difficult to move around. As I was transplanting them outdoors, the wind blew, 'snap', I lost one. It blew again and I lost another.

I've managed to get nine of them sown in the garden into the plot we've prepared beside the shed. I've left plenty of space because the packet says these guys go large, 18in apart in this case. Three more went into the raised salad bed which I built in the back garden last year. Meantime I've sown the tomatoes against the back of the shed and more in containers on the sunnier patio. Some went to the back of the fence on one side. Last year I bought a few sections of logroll for about 40 quid. These are foot-high logs, split in two down the middle and then wired together to make a flexible boundary.

After forming them into a number of shapes and finally settling for a kidney (Her Outdoors says it's a big love heart, but it's a kidney), I pegged them into place with short wooden stakes. I filled it in with a mix of topsoil, compost and manure and levelled it all off. Into this went some herbs, chives and some lines of salad seeds.

Using the rake handle to make a line, I ran my finger alongside to make a shallow depression, sprinkled the seeds along, covered it up and marked them with one of those plastic stick-in-the-ground, picture markers that come with some packets. I need to know what's what when it starts to sprout. Sure enough, within days the lettuces, mixed leaves and rocket are above ground. I wish all growing was as easy as this.

As we push into June my food-growing project is teaching me that each change in weather and season brings on a new set of obstacles and challenges, new pests, new threats and new disasters. When they accumulate, it can be difficult not to develop a siege mentality. This, I will learn, becomes the toughest time of the year for the urban food grower.

Following a particularly bad run of late, I almost felt like throwing my hat at the whole thing. Because after weeks of drought it rained and overnight the slugs and snails descended on my crops. Worst hit were the courgettes, with the forces of the night reducing most of them to leafless stumps.

The second-last week of May brought freak winds which absolutely decimated the newly installed dwarf beans and petits pois, beat up the outdoor tomatoes and knocked over the seedling tent.

Lovingly weaned in the nursery (the kitchen table), the dwarf bean's leafy vines are everything that is fresh, lush, green and wholesome in edible nature. Right after these prize specimens went into Plot 34, one night of freak winds reduced them to leafless stalks flailing around the bottom of my cane frame. The sweetcorn was also completely creamed. Ditto the petits pois and more than half the squashes, even despite the fact that I used twigs to pin them down as protection against just such a disaster. Those tomatoes that had been placed outside were battered to within an inch of their lives and most shed nearly all their leaves from the shock.

But worst of all for morale was the seedling tent tip-over. The 5ft-tall framed tent with four shelves was hugely useful for starting off and hardening up tender plants. I put it outside on the patio along with hundreds of seedlings.

Recently, upon being summoned to inspect my younger brother's newly purchased version, which he'd left freestanding in the middle of his patio area, I advised him to put it somewhere where it would be protected from the wind and more importantly, to ballast it down with something to stop it from taking off in a gale.

My warnings met a wall of mumbled "yeah, yeah, yeahs" and he decided to leave his as it was, unsupported in relatively open ground. My own, on the other hand, had been well-ballasted and placed in a corner flanked by a heavy flowerpot. Unfortunately, the enclosed patio must have generated some sort of unnatural cyclonic lift because I woke up one morning to find the whole lot on its face, three or four feet from where it had stood. Of course my brother's stayed standing all through the season.

Thus overnight, four shelf-loads of 200-plus seedlings became a great big plastic-coated compost heap mixed through with dozens of empty (but neatly and meticulously labelled) pots and countless submerged seedlings.

In the same way that all babies look the same for a time, so too do most seedlings before they've added their second set of leaves. This is why you should always label your pots. I couldn't tell a Californian Wonder bell pepper from a Marmande French heritage tomato. There was nothing for it but to sit down and, one at a time, pot the whole lot up again, unidentifiable and otherwise. It took from midday until 7pm that Saturday.

Food growing really does have its setbacks but if anything it teaches you not to give up. Because just a few weeks on from this disaster the general outlook was good. While we had been running around putting out fires, plenty of plants had been quietly growing. The allotment and the garden are now making their first impact on our diet. Last week I grabbed a handful of fresh rosemary for the lamb dinner and went outside to fill a bowl with just-picked mixed salad leaves, different lettuces, mustard, rocket and chives. I replanted more beans and peas, and a new batch were by now fast pushing up. They tasted divine.

It has been just over three months since the project started and after wandering about and taking notes, here is the first quarterly progress report from Plot 34 and Plot 34a (my garden and windowsills).

Fruit trees

Six blackcurrants, three raspberries, three blackberries, two tayberries, two redcurrants, two gooseberries and one blueberry. All survived planting. We have a few raspberries coming on, but because all the fruit trees went in as juveniles, it will probably be next year before we get a proper crop.

Rhubarb

Four batches of tubers went in. One died. The remaining three have had their leaves holed by caterpillars, but are otherwise doing nicely.

Onions

A hundred onion sets are looking good—that is, when you can see them over the sea of chickweed that has risen up around them.

Red cabbage/green cabbage

The stars of the allotment. Bought in a bargain bucket in Lidl, they've surged to about 1ft in size. About twenty of each.

Brussels sprouts

Of the dozen plants that went in, about a quarter are starting to look ropey of late, with soft, droopy leaves. We're fearing the dreaded vine weevil or some other sort of root muncher.

Sweetcorn

Planted into Plot 34 and blitzed by wind. All 12 are brown bread.

Dwarf beans

All plants grown at home were destroyed by winds. We've planted the surplus bean seeds directly in the ground. They're coming up now, but might be too late to crop properly.

Petits pois

See dwarf beans.

Carrots

Two packets of seeds have been sown into a good-sized bed. Almost all have come up. They'll need to be thinned soon. Again, because they were sown late, there may not be enough in the growing season to get them beyond the baby carrot stage.

Squashes

Six types of squash seedlings are ready to go into Plot 34 including pumpkin, Turk's Turban and butternut. They are susceptible to being moved and at a risk of being eaten by slugs.

Lettuce and salad

There are six types of lettuce growing happily in the back garden in a raised timber bed that seems to have kept the slugs and snails away.

Herbs

Also in the raised bed, doing well and contributing regularly to the table are parsley, sage, rosemary, thyme, fennel and oregano. Window boxes have spearmint and lemon balm and chives.

Swiss chard

This one's the unexpected star. On just five plants, the leaves can be picked and picked again.

Tomatoes

Four types. The cherry wonder, Gardener's Delight, is already 3ft up around the shed and in two places on the patio. The three remaining Ailsa Craig regular tomatoes are also outside although still only 6in high. More Ailsas, the French Marmande variety, and an F1 hybrid are still in the seed tent and awaiting new homes.

Cucumbers

All plants bar one were wiped out in the seedling tent massacre. One crippled plant is struggling on in the raised bed.

Strawberries

Having had the strawberries obliterated by slugs before, these ones went into an upright terracotta container. Large fruits are on board and should be ripening soon.

Courgettes

Half of my dozen plants were wiped out by slugs, two more look like they won't make it. But four healthy courgette plants are enough to keep a family in these versatile fruits for four months. I have been fertilising the flowers with feathers in case the bees don't make it!

Peppers

Various hot chillies, jalapeños and bell peppers have been planted on the windowsills inside. Half have come down with some odd disease that has caused the leaves to break as if under attack from caterpillars. Having sprayed them with insecticide, I can confirm there's nothing eating them. Jalapeños are beginning to form.

We're getting there at last.

Chapter Three

God's Little Creatures...
And How to Obliterate Them

Under cover of night the forces of darkness swept in. Having waited patiently for the first rains, they finally slithered forth en masse from under the thickets and the destruction left in their wake was total. Casualties amounted to 90 per cent dead or maimed and where once there was life in its prime, nothing remained but a clutter of dissected limbs amidst intertwining trails of pus. Those left alive had been so badly mutilated that most would be lucky to pull through.

I stood surveying what was left of my 12 courgette plants in my first summer growing food and the sight was my introduction to what a full-on pest attack can do.

Before I took up urban food-growing I believed that nature's little creatures, or pests, took a little nibble here and a little nibble there from the occasional leaf. And sometimes they do. But now I know that far too often they're working away busily under the ground where you can't even see them, until one day your entire crop of one type completely collapses. Sometimes, as was the case with my courgettes, weather conditions contrive so that they just sweep in and decimate almost everything in one go. Believe me, the 'live and let live' philosophy most city-dwellers have with God's little creatures ceases to exist on the event of your first blitz. The gloves come off and you adopt a farmer's ruthlessness once you realise that pest attacks can wipe out weeks of your own hard work and effort. That's what makes the war personal.

God's Little Creatures...And How to Obliterate Them

In more than three years of allotmenteering I've learned that everyone who grows food should accept as a fact of life that around 20 per cent of their work will be for nothing—nothing but the pest's gob. You can actually drive yourself crazy if you don't accept this tenet from the beginning. Also you will need to accept that perhaps 10 per cent of your allotment or vegetable garden schedule should be devoted to battling pests, whether that means putting down sheets to prevent cabbage fly penetration or sieving through the soil in planters to remove the dreaded vine weevil. Because if you don't put in this work, you'll have nothing at all for your table.

As a youngster, I had the typical young boy's indifference to insects. I would torment them the way that only small boys do. I crushed woodlice. I'd sit by an anthill squashing each unfortunate as it came out. I singed them with sunbeams through a magnifying glass. My favourite was the old "how-spiders-get-deaf-if-you-pull-their-legs-off" joke. You pull their legs off, shout "Walk!" and of course... they don't. What is it about little boys that makes them want to play God(zilla) with insects? Perhaps it's inherited memory or instinct left over from times when children probably did spend long hours painstakingly removing insects from their family's crops.

But as an adult, I've tried to make amends for a childhood of wanton insecticide. Like most little boys, I changed my ways on growing up (well most of them) and until I started growing food, I was always the one who escorted the spider from the plughole safely outside before Her Outdoors could pelt it with a newspaper. Stupidly I've since realised that I've also escorted pot-plant-decimating vine weevil beetles back outside...to the patio!

—"There ya go little feller..."

I'd even been trying to instill a respect for insects into Plot 34's self-appointed Head of Secret Tunnels (HST). I rattle it off.

—"Why do we not squash ants for fun?"

—"Because they're God's creatures and they have a right to life just like everyone else."

—"Exactly."

So it was a touch difficult, then, when he recently caught me gleefully whacking a pile of snails, one at a time, into the field behind our garden using a spade as a bat.

—"What are you doing, Dad?"

—"Er, helping the snails get into the field."

—"Cool! Can I have a go?"

The other thing I've learned since starting an allotment is that it's so easy from an armchair viewpoint to be anti-chemicals and pesticides. Now I wonder how on earth did people eat at all before they were invented. And I thank God that we don't have locusts—yet!

In truth I really did try to stay away from the top-shelf chemicals and heavy-duty pesticides. I tried to avoid them where possible but I found myself resorting occasionally to drenching everything in nasty blue slug pellets while applying tiny pinpoint doses of Round Up to those dock plants whose roots seem to start in Australia.

It can't be good for the plants, and it's certainly not healthy for the resulting food. However, had I not used the blue slug pellets in particular, I know that there wouldn't be a basil plant, a lettuce, a courgette or a strawberry plant still standing. Pests start right in with the first produce of the year and from then on they just don't let up right through to winter.

It starts with the local gang of rag-tag magpies, who, in between winding up the cat and terrorising the local songbirds, pluck the unripe strawberries off the plants for the sheer hell of it. So you buy bird-netting, which keeps them off, but also makes picking the berries an exercise in escapology. Then the plants fall over rootless, their underground parts devoured by vine weevils.

My personal list of adversaries to date includes slugs, snails, cabbage flies, vine weevils, grubs, aphids, mites, caterpillars, birds, rats, rabbits and even cats. Then there's the ones you won't see arrive without a microscope—most notably potato and tomato blight spores. For every food plant, there's at least one pest, and some have several. Then there are the other diseases, club foot for root crops, onion white rot, and various assorted fungi and rots.

For three years I've had an ongoing battle with a long yellow maggot, which despite all my efforts, remained unidentified until very recently. It turned out to be the larva of the click beetle and it's commonly known as a wireworm. It has claimed at least 40 per cent of the crops in the raised salad bed each and every year by eating the root from below. The first you know about it is when the plant suddenly collapses, completely rootless. When I finally identified it, I discovered that it can live for up to five years in the soil. Looking for a solution to the infestation, I discovered that effective chemicals are either banned altogether or not safe to use with food plants. My only option was to sieve every inch of the soil and take them out by hand.

Years ago birds and carnivorous insects would have put paid to many of these pests, but thanks to man's sustained use of pesticides on crops, the insect numbers have been decimated and many birds no longer trust spots in which man grows. Chemical fertilisers have also put paid to nematodes in the soil, the tiny naturally occurring micro-worms which prey on so many grubs, maggots and larvae. This, and the concentrated nature of much commercial and garden growing, means the conditions have been made rife for an explosion in pests like vine weevil and wireworm. Not surprisingly, in recent years science has looked towards nematode-based products to provide an effective and natural solution.

Slugs and snails are right on the top of my deathlist. While other pests tend to focus on specific types of plants, the slimers will massacre almost anything and everything. In the past few years, weather patterns seem to have changed in these islands with long wet summers and wet mild winters, creating ideal conditions for them to move about and multiply. Because of this, I'm guessing their numbers have soared way above what is usual. Once I picked sixty full-grown snails from the foliage of one single patio climbing plant.

Usually the first nibbles here and there give you time to react with due reason, time to reflect that there's a place in the world for all of nature's creatures, time to consider that they're just doing their slimy, leaf-munching thing. It gives you time to conclude that the least they deserve is a happy death sloughing down in a beer trap, which is both humane and considerate to the environment. Indeed if I had to pick a way to go, the old falling-drunk-into-a-vat-of-beer scenario might just be it.

But the slug/snail attack our courgettes experienced in our first year when a night of rain followed a long drought was the invertebrate equivalent of the Tet Offensive and marked the abrupt end of my love affair with this particular tranche of God's creatures. After being confined to quarters by drought (they don't like sliding over dry ground), the buggers had obviously been very hungry indeed.

The slimers had probably done me out of 180 courgettes in just a couple of hours—and that's a whole lot of dinner!

Ironically, I had prayed for the rain. It hadn't spilled properly since St Patrick's Day, and the plants had been feeling the effects. Before the rain a few slugs and snails actually cracked and made a desperate break from cover for the seedlings sat across the sun-drenched patio, despite the dry ground—I'd noticed erratic shimmering trails ending in little dried-out corpses. The smell of young basil must have been driving them mental to cause the occasional banzai charges which saw them run out of juice and get frazzled.

But following the great courgette massacre, it was retribution time. "Sod the beer traps," I thought. "There's no way these bastards are going out singing."

I stormed indoors and broke open that arsenal of domestic toxicity—the under-sink cupboard—and reached right to the back, to grab the big, chunky bottle of old-fashioned, nasty, Day-Glo blue pellets. Off I went sprinkling showers of Dr Death all round the shed.

Now I can already hear the boos and hisses from the greener gardening brigade. Their main gripe against the slug pellet is its unnatural chemical make-up, and there's also some worry that they kill birds.

To those with hackles raised, I say this:

1. I don't care what you say, the environmentally friendly white pellets melt overnight in wet soil, a bit of a problem considering that wet soil is what most food plants require to grow in.
2. Tending beer traps equals bedpan duty in an old folks' home.
3. My cat also kills birds, so they don't tend to socialise in my garden anyway.
4. I have no intention of stalking slugs with a flashlight at midnight in order to bag them up and freeze them. (I also freeze my own sprouts and am just ditsy enough to make an erroneous selection from the freezer which could have truly disgusting consequences.)
5. Blue pellets work. Really well.
6. I like my beer far too much.

Now the greenies chorus: "Nematodes! Use nematodes!"

God's Little Creatures...And How to Obliterate Them

As I mentioned earlier, nematodes are a fast-developing form of biological warfare. The idea is that you buy a solution that spreads tiny living parasites in the soil. Nematodes climb inside the slugs through the little hole in their flank and eat them from the inside out. But while all that sounds suitably nasty, nematodes are also expensive, I have a clay soil which isn't convivial to the 'todes' and finally, they take a while to kick in. I needed instant and reliable firepower.

Sometimes I think humankind seriously underestimates the resourcefulness and ingenuity, if not the intelligence, of other creatures, not least slugs and snails. One recent damp evening, Plot 34's self-appointed Head of Secret Tunnels (HST) and I were busy on a snail roundup when HST suggests it would be good sport to race a couple of the little blighters. So we settle on the top of the circular mosaic patio table as a suitable racetrack and each of us then picks out our respective racers from the slew just gathered.

I choose a rather large one, while HST cleverly opts for a small, skittish animal, constantly looking about. We place our contenders in the centre of the table and decide that the winner will be the first snail to get his entire body over the finish line, the outer circle of the table's mosaic pattern. (The great thing about having a young son, by the way, is you get to do all this stuff over again.) HST puts his head down close to the two invertebrates, then shouts aloud: "Go!"

Slowly, obviously, my snail starts to come out of his shell. HST's snail doesn't do much, but his eyes, out on stalks, are still moving around like bobbers, sizing its options. My snail soon clears the starting spot. "Ha ha!"

HST's nag breaks into a sprint (snail version, you understand) towards mine, then begins to climb up onto the bigger animal's shell. When it's perched entirely on top, it stays there, as my snail goes for broke, apparently unaware of his passenger. Twenty minutes later, my gastropod is slithering across the finish line ten inches away. However, because HST's racer is smaller, and still perched on my racer's shell, he's actually the first one to get his entire body over the line and therefore he/she (they're hermaphrodites) wins.

HST is triumphant.

—"My snail is more cleverer than yours!" he shouts, and

declares that if he weren't a person, he'd like to be a snail, because snails "can do whatever they want except ride bicycles".

Now while there's no point in even suggesting our smaller snail deliberately planned its hitch-hiking tactic, there are many more simple feats you or I can witness that can only be explained through nothing other than gastropodic guile and genius in the extreme.

Later in the week, I'm in the plastic greenhouse (which we acquired in our second year a-growing) and I notice my three melon plants, previously in rude health, have now disappeared. Closer inspection reveals three stubby stalks at soil level. How did the critters get in? Surely they can't open zips?

The greenhouse is sealed all round, apart from a small hole in the plastic sheeting high up in the apex. I look around, and sure enough, there are more of them hiding around the place—three stuck out of sight under a tray of chillies. I dispose of them by dropping them into the watering can. That's nine quid they've just eaten. One melon eventually recovers, but we need at least two to cross-pollinate and produce fruit. Murphy's Law.

The next day, three of the courgette plants in the greenhouse are gone. The following day I lose a load of basil seedlings, transformed into a little forest of leafless stumps. Blue pellets time again.

HST's 'cleverest snail' theory continued to resonate in that little space at the back of my head from whence right stuff of instinct always whispers. How did they know where the tiny entrance hole is? Wouldn't they have had to slime all over the outside of the greenhouse to find it? Then they would have to find their way onto the racks and slide along thin-wire grids to get to the seedlings. What's more, how can they find their way straight to the melons which were their obvious preferred target as little else was touched on that first night?

When I next water the seedlings, the basil tray, despite containing a minefield of lethal blue dots, has a fat black slug right in the middle, munching away contentedly like a grazing friesian and surrounded by headless seedlings. How did the little git manage to pick his way through the pellets?

At night, when my entire crop of seedlings is most pressing on my mind, I have visions of snails abseiling down the inside of the greenhouse, targeting the best food spots. Thinking too much into this stuff can drive you bats!

God's Little Creatures...And How to Obliterate Them

During another warm summer's night, I'm sitting outside on the patio and I see a handful of slugs inching painstakingly up the outside plastic coat of the greenhouse tent to where the hole was six foot above the ground. And they're heading straight for it! They KNOW where it is! They REMEMBER! Or else they've been TELLING ONE ANOTHER! They couldn't ALL have found this one hole completely by accident. I mark mentally the space the lead slug covers in a half hour and then I do the math.

Based on my calculations, it will probably take this slug about six hours to get inside to the food and then get out again before sunrise. Maybe they can smell the plants? But surely not through one small hole the size of a 20c piece?

That night I go on to Google and search 'snails' and 'slugs' and 'intelligence'. And there it is, courtesy of none other than Charles Darwin, the expert on all things evolutionary.

I note that in his work *The Descent of Man*, published in 1871, Darwin described an experiment in which two snails that had been kept together for a time, one quite sickly (don't ask how they knew that!), were placed side-by-side in a small garden with very little greenery in it. After a while, the healthier one disappeared next door into a well-stocked garden. After a day's absence, it returned to its sickly friend, and both followed the same route back to the food stocks. The conclusion was that Snail One came back to tell Snail Two where the food was.

I knew it! The word is being spread in the slug world: all-night seedling party at the garden of No. 51—all you can eat, come on down! Later in bed, my imagination freewheels further and I am picturing a gastropodic Alfred Hitchcock *Birds* scenario. What if they turned on us? At least we'd have no problem getting away. But then maybe HST is wrong; maybe they really can ride bicycles!

Not surprising then that in the wake of the great Plot 34 snail-and-slug cull, they made an attempt on my life. Chowing on a tasty salad in a well-known city café eatery soon after, I almost choked on something crunchy. Giving it an investigative prod with the side of the tongue, I sensed... movement. Aaagh! I spat out a live snail, minus a load of shell—the bit I had just swallowed. Now here it was held between two fingers, all stretched out, dazed and peering at me with its stalk-top eyes. My stomach began to heave.

Given the legions of snails I'd been despatching, snail kind could perhaps be forgiven for trying to take me out with a kamikaze. ("Get into his mouth and wedge your shell in the windpipe. If they catch you bite on the blue pellet...")

Suitably shaken, I asked for the manager, a far-too-cool, well-coiffed, tanned-up David Ginola-type, complete with the mandatory Clairol shoulder bob.

—"Shows ze salad ees fresh," he offers.

I kept looking at him, incredulous, the snail held aloft, by now fully extended from its broken home and leaning towards Ginola as if it too awaited his response.

—"I heet zem all the time," he continues wryly, giving it all the Gallic disdain he can muster.

And after his particularly continental take on the old "or everyone will want one" joke, I thought: "Okay, Ginola, that's a decent freebie you owe me, 'cos the state of damn well near choking on a live mollusc in a reputable eatery is worth a whole heap of compo—should I thus feel inclined." Instead I smiled.

—"But I'd say you cook them first with garlic butter?"

The held out snail is drawing the attention of other diners.

—"Free coffees?"

I kept looking at him.

—"Free coffees ... and I take the salad off the bill?"

I nodded. Perhaps he remembered he was in Ireland, compo country. "Your honour, since the shock of ingesting the snail, my client has become depressed, suffers recurring nightmares, loss of sleep and appetite and has been forced to give up work and rollerblading." Off strode Ginola to the food counter to hand the slimy one over to the chef, presumably to marinate it up for his own lunch.

—"That was nice of him," says Her Outdoors sitting opposite, her eyes following Mr Fragrant while I wiped the goo from my gob.

Meantime, our conversation in our office has drifted towards Gordon Ramsay, who apparently has recently had his children out picking snails from the garden to be cooked. Yes, it seems he and the French do use ordinary garden snails for l'escargot in garlic butter. This nugget of information has me looking at the hundreds of dead empty shells piled up over at the courgette patch and wondering. Whether I could stomach such a solution is quite another thing.

God's Little Creatures...And How to Obliterate Them

Not far behind slugs and snails in the bumper book of pest bother are the assorted weevils and maggots which get themselves into the soil and eat your plants from the bottom up and from the inside out. The trouble with these guys is that you don't know they're there until your plants are pretty much dead. Usually they result from eggs laid by either beetles or flies of various types.

My nemesis on the patio is the vine weevil, a horrible little grub which tends to completely infest patio containers and eat roots. They're particularly fond of strawberries and, as the name suggests, vines. Most recently, my valued grape vine, which seemed to be getting into its stride after two slow early years, stopped budding all of a sudden. The answer to the problem was to be found tucked in among its support sticks—a load of salt-and-pepper, gray-black beetles with big feelers, the vine weevil adult. The roots were eaten and a vine, for which I had paid about 20 quid, was now dead.

A little while ago, I was emptying out a window-box container full of compost which had held chillies in the previous year. I was breaking up the compost on the ground beside the garden strawberries when to my horror, it revealed itself to be full of fat white grubs. Tipping half a century of vine weevils at this spot was akin to slipping a dozen piranha in with a goldfish. I had to reload up the compost, picking out the white grubs one at a time with Her Outdoors' 'good' tweezers (if you're reading this, remember that I did boil it afterwards and whatever you say, it's still perfectly usable). Then I noticed the more difficult-to-spot brown ones which had almost made the transformation into adult beetles. In the end I half filled a large yoghurt carton and counted sixty-seven from a container which had four plants.

But in some ways I've also been lucky. Thus far I've managed to dodge an attack of carrot fly which, by the hushed tones in which it's described by more seasoned allotmenteers, must be quite a blitz. Like the cabbage fly, its carroty cousin can similarly render an entire carrot crop useless from the root up. Experienced growers seem gob-smacked that I've managed to go three years without a visit. Personally I put it down to three factors. First our allotment is high on a windswept site which might not suit flies, which like to hover at a low level. Secondly, I have learned to always grow onions beside my carrots and whenever I pull up some onions I crack up the foliage and drag them back and forth over the carrot tops. I have read in a number of books that carrot fly hate the smell of onions and most sources recommend the 'companion growing' of onions alongside carrots. Companion planting is one of the more traditional handed down pest control methods learned from nature which involves situating two or more plant types together in order to provide benefits for both which they wouldn't have otherwise had on their own.

The more experienced growers at the complex tend to plant marigolds around crops vulnerable to aphids because aphids hate the smell of them and, secondly, they attract hoverflies which in turn eat the aphids.

I read that it's best to sow carrots as thinly as possible so you don't have to thin them out for overcrowding when they grow larger. The carrot fly can smell broken carrot foliage literally from miles away.

I have been less fortunate, however, with both the vine weevil and the cabbage fly. Cabbage is one of those plants, like strawberries, which seems to draw in just about every pest there is. In three years of growing cabbage I haven't had an unmolested crop yet, excepting the inedible-to-all-species, black rubber things I got at Lidl. In Year One all the regular cabbages were wiped out completely. The pest in question looks like an ordinary house fly and it lays its eggs in the soil at the base of the cabbage. Once they hatch, the little white maggots burrow down in numbers and attack the root of the cabbage with the end result that they get flat looking as if someone let the air out, and simply fall over, minus their root. The little buggers can produce three generations of egg-laying flies in one season. So in my second year, being aware that the fly would be hatching from the old cabbage patch, I moved my cabbages to another bed. Crop rotation is well and good, but given that the pest in question is airborne, it can surely cover a 30ft jaunt to my cabbages.

Internet research suggests 'cabbage collars' at a quid fifty a packet. Yes folks, collars for cabbages—discs made of loose plastic with a hole in the middle for the cabbage to grow through. Surely this is taking a passion for growing to ridiculous degrees? I will, however, admit to digesting this concept and then spending a single evening cutting out cabbage collars from black plastic binliner sacks. Instead I settled on the alternative of a roll of weedproof overlay material, a black cloth sold in garden centres which goes on the ground, lets the water through, retains it, keeps weeds down, but more importantly, it stops the cabbage fly maggot from burrowing down to the roots. I laid it on the ground, anchored it and planted the cabbage through tight enough holes in the sheet. And it did its job.

The cabbages soon grew fat and heavy and became the pride of my allotment. But having sorted out the enemy below, I forgot completely about the massed airborne threat. I arrived to my allotment one day in July, exactly a week after a neighbour was admiring them, to find all of them completely shredded to ribbons. The suspects? Freddie Krueger making coleslaw? White stains on the fence showed evidence of a very large bird attack indeed, most probably crows or pigeons who are known to have a taste for cabbage.

Bird netting was then purchased and installed above the savaged cabbages at yet more cost. In time, in reaction to being partially shredded, my cabbages mutated and each grew between two and four new heads each on the same stem, albeit smaller, stranger, but still perfectly edible. The bottom line though is that the cost of seedlings, the protective carpet below and the roof above meant they had been far more expensive to grow than just going to the greengrocers and buying them.

Strawberries too are a favourite target of everything that lives. The plump crimson berries are Mother Nature's fruit seducers so it's not surprising that they have many fans. They're put upon first by the raggle-taggle magpies who pick off the unripened green berries just for sport. When they do turn red, the strawberry season opens for other birds, slugs, snails, wasps, ants and weevils. You put a load of protective netting over them and then, as I said before, you need a degree in escapology to pick the ripe ones.

Our dozen plants, which were nicely planted up in a multi-pocketed can, simply shrivelled and died thanks to the efforts of an army of vine weevils. That was 30 quid's worth of plants gone straight into the guts of the evil weevils.

It's particularly disheartening with strawberries simply because they're the first food crop of the year—the first signs that your efforts have been fruitful. Losing them is like training hard for months for an important match and then being sent off in the first minute of the game. Before the forces of pestdom did their

damage I had managed to take two beautiful and fulsome looking strawberries inside. I handed one to Her Outdoors who rinsed
it, popped it into her mouth and then gushed forth, sighing about
the perfect flavour, chewing, savouring, oohing and aahing, and
then swallowed it.

Having the one with a slight blemish, I decided to shuck the
bad bit off with a knife before indulging. But the cut uncovered
a ball of tiny green caterpillars inside who, upon realising the jig
was up, scrambled off their strawberry and leapt to the floor like
the proverbial rats. As I chased them around with a piece of cardboard and a plastic cup, Her Outdoors was already running to
the loo, hand over mouth. That's another side of growing your
own food—thanks to the pests, some of it is likely to contain
unexpected additional proteins, a factor which can easily deter
the overly squeamish.

On one hard day's digging at the allotment I had to rub my
eyes to prove I wasn't seeing things. But there was absolutely no
doubt about it—the tuna, sweetcorn, lettuce and onion roll I had
packed for my lunch had leapt out of its plastic carrier bag and
appeared to be making a break for it. From where I had been digging, I heard the bag rustling and looked up to see it bouncing
about. Then the bag fell sideways, and the roll leapt out and
began moving up the hill in stiff little increments.

After hours of hard labour in the blazing sun, I hoped this was
heat exhaustion, because the alternative was some sort of con-
temporary gingerbread-boy scenario which was just too much to
deal with given the week I'd been having.

After wiping out the sweat that was stinging my eyes, I saw
the brown fur and determined the true force behind my peram-
bulatory panini. A dirty rat! I lobbed a stone. "Gerroff!" I shouted, hoping he would realise I was far bigger than him (rats and
wasps seem to have a serious problem with interspecies size dif-
ferential). He scampered about 20ft, stopped and looked back
like he was fixing to return for another go. My banana was half-
eaten, and the roll, a few feet away, had the top nibbled off it, but
at least the custard creams were intact.

This wasn't the first time I'd met our new allotment roomie. A
week earlier, I had noted a lot of rustling from our neighbour's
wooden compost bin and tool store. The incumbent revealed
himself to me, sitting there brassily in the open and sniffing the

air, as if to say: "Hi neighbour, I've just moved in to No. 35. We must do lunch some day."

Our *Rattus norvegicus* seems slightly larger than average: about 18in from nose to tail end, and probably weighing in at a pound and a quarter. In cities they tend to be smaller due to the confined spaces they move in. In the open country, they are creatures of the field and will roam further and eat more.

However, when it comes to getting rid of them, be warned: rats are the world's greatest survivors. They weathered a whole mess of atomic bombs on the Bikini Atoll island in the Pacific when the Americans were running their nuclear tests in the fifties. That's how tough they are to get rid of.

Unlike snails, it's been conclusively proven by science that rats do "tell" their buddies fairly complicated stuff—one of the reasons why exterminators keep having to change the poisons. ("Whatever you do, don't eat the red ones!") And recently scientists proved that rats are among the few animals, along with humans, dolphins and some primates, which are capable of metacognition—the ability to think about thinking ("I think, therefore I am?").

Getting rid of a rat means you have to start thinking like one. A survey of some older growers reveals the best solution. I need to ask a hardware shop about a current poison that the rats haven't already heard about. Then I need to buy or procure a length of pipe or plastic tubing and a jam jar. I need to get some masking tape and attach the jar to one end of the pipe. The pipe prevents birds, rabbits and other, larger animals being harmed. The idea is that you leave the pipe out for a few weeks along a route you know the rat uses. The rat then becomes familiar with it. Only then place the poison in it.

Poisons are cruel as rats die slowly, so it might be worthwhile looking at some other traditional methods. Coat a sheet of cardboard or wood with a non-hardening glue or gum (my granddad used a substance called Dack), and bait the centre with butter or bacon. Be prepared to then dispose of the trapped rats humanely.

Back at the allotment, a neighbour tells me that our rat has already been attacking his potatoes. It tunnels horizontally into the furrows, and filches out the spuds, rolling them off to eat them under a cracked upturned flower pot. Now that he mentions it, a number of my carrots were attacked, but I had blamed the bunnies. Did the rat intend to frame the rabbit? Rabbits, of course, are another prime pest on allotment complexes and have wiped out large numbers of plants at those plots located at the very top of the hill. Rabbits hoover up just about everything green on the surface and can naturally dig for what's underneath. It takes chicken wire sunken a foot or so under the ground to keep the burrowing raiders out.

Apart from my sandwiches, rats filch one fifth of the entire world's food produce every year, putting them right on top of the global wanted list. And allotment complexes will always have them—so it's a matter of control rather than elimination.

As the day wore on, I decided Mr Rat had to go. I had a bottle of Roundup, a vicious weedkiller which I had deployed only on the most stubborn of dock plants. The label was full of nasty symbols and red Xs so I scanned down the warning list: small children etc... wash hands...poisonous to... pets and animals. Bingo! I drenched my last custard cream in the stuff and put it under a birdproof sheet of plastic. Let's see if he can really take the biscuit! Next day, no sign of ratty, nor the cream-sandwich biccy and pretty soon I'm starting to feel a bit guilty. As I water the plants, there is not a sound from the box in the corner and I imagine him withering away down some dark hole or other, and feel even guiltier.

Until I make my way back to the water tap, and there he is, sitting on his hind legs, sniffing the air. "Howdy neighbour, got any more of those fine custard creams?" he seemed to say.

Our cat is a useful deterrant to those rats which otherwise might have a go at our compost bin. But he was far too busy making a pest of himself around the salad bed. Oscar (named because when we got him he was wild) is so big that people stop in the street to exclaim "Good God is that a cat!" He's the sort of size that generates those big-jungle-cat-at-large myths. About twice the size of some cats, he's unafraid of most dogs and sunbathes in the middle of the road.

And because cats bury their faeces, my raised bed with lovely crumbly compost is Villeroy & Boch for feline ablutions, a fact not lost on Oscar with his outsized contributions.

Long wondering how a half a dozen small lettuces were being removed from the salad bed time after time, I looked out the kitchen window one day to see the cat crouching mid-business in a freshly dug hole that cut across at least two rows of mixed-leaf salad plants.

A loud knocking on the window vigorously accompanied by loud delivery of assorted expletives served only to raise that look of abject disdain cats tend to deploy when a meagre human dares to try and cramp their style—he sniffed, looked away and continued right along with what he was doing.

An internet search showed that there are various methods traditionally used to deter cats from browning off in your greens. I tried three, none of which worked. The time-honoured sprinkling of pepper and scattering of orange skins (cats supposedly hate citrus) both failed. So too did placing plastic bottles filled with water all over the place—the preferred front lawn deterrent of ultra-vigilant Neighbourhood Watch types who keep the factory plastic on their sofas and confiscate children's trespassing footballs.

The bottle gig is based on the idea that cats don't like their own reflections, or some such twaddle. But bottle-loving busybodies should watch out—a news item I found in the same online search from the *Japan Times* told of a man who burned his house down on account of a 'nekoyoke' (translation: scare-cat bottle). Apparently it focused the sunlight much like a magnifying glass into a concentrated beam on the curtains on the inside living room window of his house, and set them on fire. As unlikely a story as the 'nekoyoke' is a solution methinks.

In my case, the answer did come Japanese style, but from a bumper packet of two hundred barbecue bamboo skewers. Thus, ensconced in a giant log-lined porcupine fortress, the salads are growing magnificently—particularly the mixed leaves. Make sure you keep children well away from it though.

What you might find surprising is that plants can also catch pests indoors. I've had caterpillars and mites on my windowsill plants among other things. The chillies in the house got some sort of tiny spider mite that covered them in webs and caused the leaves to close while those in the greenhouse got a bad dose of aphids. One day there were a few, the next day they were clinging on in thick layers, aphid on aphid. This is because aphids are the world-champion reproducers. Some have the ability to reproduce telescopically—like Russian dolls with the baby in gestation already having a baby inside it and that baby already having a baby inside it and so on.

Sometimes incorrectly called greenfly, they are the vampires of the pest world. One or two don't do much damage, but get a few hundred on the job and pretty soon the leaves will corkscrew and the plants get sick. I use a spray of soap and water to get rid of the suckers.

Back outside again and aphids are rampant, particularly in warmer weather. Now I was surprised to learn that some people try to deal with aphids in their gardens by ordering ladybirds (which eat vast numbers of aphids) off the internet. The ladybirds come by post in a box and cost about 15 quid sterling for 25 if you buy them in the UK. Now I don't care how green and earth-lovey this concept is, anybody who pays cash for a box of flying insects and then releases them into a garden needs their head examined. Short of enclosing the whole garden in a tight mesh enclosure net, what's to stop them all just flying away? Despite this rather glaring flaw in the imported ladybird logic, apparently there are still plenty of customers out there for the mail order packs.

Instead of purchasing them on eBay there are plants you can grow to encourage them and other beneficial insects to come into your garden and stay in residence. The other visitors you are aiming to attract are lacewings (their green grubs look like little crocodiles), hoverflies and wasps. A mixture of sunflowers, marigolds, fennel, dill, coriander and mint will keep them coming.

Pretty soon as a grower you notice that the insects you hated (like wasps) suddenly become your allies, while those you always loved, like the cabbage white butterfly, turn mortal enemy. Though the lovely flouncy white butterfly might bring a surge to your heart as it soars and flutters about on a summer's day, I am more likely to batter it to a butter pat.

Because while they might bring a lift in your spirits, they also bring squillions of eggs to my greens which in turn hatch into an army of caterpillars capable of eating plants so fast, you can actually see the leaves disappearing before your eyes.

So when help comes unexpectedly you welcome it. One day in the garden myself and HST were confronting half a century of scoffing caterpillars when, from above, the cavalry soared in, attacking like tiger-striped apache helicopters. Three wasps swooped in on the stricken calabrese and began plucking the caterpillars from the plant, one at a time, biting their heads off, and dropping the still writhing carcass to the ground. Within minutes, three wasps had eliminated the whole lot. When it comes to insecticide most foul, wasps leave any juvenile Godzilla in the ha'penny place.

While a wry humour may often prevail between fellow growers on the subject of insect attacks, blight is never a joking matter, perhaps because of our history and the 1847 potato famine. Take a look at the nineteenth century painting by Daniel MacDonald, *Discovery of the Potato Blight*, an image often displayed in history books. It shows the reaction of a family to finding rot in their year's store of harvested potatoes. A young mother is sobbing uncontrollably, her infant dropped to one side, her husband is blank and numb, the older patriarch, having experienced it before, seems to have lost his mind completely and is appealing skywards to heaven. Even the youngest children depicted seem to understand the consequences for their family, which history tells us was starvation or immigration.

The Famine is the one event we all remember from our school history curriculum. Its influence and inherited memory still pervades in the national psyche 150 years later. As children we're told it's a sin not to clear our plates. As a nation we are consistently among the highest per capita donators to famine causes abroad.

It ultimately halved a population of 8.2m to 4.3m and scattered our people around the planet. Before the event, Ireland was home to one third of the population of these two islands while sixty years later, that figure lay at just 10 per cent.

As a city slicker, encountering a blight for the first time brought an unexpected chill to my bones, not least because the damage was so complete up at our allotment complex. Even without the poignant history behind it, there's something seriously macabre in the workings and effects of *Phytophthora infestans*.

From the top of the hill, the scene below was one visibly pocked with devastation. In the first year I didn't grow any spuds, being put off by the talk of 'chitting', 'earthing up' and 'first and second earlies'. But because planting potatoes is a recognised way of breaking up new growing ground, most allotment holders had not only planted them, but some had taken up more than half their allotment with spuds. Where the bushiest lines of potato vines once stood, there are now masses of grey and black withered stalks and in some spots where the potatoes had been dug, the deathly awful smell of rotted tubers.

The guy next door to me had split his crops between potatoes and cabbage and, because blight followed cabbage fly on our complex, almost all of his crops were now completely inedible. This is the sort of complete wipeout that many food growers dread.

Our plot remained mostly intact in its first year, with some of our crops hit hard but most doing well for us. We grew potatoes the following years and got blight every single time, despite the use of the traditional copper-based fungicide.

But I did learn something from our neighbours, who, as soon as blight hit other plots, immediately cut their potato foliage right down to ground level. The trick is to catch the blight in time given the fact that it only takes three or four days to completely corrupt your crop. We used this tactic a number of times with the result that our potato crops were undersized but we never lost one.

Allotmenteering helps to bring home to you the notion of food as a living thing that needs nurturing and protection in its own right, and we sometimes forget that, like all life, plants are just as prone to their sicknesses and pandemics. Small disasters can be taken on the chin, but larger wipeouts like blight are tough on morale as well as on the pocket and if you want to grow food, you will need to accept the pest and disease factor.

What it drives home to the newbie food grower is not only a newfound respect for food, but also an understanding of the precarious existence of those less fortunate in the world who, like our ancestors, rely on the success of their crops for absolutely everything.

Allotment Diary, Year One

Late June/July

By late June in Year One, our five surviving courgette plants from the great slug-and-snail massacre had sprouted big and bushy in the garden. And in contrast to their delicacy upon transplanting, they had transmogrified into big, bushy, spiny monsters with leaves the size of saucepan lids and little thorns that give a nasty sting if you catch on them. Last year when our garden courgettes reached this point they began flowering and shooting out fruits at such a rapid pace that we'd trouble eating them all despite ploughing them into all manner of stews and bologneses.

So far this year, there's been plenty of flowers still but no courgettes. We also noticed that there aren't too many bees either. Some blame a parasite that has hit the population hard all over the world. Bees, of course, are needed for pollination. Each plant produces some male flowers and some female. Pollen needs to be taken from the male to the female to fertilise it. On a courgette, the female flowers are supposed to have a bulge underneath, while the males do not. When the flower is properly fertilised, the plant becomes 'pregnant' and the bulge blows up into a courgette. Sometimes in days.

If the flower isn't fertilised, it just drops off. The flowers can be eaten raw in salads and, in the Mediterranean, growers like to batter and deep fry them. But with our flowers continually falling off and still no sign of fruits appearing, I'd taken it upon myself to do the job of the bees—with a paintbrush.

The tricky bit is the weather, which has been pretty grim of late and dark days keep the flowers closed up tight. The rain has been pelting down, which makes matters worse again because it knocks off the flowers before the job is done. It took a week or two of running out in the rain to tickle flowers before they closed up—but finally the fruits of my labours appeared and before long, we hit pay dirt.

Later that month we were caught off guard by the broccoli, or calabrese to be precise—broccoli is purple and has much smaller heads attached while calabrese (which we call broccoli) is green and comes in big heads the size of your hand.

We hadn't been up to the allotment for two weeks because of poor weather and car trouble. Then, suddenly, from being about as big as buttons, the heads had swollen to the size of saucers, and some were starting to go to seed. Calabrese heads are in fact immature flower buds. When they 'go to flower' or 'to seed' they become fragmented and inedible. What this meant was that the whole lot had to be cut then and there—in another week they'd be useless. My research tells me that cutting the main heads should spur the stalks to produce again, with numerous smaller ones. Many plants which have their seed or flower heads removed prematurely (for the plant) will strive to produce again in the same way that deadheading roses or dahlias brings on more blooms.

Our self-appointed Head of Secret Tunnels was eager to help with the harvest. As I cut, he followed me and bagged it up. Afterwards he asked for some calabrese for his dinner. Job done. One of the aims of involving him in our allotment was to educate him about fresh food because he's a particularly green-shy eater.

The two sacks of fresh calabrese mark a major victory for Plot 34. It's expensive stuff to buy and it's also very good for you indeed. But now we've come up against another problem—that of storage. Calabrese is one of those foods that perishes quickest, turning flat just a day or two after being picked. I learn that to counteract bumper crops like this arriving all in one go, you should 'stagger' planting by sowing some seeds one week, more seeds the next and so on. Unfortunately I'm forced to give away a load of our calabrese because there's no room in the fridge-freezer for all of it. And we're going to have to buy a chest-freezer as more crops mature and we require more freezing capacity to store them—another unforeseen expense. But our calabrese tastes divine. The two sacks must be worth about a hundred quid or more at current prices and we only paid a fiver for the juvenile plants in Lidl. Now this is what being an allotment holder is all about!

As we push into July, the carrots are doing really well without too much interference and they taste great. Everyone who's been given a batch as a present enthusiastically agrees. Straight from the ground is the best way to eat them, after a rinse under the allotment tap.

The blue/black cabbage is royal, the onions, laid out in raised furrows, are expanding nicely, and the pumpkin plants are spreading out and blooming with a vengeance. The petits pois will soon be ready for harvesting.

We're also relieved of the continuous remedial work of digging and the constant care we gave those less successful plants whose slow demise occupied us when we weren't busting sods. The casualties have included the exotic squashes, the wind-blitzed corn, tattered green beans, and the badly eaten green cabbages (cabbage fly) and sprouts (caterpillars).

This enforced downtime, along with the accompanying restlessness, has shown me how much exercise I've been getting since March—without knowing it. I'm fit and missing the endorphins of the heavy digging and weeding we've been putting in these last few months.

As July nears its close, our tomatoes are not doing so well. To me, tomatoes are the best example of why it's great to grow your own food. So it is disappointing that, in this erratic year of drought followed by torrential downpours, outdoor tomatoes are well behind.

Even though I gave away bags of tomatoes from last year's crop, they still lasted me until February this year. They started cropping in July, and the last usable fruit was picked off the vines in early November. We froze the small cherries, and cooked the larger varieties into gallons of pasta sauce, which was then frozen. The green ones left on the vine in December went to my uncle, who made them into a spicy chutney.

But in this awful growing year I'm still a long way from chutney, so once again, it's on with the raincoat and out with the watering can to get a drink in a downpour to those tomatoes I've got sheltering under the jutting house gutters.

Meantime the lovely green cabbages, which had been doing so well, went down to the cabbage fly larvae after we'd eaten only one or two of them. A complete wipe-out. Every one that I pull up has its roots in various stages of decay.

Chapter Four

Food For Thought

After growing a huge variety of food at home and on my allot-ment, I realised it all tasted so much better than any shop-bought produce. I sought out relevant newspaper and magazine articles and I scoured the internet to find research, studies, university papers and reports from all over the world on the subject. As I ploughed through the material, a disturbing picture began to build of how we have changed commercial food-growing through the last forty years or so and how we have changed our treatment of the food plants.

Primarily my research showed me how big business has applied a series of processes and treatments to our grown food through the past two generations, which have not only dulled the taste and the nutritional value of our bought food, but in the long run, may ultimately threaten our very future. Apart from the arti-cles I sourced on specialist clippings websites which require paid membership, most of this information is widely available to any-one with a home computer and a willingness to look for it.

Sit through the dinner scene from the schlocky 1973 sci-fi movie, *Soylent Green*—perhaps the first film to ask where unre-strained consumerism and global warming might lead.

Based on the Harry Harrison novel *Make Room! Make Room!*, Richard Fleischer's cult curiosity is set in 2022, on an overcrowded Planet Earth where global warming, big industry and the destructive farming practices employed by commercial food-producing multinationals have long ago destroyed most of the plant and animal life on earth. As a result, the population is reduced to living on a ration of colour-coded vitamin and protein wafers manufactured by one all-powerful multinational, Soylent Inc. Only the extremely rich can afford to eat 'real' food.

One of the film's most memorable scenes is when the corrupt cop, Thorn (played as hammy as only Charlton Heston can), and Roth, his septuagenarian sidekick (Edward G. Robinson), sit down to savour a haul of 'real' food that Thorn has stolen from a rich businessman's house. The stash comprises two small, sad-looking apples, a single tiny slice of beef, a soggy stick of celery and some brandy.

But with real food being such a rarity, the pair are so delighted with their sorry haul that they sniff ecstatically along the length of the floppy celery stick as if it were the finest Cuban cigar. Each mouthful of their meal is smelled, the aroma savoured. Then it's chewed slowly by both with an accompaniment of eye-rolling, much vocal appreciation and high-fiving. Thorn, the younger man, has never eaten real food in his life and the meal sparks the much older Roth to yearn for the "old days when you could just go out and buy an egg".

When I saw that film a few years ago I didn't see too much difference between the sorry stick of celery on the screen and the stuff I'd just bought in a convenience-chain shop that day. The shop's answer to my complaint about its soggy celery was: "If you don't like it, don't buy it." My option: buy the rotten food or do without. The vegetables amounted to little more than borderline compost.

Try returning a rotten bag of potatoes to the supermarket in which you bought it. A decade ago, the supermarket manager would be gushing in his regret and would not only replace your potatoes on the spot, but would also be liable to give you a voucher to compensate for the inconvenience. He or she would probably thank you for pointing out the problem and assure you that the supermarket would do its best to ensure that this didn't happen again.

Today if you bring back that same bag of rotten tubers, a pimply-faced teenager grunts and points back at the same display, urging you to replace it yourself. There's a perfectly good chance you'll simply exchange one bag of rot for another. Because things have changed.

Food For Thought

Ryanair was one of the first big companies to begin a mass corporate ejection of the old 'customer is king' tenet. When Michael O'Leary boldly declared that Ryanair would be charging a fee for the handling of wheelchairs used by the disabled, professional PRs everywhere winced and held their breath. Ryanair initiated a long succession of other blatant measures which almost seemed intended to rile customers, even at one point threatening to charge them to use the bathroom on flights. But Ryanair lost no business whatsoever. The airline realised that it ran a budget business where price was the main consideration and its prices were so attractive that travellers would continue to fly with Ryanair regardless of what was served up to them. Big business everywhere sat up and took notice.

The new philosophy became: "So long as you offer a cheaper product, you can treat your customers as you like." The thinking spread across a rash of big companies in cost-led businesses in all fields. All realised almost overnight that massive costs could now be slashed and vast amounts saved, particularly in the realm of customer services and PR.

A friend of mine who works for one of the largest grocery retail chains in Europe has been a fresh food specialist on the supermarket floor for more than twenty years. He explained to me what's been happening.

—"Supermarkets used to employ people because they had a specialised knowledge in greengrocery. This was something you had to learn over time and pick up by experience. Each type of fruit or vegetable has different handling and display needs. The shop needs to know to store each item properly and how to place it on the shelves so it doesn't bruise or rot. There are some food types that you shouldn't put together on a display and many you shouldn't ever put under air conditioning. Berries should be stacked diagonally so they don't crush. Some foods can't reach freezing temperature and others need to be kept cool at all times. But supermarkets have been busy cutting wages, costs and conditions. What it means is that most of the people who work at greengrocery these days actually know very little about these things. Some in fact know nothing at all about greengrocery."

He says that each year more food is sourced from further and further away. The decision, based on cost, means that the food usually arrives in poorer condition than produce sourced closer to the outlet. He asserts that he has even been aware of produce which had already been frozen in another country, then shipped here, thawed out again, and served up on the shelves as 'fresh'.

But you don't need a Deep Throat in the supermarket/convenience shop business to realise all this. You can go and see this for yourself any day.

I have inspected carrots on display in leading brand supermarkets which have more black spots than a Dalmatian and are so soft that you can bend them end to end without breaking them. I've seen addled avocados with sturdy Mohawks of fur mould. I've purchased potatoes so full of rot that you have to throw half the bag's contents away. I've bought tomatoes which look lush and red at the checkout, only to see them collapse in themselves in the fridge within 48 hours.

But then there's the opposite to rapidly perishing foods—the stuff that eerily refuses to rot. Conduct a little experiment to see what I mean. Buy some of those blown-up, heart-shaped strawberries at the supermarket, the pumped-up ones that look like they're on steroids and seem about to explode. Place them in your fridge and leave them there. Check them two weeks later, and what do you notice? They're still there, still blown up and bloated. They're not rotting away. There are certain types of Chinese pears, rounded and more watery than European versions, which I have had in my fridge for three months without any sign of degeneration. Why is this? Perhaps, like many fresh fruits, they've been shot with ionising radiation, a process which kills all microbes, bacteria and fungi, but which also arrests the natural perishing process. It's just one of the methods used to prolong shelf-life in modern fresh food processing.

When fruits or vegetables leave the ground or their host plant, they're supposed to start dying. Degeneration is a natural part of what they do. If a human body behaved like this, we'd call it a miracle and put it in a glass box on public display. In short, food which fails to rot within a given time is even more unnatural than that which is already perished when you buy it.

Despite the fact that fresh food can usually be grown in better conditions only a few miles away from the point of sale, labour and other costs mean that today it's often far cheaper for a supermarket to import much of their food from hundreds, and sometimes, thousands of miles away. Labour has, in recent decades, become the highest cost of food production. This means that in the quest for tighter margins and higher profits, the super-markets have squeezed local home-based growers more and more, putting them out of business one after another because workers in less-well-off countries with poorer labour conditions can produce the same food, albeit at a lower quality, for far cheaper.

But again we only have ourselves to blame because we as customers always put cost first, without considering what we might be actually getting on our plates for the savings we make. We still believe that if it looks okay, then a carrot is a carrot is a carrot.

Not only do we want our fruit and veg cheap, we also demand that they come completely unblemished and in a uni-form shape and size. A commercial cabbage grower in north Dublin (who recently went out of business) told me that in his last year of trading, the supermarkets would not accept his cab-bages because they were slightly undersize. It had been a poor year, the growing season had been shortened and all his cab-bages happened to be that size. In the end he was forced to cut his prices and offer two cabbages for the price of one in order to have them accepted.

Each year the supermarket had cut his margins, as they did with other indigenous growers, until the cost of paying a labour force to harvest and process his cabbages became more than he could actually earn. Now his fields, only miles from most of the biggest food shops in Dublin, are going fallow and the same supermarket chain is bringing in its cabbage from much further afield.

A grower of carrots I talked to confesses that the supermar-kets have squeezed his margins so tight that he has been forced to forgo correct treatment of his soil. He doesn't have the money to pay enough people to properly fertilise and replenish it.

—"What it means is that the following year's carrots won't have the same mineral and nutritional content in them even though, to all intents and purposes, they might look exactly the same. I don't blame the purchasers from the supermarkets, because they lose their jobs if they don't get the same margins as everyone else."

So who do you blame?

As with the lead-in period to the world banking system collapse, everyone is busy just holding up their corner, doing what they have to do to keep their market share, and to keep their jobs. Supermarkets rightly claim they are serving the customer's demand for cheaper produce. Customers equally argue that they need to shop around and buy cheap to make a little money go a longer way.

But as our grower points out, 'the carrot is a carrot' logic just doesn't stand up any more. The reality is that 'fresh' food is becoming so much more debased as time goes on because supermarkets continue to look for cut after cut on behalf of their shareholders—and their customers. They have also reached a point where a handful of chains so dominate the market that they can dictate pretty much what they want to the country's growers. Like Ryanair, because they supply the cheapest food around, they reached the point long ago when they started also dictating to their customers—the point when there is no longer any risk of losing custom if they lower the standard of the food on their shelves. This is where my soggy celery, blackened carrots and hirsute avocados come in.

Lately we've seen Irish potato growers break into a meeting of senior Tesco executives to protest that the chain is buying more of its spuds from outside the country. The very fresh food we eat most of, and for which our climate is most ideally suited, is now being imported. So are Irish farmers ripping us off? Are Tesco right to go abroad for spuds if they are cheaper to the consumer? And what difference does it make anyway if our spuds come from Dublin, Lancashire or Timbuktu?

According to David Joachim, co-author of *The Science of Good Food*, 'fresh' broccoli has usually lost 80 per cent of its vitamin C levels from the point of harvest to the point of purchase. Canned food has usually lost more than half its nutritional value due to heating processes and chemicals used.

As the food we eat starts to come from further and further away, those who make a living from cooking good food have responded. The deterioration in the quality of 'fresh' food sold in shops and markets is the reason why so many world famous chefs have in recent years publicly expressed a new preference for using frozen vegetables over so-called 'fresh' produce. These have included Heston Blumenthal and Marco Pierre White.

Food which has been frozen shortly after it has been harvested does indeed stand a better chance of retaining most of its nutrients compared with shelf-stocked 'fresh' fruit and vegetables. However, this assumes that the food which has been frozen was high in nutrition in the first place simply because it was frozen while fresh. So let's examine what happens to our food before it reaches us.

First it is fertilised artificially. Most farms use artificial fertilisers and most of these come from oil. Food is likely to increase in price in the coming years as the fertiliser necessary to produce it soars as oil supplies begin to dry up and more competition develops for existing stocks. Recent research suggests that artificial fertilisers replenish only primary plant foods in the soil and not the micronutrients and other peripheral minerals which scientists now know are also vital for producing the nutrition we need in our food.

Food crops then generally undergo a range of processes to protect them against pests and moulds. Chemicals and pesticides are deployed and their toxic residues will still cling to our food even after it has been harvested and cleaned. Mass commercial growing processes today usually involve the use of more chemicals—pesticides and herbicides—than ever before.

In fact, on many commercial farms a cycle has started to build. Chemicals used to treat pests will kill them off but will also kill beneficial insects and micro-organisms which are key to keeping pest numbers down in the first place. It also causes the pests to develop resistance. These factors in turn lead to the need for more, and stronger, chemicals.

Those everlasting strawberries you buy which refuse to rot may have been exposed to ionising radiation. Blasting fresh produce with radiation has become an effective way of lengthening shelf-life. The irradiation process kills all insects, moulds and micro-organisms, and also switches off the natural perishing process. Do we really know the long-term effects of eating irradiated food?

Apart from adverse effects on human health, over time the chemicals used also effect the make-up of the plants themselves.

We know that people who get no exercise become unfit, unhealthy and eventually so weak that they are unable to fend off illness. We also know that exposure to germs in small amounts provides us with another form of fitness—the strengthening of our immune systems. An immune system with no bugs to fight similarly becomes weakened.

If a chemical spray is used to remove the plant pests, the plant no longer needs to develop its own means of fighting those pests in the first place. Remember that through natural adaptation, all plants survived perfectly well before mankind started squirting toxic chemicals at them. Indeed, certain trees repeatedly attacked by a particular pest have been shown to develop their own chemical deterrents in their sap as a direct result of these attacks. Scientists even proved that plants attacked by a certain insect will be stimulated into producing and emitting chemicals designed to attract a predatory species which then preys on their attacker.

In contrast, generations of plants which don't have to fend for themselves any longer lose their ability to do so and thus become as dependent on us as a dairy cow. Meantime their pests use their own adaptation skills to gradually build up immunity to our artificial pesticides. More interesting still is the fact that recent research has revealed that those natural pesticides and deterrents which the untreated food plants produce are highly beneficial to the people who eat the plants. Reports that followed the research findings suggest that those foods which come to our table with a nibble or two are brimful of these naturally occurring substances, which in turn fight illness in our own systems. Of course, supermarket foods don't come with nibbled holes. They come with different types of chemicals.

We are also increasing the co-dependency of plants through a range of other interventions. Let's take the selective breeding process that has been going on ever since mankind started farming, but which has escalated into overdrive in the past three decades.

Just over a year ago Tesco announced to great applause that it would soon be marketing 'ugly fruit' at cheaper than normal prices. To understand what an 'ugly fruit' or an 'ugly vegetable' is, we must consider something we mightn't have noticed already about supermarket produce. That it is homogenous! That a tray of apples today comes with all the apples in the same size, in the same shape and in the same colours. So too do the carrots, swedes and just about everything else you buy at a supermarket.

Of course they don't grow like this naturally. Like people, food produce should naturally come in all shapes and sizes, with marked differences even off the same plant.

Recently the EU lifted a series of rules it had made twenty years previously which demanded that fresh fruit and veg come in standard shapes, sizes, colours and consistencies. The EU had in fact devised a complex, set menu of stated sizes, shapes and dimensions—a complete list for each food type. Remember the 'straight bananas' controversy? The problem now is, after two decades of buying uniform foods, we the consumers have completely the wrong idea of what 'real' food looks like. We are now implicitly programmed to believe that all 'good' food is supposed to look uniform. Thus an apple which was just an apple thirty years ago, has now become an 'ugly' apple. Tesco's initiative involved stocking fruit and veg of all shapes and sizes, the sort which had been banned in all EU countries for that period. This food was sold at reduced prices, thus suggesting implicitly to the buyer that it is substandard in the first place.

If we made a similar rule for people, then the EU's ruling might have been akin to deciding, let's say, that only blonde-haired, blue-eyed midgets could become lawyers. After two decades of enforcement, a relaxation of this rule wouldn't mean that clients would start hiring tall, brown-eyed people to represent them in court. Because after two decades of every lawyer being blonde, short and blue-eyed, we would innately believe that this is what a good lawyer looks like.

The unexpected effect of twenty years of regulations against 'ugly' apples and other produce in such a huge population area and market as the EU has not only completely changed the consumer's perception but it has also meant that commercial growers who wanted to sell their produce in the EU have had to go into overdrive to ensure that they choose not only those food plant strains which conform with those appearance traits, but also that they invest in the long term, in machinery and processes which can deal with the sizes and shapes demanded.

. Back when Disney made *Snow White* in the 1930s, few apples looked like the great big shiny red one with the heart-shaped crown and squared bottom with which the wicked witch poisoned Snow White. This apple was a creation by Disney artists portraying what they believed would be the most desirable and tempting looking apple possible. Today this type of apple is the norm because mankind has 'remade' his apples that way. He did it just the same as if he were a Disney artist, redrawing and repainting it, but using selective breeding and other genetic tweaking processes instead of ink and a paintbrush.

Selective breeding, whether in plants or animals, has its upsides and downsides. Thus we take all the trees which produce only larger apples and cross them only with other trees which produce similarly larger apples. Many different qualities from size to taste to colour to texture to pest resistance can be selectively bred. The downside of highly selective breeding is that it is unnatural. It doesn't occur in nature. Nature encourages difference because difference enables survival. What we are doing in selective breeding of food is producing mutations which would not occur naturally.

In humans it is good, for example, to have people who are thin but who can run fast as well as people who are slow but strong. Humanity would have had a lesser chance of survival if only the thin runners survived at the expense of the stocky, strong individuals. Imagine then for a second that we took the selective breeding of humans to such a fine degree that we decided only to let sensitive musicians have children? Bred only with other sensitive musicians? That's what we're doing to food plants.

Nature treats sameness as a mutation which needs to be ironed out, and for good reason. But we're doing the opposite with our food.

Take the much loved bulldog. His big oversized flat head and jowls, his outsized shoulders and tiny back legs originated from nothing else but the human need to make dogs fight against one another for entertainment. Selective breeding over generations brought on the physical traits in certain dogs which were most useful for fighting other dogs. These happened to include big powerful jaws, strong front legs, and pliable facial skin. Today we have a 'pedigree dog' which is in reality an extreme mutant that nature would never have permitted. The bulldog suffers immense problems as a result—its outsized and flattened head means this breed is hugely susceptible to breathing difficulties and respiratory illnesses. The bulldog is recognised today even among those who love the breed for its excess snoring, farting, drooling, respiratory infections, high vet bills and short life span. Nature doesn't inbreed (it interbreeds) and this is why the happiest, most intelligent, healthiest dogs are mongrels.

The same principles apply to food plants which is why today our supermarket baskets are already stuffed with weakened strains, the food world's versions of bulldogs, dachshunds, chihuahuas and pugs.

Much of this selective emphasis on mutation of the plants (like deep red colouring for the plant instead of a big head for the bulldog) has been led by the consumer, you and me, because we consumers always want the Disney apple and, in turn, the supermarket buyers will only buy those types from the growers. Over time, the changes in the food plants themselves have been so huge as to make some of them completely unrecognisable from what nature originally created.

For example, consider that carrots are orange today only because we made them that way. They were originally pale yellow but then in the seventeenth century an orange mutation became fashionable in Europe, to the degree that everybody wanted orange carrots. A few hundred years later and most carrots are orange because the original butter-coloured vegetable strains were bred out. Today the mutant has become the norm. We don't know why nature made carrots yellow in the first place but we can be sure that she did so for a damn good reason.

And while big business has interfered with the strains of our food plants to please the consumer, most of the changes have been made to suit its own more selfish needs, allowing alterations which actually work against the consumer's health and well-being.

A car manufacturer will produce more black cars if the consumer wants black cars. But if that manufacturer wants an even bigger profit, it might also start adding cheaper plastic parts to replace more expensive metal equivalents while still charging the same price. The result is a less solid car which isn't in the best interests of the buyer, but one which might come into being because it makes the manufacturer loads more cash.

Those traits which growers have developed to increase their profits are found in those modern plant strains which have been developed to produce larger fruits or vegetables, which produce them in greater numbers, which produce versions which are more pest and disease resistant and strains which last longer in transit and in storage. There is strong evidence to suggest that a concentration of these qualities along with the consumer needs (uniform shape, attractive colour) means that other, more consumer desirable qualities such as taste and nutritional content have suffered. In fact, outsized versions of fruits and vegetables generally contain far less nutrition.

And in their quest for 'super' food plants, forty years ago they went a step further and embarked on full-blown plant cloning. They produced the F1 hybrid, a plant which has been cloned from a selection of others. Cloning has allowed newer, stronger, more disease-resistant strains to come to market.

What's wrong with this, though? Surely that can only be a good thing and demonstrates evidence of how man's ingenuity can triumph even over nature? The problem with a clone is that, as a hybrid between two intensely inbred strains, it cannot actually produce another plant from seed which can in turn reproduce. In effect the seeds from clones create impotent plants. Here the clone or hybrid strain has become 100 per cent reliant on mankind for its reproduction process, i.e. the cloning process. The seeds from a hybrid plant can be sown and will indeed produce another plant but that plant in turn is flawed, non-vigorous and incapable of producing reliable food.

So we have taken another step on the road to Soylent Green, by making F1 hybrids which require human care for their very existence. They could not survive in the wild. But it gets worse again. Because the hybrids have proven so popular since their launch forty years ago, they now account for most of the food producing plants in the world today. Having turned the poor carrot orange, now mankind has made it sterile—80 per cent of the carrots consumed in the world today are from hybrid plants. The same story is true to some extent across almost all food types, fruit or vegetable.

The handful of multinationals who produce the world's seeds have in fact pushed hybrid seeds for another highly profitable but hugely consequential purpose. If growers can no longer collect some of their seeds to sow again the following year, then they are forced to buy new seeds each year from the corporation. In turn the corporations will put all their efforts into developing the most productive strains in those lines which prove the most profitable—the F1 hybrids. Through use of the impotent clones they have succeeded in creating monopoly markets. The result is that few growers in the world today harvest their own foods, save perhaps some in Third World countries where farming has remained absolutely basic.

Meantime as we twist and tweak with our impotent hybrids, those old-fashioned strains, which are actually capable of reproducing by themselves as nature intended, are fast becoming neglected and extinct as a result of the continued growing popularity of cloned varieties.

In these circumstances what are the eventual consequences of a slip-up, meltdown, or mistake made by those small numbers of multinational seed corporations who, backed by international governments, are pushing the F1 hybrid agenda? If bastardised, mutant clones replace natural plants, which can reproduce by themselves without our help, the possible repercussions for humanity are obvious and immense.

Dolly the cloned sheep died early in her life and it has been widely speculated that this happened because she was "born aged," that the tissue she was cloned from had been taken from a sheep already in advanced years and thus the tissue she made as she grew was also somehow pre-aged.

As we know, corporations and scientists also make mistakes. But the roads we are taking with our foods might not, in the end, be ones that we easily can back out of.

And we're not yet finished with the Frankenstein fooling that humanity has inflicted on the food-producing plants these last forty years. The latest twist is genetic modification—tinkering with a plant to change its very genetic make-up—to tweak its very genes, or to add additional ones, sometimes from other species entirely. The end product is better known as a GM food.

Such is the worry about GM foods that they are currently banned from many parts of the world. Genetic modification is the introduction of alien genes not naturally found in a species or even in a group (animal genes might be introduced to plants or vice versa) with the intention of producing a desirable quality in one or the other. We already know that GM food plants can cross-breed with other non-GM varieties in proximity. And though GM foods are not with us long enough (the first tomato became available in 1994) to truly evaluate whether they are dangerous, the fact that they have crossed accidentally with non GM crops—and continue to do so—means that if they do turn out to be damaging, then the genie may already have been let out of the bottle.

There have already been allegations that early problems are showing. It is alleged that soy allergies have soared by 50 per cent in Britain since GM soy products entered that market. There have been allegations that shepherds in India have lost a quarter of sheep that have grazed on GM cotton plants when none died eating non-GM versions.

Of course if we can genetically modify our food plants in a completely safe manner to increase food quality and quantity, then that would be a great thing. The big GM question is this: can we really trust profit-driven multinationals to tinker around with GM on a huge scale when we can only be sure that (a) we don't yet understand the consequences and (b) we know GM plants can interbreed?

Thus far in our journey, we have taken our humble plant, inbred it mercilessly to change the colour and shape of its fruits, we have hothoused it with oil-based substances, doused it in toxic chemicals, we have cloned it, showered it with radiation, sterilised it and finally, we have introduced animal genes into its make-up. Are we finished yet?

Let's ask a few final questions: What has all of the above achieved? The black and orange carrots which can bend end to end at the local convenience store? Have we seen an end to starvation in the Third World as GM proponents have claimed? Nope. Bigger corporate profits? Certainly yes. The vastly increased risk of a world ecological disaster on an unprecedented scale? Absolutely.

Professor Tim Lang, of the Centre for Food Policy in London, believes it's an issue of consumer rights. He has said: "We think of an orange as a constant, but the reality is that it isn't."

Lang unveiled a study which shows that today you would have to eat eight oranges to get the same levels of vitamin A that your grandfather obtained by eating just one. You would have to eat five to get the same level of iron. British studies have suggested that fresh food on average contains about half the levels of minerals that it did fifty years ago. Studies in America and Canada have showed a similar loss.

Health Canada (a federal department), showed that in a half century, a typical potato has lost 100 per cent of its vitamin A, 57 per cent of its vitamin C, 50 per cent of its riboflavin and 18 per cent of its thiamine. Much the same story was proven across twenty-five assorted fresh fruit and veg types analysed.

The *British Food Journal* published a report that compared mineral levels in fresh produce between 1936 and 1987. Copper levels were down 81 per cent, iron was down 22 per cent, phosphorous down 6 per cent, sodium down 43 per cent, magnesium down 35 per cent and calcium down 10 per cent. The UK-based expert nutritionist David Thomas believes that these reductions are a direct result of modern farming practices using massive amounts of fertilisers on the soil which encourage plant growth at the expense of mineral content. Mr Thomas has said: "We are made up of these substances. If they are deficient then the body cannot cope as well as it would otherwise."

So perhaps we'll just have to eat more of them to get the same level of nutrition? But it turns out that doing that might actually be very dangerous. Because in the case of the orange, as with other types of fruit and veg, the levels of some nutrients have collapsed through a fifty-year period, but others have actually remained the same. Your orange for example, has exactly the same amount of vitamin C as your granddad's. Eating ten oranges to get the same vitamin A will also give you ten times more than the normal dose of vitamin C. Vitamin C isn't toxic in high amounts, but some minerals which have not reduced in many foods certainly are.

For a more grass roots view, my Dublin-based commercial carrot grower adds: "I know the carrots I am producing today are not as nutritious as they were even a few years ago because I cannot afford to treat the soil the way I know it should be treated. Something has to be done soon or what we'll end up buying for our children is a big bag of water."

So how might that reduction in nutrients along with the interference of chemicals and other procedures in the processing of our food be affecting us?

Tim Lang of the Centre for Food Policy in London points out that because plant breeders have been trying to develop fruits and vegetables that look nice, resist disease and can stand long shipping journeys without decomposing, they are less and less concerned about the nutrition and minerals in our food. He claims that as a direct result of this reduction in quality, more and more people are dying from chronic degenerative diseases such as heart disease and cancer than should be. Lang, like many other nutritionists, believes we have helped to create high levels of degenerative diseases ourselves by so quickly debasing the nutritional value of our food over a short period.

Research published online by Donald Davis, a senior researcher at the University of Texas, who was studying the disappearing nutrients from forty-three common fruits and vegetables over fifty to seventy years, shows that the higher-yielding the crop, the less the amount of cancer-fighting chemicals and antitoxins (phytonutrients or phytochemicals) contained in it. Food scientists are only just beginning to understand how valuable these phytochemicals actually are.

Levels of mental illness, sterility, attention deficit disorder, asthma and many other conditions have also surged in tandem with the rise in tinkering with our food plants, although these conditions may be linked to other factors. In the same way that medical experts noticed a spike in lung cancer deaths among smokers in the 1950s, but couldn't conclusively prove their prognosis that cigarettes were the cause, so too do many scientists around the world believe that many of mankind's modern illnesses are linked to what we've done to our food.

What we can certainly say, however, is that our reliance on the 'system' and its profit-motivated, unscrupulous methods means the carrot we eat today has lost its taste, its mineral and nutritional content, and is even less likely to arrive with nutrients after a week in transit, another in storage and another on the shelves right under the air conditioning.

Finally there is the not-so-small matter of food security. *Soylent Green* opens with scenes of food riots—something we have experienced around the world in recent years when basic food commodities like rice and wheat saw their international prices suddenly surge.

The effects of two, newly enriched, massive economies like China and India competing now for meat, grain and indeed a limited amount of world oil stocks, has increasingly threatened stability worldwide. The result has been periodic spikes in food prices, which experts believe will become more frequent as time goes on. *The Economist*'s global food-price index rose by a frightening 70 per cent in the year to March 2008 when rice found itself at a twenty-year high, when flour prices jumped 46 per cent in twelve months, the price of potatoes increased 12 per cent over the year and the price of milk rose by 33 per cent.

The world experienced a food crisis between 2006 and 2008. Poor growing conditions cut the stocks of world food while rising oil prices also impacted on its price. As I pointed out earlier on, oil is the key product used in the making of most of the world's commercially produced fertiliser, which then became more expensive. The cost of oil directly impacts on the cost of harvesting because it powers the harvesting machines, and also on the transport of that food to its eventual location.

In the same two-year period the cost of rice surged by 217 per cent, wheat by 136 per cent and maize by 125 per cent. In reaction to the prices they could no longer afford, the poor rioted in countries all over the world, most notably in Bangladesh, in Egypt, in Haiti and in Yemen. In more secure countries like Russia and Mexico, restrictions were placed on the export of staple food products. In Pakistan, the army were deployed to stand guard over fields and warehouses before prices fell again in 2009.

More food price problems are in the post because the world's population is rising, commercial farming practices are destroying soils, particularly in poorer countries, and oil supplies are falling.

The overuse of artificial fertilisers and widespread poor agri-practices have led some to estimate that the world is now actually losing its soil—that agricultural topsoil is being destroyed at such a rapid rate that there are only fifty years of it left. Over-farming, loss of protective ground covers and lack of humus have made soils unproductive. It means we are now running out of the very food that our food itself needs to survive.

Good soil needs time to regenerate itself, it needs to 'rest', something that modern food production processes do not allow for. And while the heavy use of artificial fertilisers does replace minerals like nitrogen, potassium and phosphorus in the soil, it also tends to disrupt the pH balance and kills those organisms which help soil produce trace minerals like magnesium, which are seldom replaced by modern farming.

Those governments which put time and money into researching all of the above factors are worried to the degree that 'Food Security' has become a new term of concern to them. 'Food

Security' describes a country's ability to feed itself through vary-ing degrees of stress-testing.

In Britain it's "nine meals away from anarchy". In the event of an emergency, the government there determined that food sup-plies in the supermarkets would be gone within days, not weeks or months. Last year Rosie Boycott, the leading British journalist and more recently head of Boris Johnson's London Food Group (set up to examine the supply of fresh food to that city), wrote that 95 per cent of the food British people eat is now oil depend-ent. We can assume the same goes for us. Cut off the oil and it doesn't get delivered. So what happens then?

The concerns are obvious here in Ireland where we haven't even bothered commissioning serious research on food security.

Ireland, like Britain and many other First World countries, is fast reducing its food security by importing more and more from abroad while at the same time driving hundreds of local growers out of business each year. This means the developed nations are slowly losing the agri-skills needed to grow food in the first place as farmers, many of whom are from a long line of farmers, leave the business.

It's quite ridiculous when we consider that a country like Ire-land, with one of the best food-growing climates in the world, is now importing its food needs from abroad, using even more oil and fuel to get it here. We are also becoming less reliant on Irish farming and increasingly dependent on faraway growers whose produce the system imports and puts on our shelves. Did we ever dream we'd see the day arrive when Ireland started importing milk and potatoes from outside the state?

But what happens if the system we trust in so much does actually break down? The banking system, on which business and the world economy relies, broke down; why shouldn't the sys-tem of food importation and supply to the shelves unravel in the same way?

If you grow your own food, you can overnight ditch the chemicals, pesticides, artificial fertilisers, the clones and the whole lot. You can grow heritage varieties whose seeds you can sow and sow again. Vital mineral levels are 50 per cent higher in foods which are organically grown, it's the freshest food you can eat, taking perhaps thirty seconds to get to your table from pick-ing. And homegrown food just tastes a whole lot better.

Food For Thought

This chapter is not about why I started growing my own food, but the main reason I have kept it up.

There's a twist in the ending of the movie *Soylent Green*. If you'd like to watch it for yourself, then skip the next paragraph.

The *Soylent Green* miracle synthetic food which gives the film its title, and on which humanity has pinned its survival hopes, turns out to be yet another hoax inflicted on us by all-controlling corporations. *Soylent Green* isn't made of oceanic plankton, as claimed, but of recycled human flesh acquired from the dead. The film's conclusion is that humanity ends up with nothing to eat but itself. And that even that very last act of a dying species consuming itself is carried out... for a profit.

Allotment Diary, Year One

Early September—Success!

Harvesting onions in the rain is a tricky business. Grabbing the green shoots and pulling hard doesn't work because they're far too slippery. The shoots slide all the way through my fingers and the onion is still in the ground as the rain lashes in my face. I try twisting before pulling to get a better grip but now the shoots are snapping off, leaving a haircut bulb in the ground. A skinhead onion. The best way to do it is, like the furry-toy-grab at the arcade, reach straight down from above with three fingers, grip underneath and up she comes—along with a root load of mud and assorted heebie jeebies therein. The whole lot goes into a bin-liner sack and by the time I've finished I've got a good few hundred of them in two and a half large sacks. The smell of bruised onion is overpowering and it takes much longer than expected to harvest the whole lot. But I'm delighted with myself. A result. Even though Her Outdoors isn't so sure about taking this wet mucky load in her car, plastic sacks or no.

The onions have done surprisingly well in our first year. Looking around at the other plots, I can see that they're far larger than anyone else's. The neighbours are asking how come they're so big, and I'm in newbie-allotmenteer heaven, basking in the appreciation. These onions have been like adopted kids. I got them when they were tiny bulbs. I dug the ground for them, extricated every little weed, picked out the stones, levelled it off and planted them.

Perhaps the secret to my success first time around lay in the furrows. I had turned the bed into a miniature ploughed field with ridges and furrows using a trowel. This gave them extra drainage through the wet months we've had and onions prefer the soil to be well drained. I put the onion sets in the right way up, measured the right space between them and put them back into place again whenever the birds picked them out. I surrounded them with pegged string and bits of white plastic bag tied on in intervals, like bunting, to make sure the birds stayed off. Then I watered them through the dry spells, running back and forth to the push button tap I share with next door's holder.

But the furrows weren't just good for drainage, the troughs seemed to provide the perfect conditions for chickweed, a sort of fast-growing carpet of tiny leaves that intertwines and strangles everything else in its vicinity. These I removed every second week by dredging along the furrows with my fingers. Despite all the work I am in heaven with these huge, perfectly formed bulbs. They taste incredible, albeit so strong that they give us all a minor problem with gas any time we eat a substantial amount. Farting that is.

The sense of achievement at having brought in a prize-sized crop is fantastic and if they keep well after they have been dried, I will have onions all the way through to March. Not just any old onions, but the supreme tasting caviar of the onion world. We are the champions!

We've had our near misses. A recent pleasant dusky evening saw me and Her Outdoors sitting outside on the patio alongside the tomatoes, when I noticed that one of our fifty or so vines appeared to have a few shrivelled leaves. Absent-mindedly, I picked them off. The following evening there were a few more dried-up leaves and by the next evening the plant was one great big shrivel—its foliage had completely curled and was bent over—but the tomato fruits were still there, looking apparently fine. There were some spots developing on their leaves, so I took a mental note to check the internet to see if I could find out what was wrong.

The 'matties' went outside in spectacular May weather, only to be battered by storms soon after. When the first batch of Gardener's Delight cherry tomatoes and the regular-sized Ailsa Craigs got shredded, I sowed another batch of seeds in June with the old French heritage variety Marmande, plus an

F1 hybrid that I purchased by mistake. It's not the plant's fault that it's a clone, so it goes into the ground and is lovingly cared for alongside the rest of them.

While the Gardener's Delights are only one third to halfway up the shed (they were 6ft this time last year), the Marmandes on the patio are now heading for 7ft in some spots and they are also laid down with nice-looking fruit, albeit still green. But now the leaves are shrivelling. So I consult Dr Interweb. I start browsing pictures of tomato problems. I locate a handy rogues' gallery containing assorted photos of various tomato issues. A sort of clinic for embarrassing illnesses of tomato plants.

Click: "Nope. Nope. Close but no cigar. Nope."

Click: "Ah, that's the man. No doubt about it. Same raised button-type, brown bits, yes. Same concentric lines, on the money. Okay, so what's that then?"

Click: "Aw no".

Damned blight. There I was, so smug that I didn't grow spuds in the year when the worst blight in twenty summers had wiped out potatoes all over Ireland. But I didn't know then that blight can also affect their close cousin, the tomato vine. I keyed in 'tomato blight' and 'cure'.

Click: "There is no cure for blight ... kills all within days."

The rest of the search yielded advice like "Burn the plants" ... "Ensure no loose leaves spread"... "Inform the relevant government department."

Gaaaahhh!

No matter where I searched, I couldn't find a cure.

Eventually I tried a picture search on Google with the terms 'tomato' and 'blight' and 'treatment' and came upon one product, Dithane, in a big red box. I contacted Her Outdoors at home, off work for the week, and relayed to her that the plague had struck on our patio. We needed a red box of stuff called Dithane and we needed it fast. You only have days to sort out a blight crop in potatoes, so I presume the same is true for this other member of the nightshade family of plants. The problem was that no-one seemed to stock this stuff, and most hadn't heard of it.

That evening it was apparent the plague was spreading fast and I had to pull up a whole window box load of four completely dried-up plants which were obviously alive the previous day. Worse still, there were ominous signs of button-shape reliefs starting on the foliage of adjoining plants.

The plants were placed in a bin-liner bag and consigned to the household rubbish (composting it spreads the disease further as the fungal spores can survive, and then transfer to other plants).

I rang a local commercial tomato farmer and got some sound advice.

—"You need some of the 'old' chemicals for potato blight, containing copper sulphate," he said. "Yes, you can get it in most garden centres."

Before long we were clutching a big red box of Murphy's Blight Cure. I diluted it as instructed and sprayed. Three days on and the plants don't look the best, but at least haven't got any worse. We seem to have halted its spread. We're supposed to spray every couple of weeks but the instructions say don't eat the fruit for at least two weeks after treatment.

So when exactly will we be able to eat them?

Generally, though, the tomatoes, onions and carrots have been great. We took home sacks of Nantes variety carrots in all shapes and sizes. The latter took an entire weekend to process for freezing, between washing, shaving, slicing and blanching. We're still eating frozen stocks of our bumper calabrese/broccoli harvest. We've had fantastic amounts of salads (still cropping) and a reasonable amount of fruit, though it's fair to assume that the fruit bushes will need a bit longer to mature. The herbs were good, the chard has been cropping continuously and despite the shaky start, the courgettes are still firing.

On the downside we lost most of the cabbages and the entire crops of sweetcorn, beans (to the winds), all of the squashes bar four and all the cucumbers. We had small numbers of peas and we don't know whether the rhubarb is hibernating underground or has given up the ghost completely. We've ended up with vast amounts of three foods we eat a lot of—tomatoes, onions and carrots. We've had sacks of calabrese/broccoli, which is really good for you and really expensive to buy. Ditto the salads and herbs. The sprouts have still to be harvested and are looking good and while we ended up with four bell peppers, the jalapeño and cayenne have been cropping well indoors.

Chapter Five

Social and Personal—The Allotment Community

Neat military rows of lush, green plant tops, shoots and foliage of different hues; hazel-stick bean teepees in cascading scarlet bloom, elegant ladies in fluttering summer dresses and straw bonnets filling their flat baskets with neat bundles of carrots, onions and greens. Angelic children playing in the background, the sound of their laughter mingling with the tweeting of birds and the sound of bees...Stop it now.

First off, to the uninitiated, allotment complexes don't look at all as lifestyle television or glossy magazines like to portray them. There are indeed some allotments made up of those neat rows, but these people have their own problems and for the most part a modern allotment looks like a bit of squatted scrub ground in a world disaster zone, and an allotment complex much like a vagrant camp, less neat than Steinbeck's or, if you're allowed have sheds on it, a full-on shanty town. It usually comes with lots of rough empty ground and half-filled plots—because around here, we don't wait for the ladies in bonnets to start harvesting our food.

Allotments are a sea of corrugated metal bits used to frame compost heaps, gnarly knock-togethers of scrap wood for raised beds, bristles of plastic bottles on sticks and bits of bags on strings to keep birds away, rotting carpet ends used to keep weeds down, and there's always a surprising amount of weeds because no matter what you do, you can never keep them all down. In many ways our complex keeps remnants of its heritage, as a city tip. And thank God for that!

Allotment complexes are also odd little communities in their own right where people interact, teach one another and help each other out, albeit in a very informal way. It's a little bit like being neighbours but without the houses, only the gardens. But, as I've said, the people or the ground don't look like they come straight from the garden fashion section of a glossy mag. Being mostly unfashionable and practical outdoor types who don't like to ruin their good clothes, allotment people wear lots of dodgy tracksuits, old baggy trousers, holey dirty jeans, sweat-soaked faded T-shirts and oodles of tatty hats of all sorts.

And the kids aren't angelic, they're normal. They murder each other and in turn their parents murder them as the former relieve their boredom by fighting among themselves, falling over into the veg beds and whinging to go home every ten seconds, and the latter turn the air blue with expletives and warnings about reddening the hides of those who keep whinging about wanting to go home every ten seconds.

But what you will get is plenty of the sort of old-fashioned, over-the-fence neighbourliness and genuine community spirit that you just don't find in too many places these days, not least the typical urban residential estate where neighbours pass each other in their driveways and most hassled couples hold down a job each while their children do more hours than their carers in the local crèche, where modern children also tend to spend their summers.

Since starting out, I've experienced endless examples of kindness, particularly from the more experienced growers who are always happy to encourage newbies with their plots and to dole out good advice in a diplomatic manner. These days perhaps only a rip-roaring wedding can get people of so many different outlooks and ages together so enthusiastically in one place and for the same purpose.

It's also an endless source of fascination to see how dozens of different people take the same identical plots of ground and turn them into a myriad different scenes and scenarios. Whether their holders intend it or not, each one is a unique living canvas of personality. There are old-fashioned textbook allotments of pure agriculture—honed by the no-nonsense, no-frills but ultra-efficient veg men who start digging in January and don't stop until every single inch of their patch has been turned over. When finished, these plots look just like a small version of a ploughed farmer's field. These are generally run by middle-to-older aged gents who use their patch to grow lots and lots of basic food. Their lots tend to be dissected into perhaps no more than six crop-types, with a heavy emphasis on spuds and cabbages—all designed for a year's worth of no-nonsense heaps of accompaniment to slabs of meat and gravy.

The younger holders, usually foodie types in their thirties and forties, are more likely to cultivate lots of little patches with walkways in grass or mulch laid out around them. In these they cultivate a varied palate of dainties such as artichokes, sunflowers, cardoons or squashes, the odd globe artichoke, some fussy salads and perhaps even the odd grape vine. They're the ones you see in the floral wellies or with dainty plastic polytunnels.

Then there's what we call the Butlins brigade, the big family holders who use an allotment to mix it up with their kin—all tents, barbecues, outdoor tables, plastic chairs and noise. Six sitting in chairs talking and sipping and two digging. Perhaps one well-dressed guest making a few short token attempts at weeding. Kids breaking up everyone else's allotment.

It's mostly parents, grandparents and young children on a typical complex. The teenagers and twenty-somethings are the only missing links to the generations, because being that age, they find growing food a drag. If I were twenty I wouldn't be here either. In fact it's usually when people start having children that they take on an allotment.

This doesn't mean that allotment holders are boring. One of the best things about allotment people is that when you delve a little bit deeper, you tend to find that they're the sort of people who squeeze a whole lot more out of their lives. There's a taxi man who walks the parks looking for seeds from native trees, particularly Irish oak. He plants them at home and looks after the resulting trees until they're mature. He then takes a walk in the country and plants the resulting trees, by now large and mature enough to stand a chance of surviving. He didn't tell me this, I found out completely by accident.

There's the former drummer of a band which was world

famous for a time in the early seventies. He told me that he did indeed live for a time with the dream life of limos, fame and rock 'n' roll that so many younger people dream of today. From the slick west coast sound of their greatest song—which I guarantee you will know—you'd think they were a Californian west coast outfit rather than a load of pub stomping ale drinkers then based in Yorkshire. He confided to me that their one big worldwide hit—called 'How Long (has this been going on?)'—(I told you you knew it) which is widely assumed to be about the very poignant moment when the protagonist realises his girl is having an affair, was in truth penned to express the band's annoyance when they discovered their bass player was secretly moonlighting with another outfit. I looked them up on Dr Interweb and in his publicity pictures as the drummer, my allotment neighbour is smiling as mischievously and infectiously as he does today.

There's the guy who's about my father's age who tends his patch with immaculate care; he's a refugee from a long-established allotment complex which was closed down. His patch has, at its centre, a perfect square of bowling green consistency lawn complete with a park bench. He takes a break from his crops to sprawl on the bench and study the mountains on the horizon and he disappears now and again for a month at a time to go and cycle for weeks around exotic countries.

There's the sixty-something with the grey ponytail who fills his entire allotment with nothing but a mass explosion of multi-coloured dahlias. Imagine taking the upstairs and downstairs of your house, spreading it on level ground, and filling it ear to jowl with yellow, pink, orange, purple and cream blooms. No?

Now and again you'll see items that you'd never expect to encounter in an agricultural complex.

One hard-working allotment holder's immaculate but Dali-esque patch is accessed via a nightclub-style velvet rope that runs from entrance post to entrance post with brass links. I like to imagine queues of inebriated, half-dressed patrons standing outside, protesting that they come here every week and they're great friends with the owner. His patch also includes a mirrored bathroom cabinet hung on a post, a windmill and a pair of plastic swans gracing the entrance posts.

Eccentric? Maybe we are.

Down the very end, there's a high-security allotment cultivated by a guy who has divided his plot in two and enclosed one half completely in high aviary walls and a roof of wood frame and wire. The other side features lines of wooden cold frames covered in sheets of glass. His idea is to specialise in fruit. Only his giant aviary is to keep the birds out, not in. He is located right next to the gate, gaps through which sheep from the neighbouring farm have been known to conduct raids. He might be a tech manager in an office, but out here he's a fruit grower.

Moving from our main gate up to our own patch at the top of the hill we stop, chat, nod or wave as we go. We also use a low gear to get a quick look at how everyone else's plot is doing.

—"Very good, good, very good. Wow! Where did they come out of? Very good…"

Snooping on other plots and the progress of others is compulsory, which leads to a form of light competition between holders. I've become surprisingly agitated when crops fail for me but do well for the other holders. Not so much keeping up with the Joneses, but wondering how the Joneses keep it up at all.

It doesn't help that we happen to have some really fantastic allotments in the immediate vicinity of Plot 34, which is itself on the tattier end of the scale at our complex. Unlike regular household gardens where looking good is the priority, allotments are there to produce food. So they're as neat as their holders can manage in between tending the produce. It's just that some growers do that with so much more panache than others.

Weeding takes a huge amount of time and, unless it is affecting your plants or those of your neighbours, you might just leave it alone. But any more messy at ours and we'll be getting a call from the deportment police at the council, who monitor their complexes constantly to ensure they are kept spick and span. Ours are inspected secretly a couple of times a year.

We'd probably get 42 per cent (could do better). A bare pass, but a pass nonetheless—confirmed by the fact that we were not among those targeted by a barrage of 'clean it up or else' missives following the last council inspection. But we certainly wouldn't be in contention at Chelsea.

Unlike our neighbours in our first year.

This trim and sprightly late forty-something (I'm guessing) couple maintain a patch that wouldn't raise an eyebrow were it actually to turn up alongside a Bunny Guinness creation at the

Oscars of horticulture. Their pristine beds, where veg, herbs and flowers are arrayed in undulating swathes, are actually land-scaped—blended together with the sort of fine architectural and aesthetic flair that you don't even see in the most expertly designed flower gardens. The grass between their beds is trimmed to immaculate lawn consistency. Thanks to a battery-powered strimmer.

While our peas flail spasmodically around the base of our inexpertly patched-together pea teepee, theirs are deftly racked up inside an eye-catching corral of pleasing rustic hazel. Our neighbours were among the only holders not to lose their spuds to the blight this year, having trimmed off the blackened leaves before it got into the plants. And while our corn long ago popped its cobs, theirs is by now stretching upwards. While we try to resuscitate the seven dwarves of the legume world, their beans traipse languidly heavenward, way above head height, bursting here and there with startling vermilion blooms. They even have that badge of the ultimate allotment sophisticate—artichokes, in their high-stemmed, spiky exoticness.

What makes it so much worse is that they're perfectly lovely people.

I have to confess that now and again, when yet another cabbage comes out of our ground rootless, the shredded stump yet another feast for grubs, I have the childish urge to leap the fence and jump up and down on something. But I'm told by an older grower of some considerable experience that these are perfectly normal feelings for a newbie grower to harbour—just so long as they are not allowed to break out into fully fledged sabotage. The worrying thing is that he assures me it gets worse the more years you spend growing.

I'm dreading that day we arrive to find a camera crew mooching around next door while Diarmuid Gavin burbles approval as he back-pedals through their patch, arms out-stretched, fingertips brushing longingly at the tops of their coffee-book-perfect herbs and salads.

Then he stops, chortles at the camera and whispers:

—"And in complete and udder contrast to all of dizz sheer wonderfulnezz, juzt come and have a look... over dere."

The camera pans across the fence, from West to East Berlin, North to South Korea, Texas to Chihuahua—in time to catch a couple fast retreating to a yellow hatchback that smells of onions, their hands over their faces and muttering ever more loudly:

—"No pictures! No pictures!"

Following a chat with her over-fence counterpart, the driving force behind this work of art, Her Outdoors has ascertained that our neighbour has never even had an allotment before.

"Gaaahh!"

In Year Two, this couple managed to wangle a larger plot a few 'doors' down and so we got a new next-door neighbour. He, a quiet, soft-spoken gent with a large white van, and his chatty and bubbly missus (you just know they love each other to bits) have set up shop almost in an instant. Straight away, their allotment, and one side of ours, was surrounded with green windbreak netting. Closer inspection showed it was a job very well done with thick wire evenly wound above and below and pulled taut to the dividing posts. It was a sign of things to come. Whether or not he's a carpenter, we still haven't determined, but one day there was a load of planks lying around and the next time we turned up, the entire place was a neat array of squared off and perfectly built timber raised beds with stout regimented timber frames for the fruit bushes. In between the raised beds, the weeds and grass were gone and there was a pleasing carpet of woodchips.

He's an innovative sort who's shown us how to pin the 'push button' taps back with a stone of the right shape propped under it to keep a hose running so we don't have to hang around there with one finger constantly pressed on the button to water. And he's not only lent us his hose and high-powered strimmer, but he's given us all his excess netting and wire, which, needless to say, we still haven't put up. His crops are also a great success; his only mistake it seems was purchasing the same cheapie, black, rubber, inedible, industrial-strength cabbage plants from Lidl as we did. These finally went into his compost heap, a high end kitchen-cabinet-standard, self-built wooden affair.

Other presents we've received from our neighbours include masses of assorted produce. Cabbage from the lady on top of the hill, strawberry plants from the guy across the way. Even the grumblies turn out to be decent skins once you get to know them properly.

And we haven't seen any bother or heard any bad words. There

was one family whose kids ran around screaming all day random-
ly through everyone else's patches while their parents sat and drank
beer, treating the place a bit like Benidorm. But without anyone
needing to complain, they simply disappeared after a few visits,
having lost interest. And that's what tends to happen, the faddists
weed themselves out before long and the allotments go back to
those who will use them properly. Many find that the idea of an
allotment just doesn't match the reality. For some, it doesn't turn
out like the telly suggests and four hours of weeding or digging at
a time just isn't how they want to spend their free time. And if that's
not how you want to spend yours, don't take one!

The pull-out rate was high in the first year when about a third
of our allotments went fallow. This was particularly frustrating to
me and our Chelsea Show neighbours in that first year, because
both of us had originally been given much smaller plots than we
had asked for. We assumed that the larger ones had been given
to more experienced growers and were not at all impressed when
most of the larger ones were let go wild.

If you do get an allotment, even a small one, you'll soon
realise that even a modest patch of ground can suddenly become
quite daunting when you've spent a day digging and have still
only managed to prepare a bed the size of a kitchen table top.
There's added pressure too because the weather is normally too
cold or wet or the days are too short to get stuck in before March.
At our complex you must have 75 per cent cultivated by April.
Therefore the pressure's on in those months and talking over the
wire is kept to the minimal nods and waves out of necessity.

My solution is to break it down into portions. Do a bed at a
time. Then the next one, then the next. Otherwise you'll just get
completely overwhelmed. But you do have to keep going.

Even so, mine still stays tatty like my office desk, and sometimes the neighbours think I do it on purpose:

—"Mark, we noticed you didn't get any carrot fly last year
and we only realised recently how you did it."

—"Em really? How do you mean?"

—"You left them undisturbed and let all the weeds grow
freely through them. The smell of the weeds kept the carrots dis-
guised. Very clever. We did the same this year and it's worked a
treat."

—"Em, delighted that it worked for you too."

Social and Personal—The Allotment Community

Despite Plot 34's tattiness, I do have an excuse in that I can usually only get up there one day a week. But then again, I do always try to keep the weeds from getting completely out of control as weed heads growing next door or nearby mean weed seed blown into your patch which can germinate there, adding to your own work.

Which leads to etiquette.

There aren't any hard or fast rules but there is an unspoken code. You can look at someone's allotment from outside their fence, but don't intrude when they're not there, unless you happen to know them really well. You can borrow buckets and tools without asking for them, from people you know really well, but not from anyone else. You can drive your car up beside the plot to unload, but must be prepared to reverse it back down to let others up afterwards. You don't have loud radios or make too much noise. It's a place of escape. You share. If you have a surplus of anything, be it seedlings, tools, crops, wire, buckets, compost, manure or bordering materials, you offer it to your neighbours. You always lock all the gates when you come in and when you leave. You keep an eye on your neighbours' allotments when they're not there. You keep the common areas near you clean. Like passing a car on a country road, you always lift a finger, nod or otherwise acknowledge when someone passes. Most of all, you keep the weeds down. In short, it's one of those things which runs itself well—how society should be.

But the one essential component we do all lack for an allotment complex worth its salt, is our own sheds, the construction of which has been banned outright by the council, possibly to discourage trespassing, vandalism and break-ins to the complex.

Elsewhere on allotment complexes, the shed is at the heart of each allotment—the built expression of personality and individualism which endures from season to season. And building the shed was something I had looked forward to with great relish. Generally in allotment culture, people are encouraged to build from old bits of timber, salvaged doors and glass panes pulled from skips, salvaged or blagged, which is far more in the spirit of improvisation and self-sufficiency as generally espoused by allotmenteers, than going out and just buying a boring old new shed at your nearest DIY barn.

In my younger years I had plenty of shed or 'hut' building

experience. My brother and I tackled our first project—when we were four and five. Ambitiously, we decided to site it in the fork of a big old apple tree in our garden with the idea of making a rope ladder we could pull up after us to ensure complete privacy from adults.

And while allotmenteers won't always admit it, the typical allotment shed is more of a 'hut' or 'den' of childhood than anything else. If you leave children to their own devices for long enough then they'll inevitably build their own hideaway, incorporating whatever materials are at hand. Girls call them 'houses', boys call them 'huts'.

Fast forward to adulthood and many of these lads are still poking about in huts and hideouts—this time sheds, garages and workshops. In these refuges, they find woman-free company and solace in the midst of widgets, gadgets, broken chairs, old radios, cans of oil and beer, and cups of tea.

There are three principal purposes to an allotment shed. First, it provides shelter from those heavy showers for which this country is best known, and with enough room, might even allow you a space to work in while it's raining outside. Second, it's a mini storage depot, which should save you the time and bother of having to lug the kitchen sink up to your allotment and back every time you go. Finally, and probably most importantly, an allotmenteer's shed is a sociable sanctuary in which you can sit down and take a breather from the digging, a retreat into which you can burrow and from which you can welcome your fellow growers for a thermos administered cuppa.

In Britain, where allotment culture is strongest, people get extraordinarily fond of their sheds. Some are so delighted with their creations that they feel compelled to show them off. For amateur-shed pornography, head to Readerssheds.co.uk where Brits can get them out on the internet!

If you're growing veg and want a shed, there's a lot to consider before you buy or build it. The first plan is exactly where to put it. You won't want to overshadow any of your growing land or your neighbour's, so stick the shed in the least valued and least lit part of your site where it won't cast a long shadow.

Then consider drainage. Always put it on blocks and keep the wood away from contact with earth, trees or foliage, otherwise it will flood or rot or both. Next, face it in the same direction as the prevailing wind is blowing, unless that is, you want to have yourself whacked by a flying door every time there's a spirited gust. You'll also need to consider security, because as our council fears, young lads still love to play with sheds, especially when they're drinking cider in the fields and fancy borrowing a few things. Or worse, if they've a box of matches handy and feel the need for a good burn.

If the shed is for your own garden, a lock is a good idea. It will slow down someone trying to steal from it and may put them off entirely, but whether they'll bother in a built-up area where neighbours might see or hear them is another question. However, on an unattended site such as an allotment, leaving a shed unlocked is usually the best policy because in a remote location a vandal or thief will have no compunction about breaking down a door or smashing through a thin timber wall where there's nobody around to hear, or see them.

Therefore tools stored in allotment sheds are usually hand-me-downs or second-hand expendables. Indeed you should keep nothing in an allotment shed or on the allotment site that you can't afford to lose.

All this is probably why Mother Council in her infinite wisdom has determined to ban any sort of a structure, be it rain shelter, shed or even a small greenhouse from our site. So where do we sit? We use fold-up wooden garden chairs rescued from the rubbish left outside someone's house on a special items collection day. How do we shelter from the rain? I wear a big hat and rainproofs and carry on regardless. Where do we leave our tools? The council has provided us with communal accommodation in the form of some giant iron shipping containers or other, placed a long way from our plot. It's better than nothing, but it's just a bit too far away from us to be of any practical use. We prefer to take all our tools home again.

We have, however, been moved to admire the genius of some of our fellow plot holders who have figured out ways to circumvent the rules. Downhill from us in Year One was a man who could be seen crawling on hands and knees after a rain shower, emerging from a four foot high plastic pink Wendy house complete with over and under door and a little window framed in plastic powder blue. Well it's definitely not a shed, and the council have no rules about Wendy houses.

I truly like most of the people I have met on our complex and I do believe that allotmenteers tend to have a far more positive attitude to life. Whether food-gardening brings out the best in people or food-growing just attracts more positive personalities is another question entirely.

Spend a few months with an allotment and you'll also find that your attitude to the weather changes markedly. It often seems to me that through the last two decades we've become a nation of weather worriers. Families put off plans for excursions because it's either raining to begin with or rain is threatening. At an allotment complex, people stay put and keep right on doing what they're doing albeit with a hood pulled up. In the biting cold, they'll wear warm clothes when they arrive, discarding most of them once they start working up a sweat. An allotment complex is most likely to be abandoned on a blistering hot day, save perhaps in the relative cool of the evenings when it comes to watering time.

Despite generations of us growing up seeing the outside world periscope-like from the inside of a snorkel jacket hood, and despite spending our school holidays peering through drizzled windows, and collectively maturing into masters of the indoor barbecue (guests indoors, brazier and cook under a parasol outside), we still get up in the morning, frown out the window and go: "I can't believe it's raining. Again!"

Why? We live in a temperate climate. It's what keeps the grass green. And the vegetables growing. We have one of the best climates for growing food in the world. We had rain yesterday, the day before and the day before that. We've had rain for thousands of years on this upper east side of the planet. Are we not used to it yet? Can you imagine the Egyptians waking up each morning, peering out through the bedroom shutters and hollering to Fatima:

—"You're not going to believe this, but it's blistering sunshine... Ag-ain!"?

Allotmenteers put on their coats, or take them off—and keep digging.

Food growing makes you become proactive and positive, allowing, of course, for a good moan here and there about pests and blights. You learn that you win some and lose some but at the end of the day you'll always take something worthwhile home with you. And it's not just the veg and fruit that ripens—I've turned from my more usual off blue white complexion these years to pink or even light brown because I am spending more time outdoors.

We have become a human nation of battery chickens. We need, quite simply, to get outside more. We spend our lives cooped up in (office) cubicles, our indoor existence farmed under artificial light and ventilation. We too peck buttons on machines for our foods and drinks, and like the so-called 'free range' battery hen, our handlers also let us out for an hour in the day to roam as we please.

And where suburban greens once buzzed during the school holidays with kids kicking footballs, running around and playing games, today those greens are empty in the summer months. The accepted norm of two parents at work means our children spend their summers in crèches and afterschool care—usually indoors. Then at home, bad habits see them immersed in computer games while we, their parents, do the same, taking a mental soak in the soaps or escaping into satellite football. An allotment life, even for one day a week, has shown us that soaps and football mean nothing.

Allotments are also ideal for those who don't want to kill their fellow man or woman a few times a week on a soccer or hockey pitch. Ideal for the person who doesn't fancy a five-mile run after dinner or walking the dog endlessly round the houses. They do tend to be a haven for those people who aren't team players of the locker room mentality.

But the exercise is assured—even without realising. After one particularly hard-felt digging season which stretched over two months, we reached the June/July lull and I realised that I felt strangely twitchy. A colleague in work who goes cross country running asked if I had stopped an exercise regime suddenly. He pinpointed the end to the digging and he indicated that therein lay the problem—a common one experienced by runners who have to stop for reasons of injury. He explained that strenuous regular exercise produces feel-good endorphins and when these stop suddenly, you experience withdrawal symptoms.

Dr John Farrell, medical director of Pfizer Healthcare, claims that digging burns 150 to 200 calories every half an hour—the equivalent, he says, of a workout with a punch bag. Weeding, he says, burns up to 150 to 180 calories every half an hour and regular gardening reduces the risk of heart disease by a third and the risk of a stroke by a quarter.

Then there's the meditative side. Along with Her Outdoors, I discovered, quite by accident, that weeding on a large scale—and we've done so much of that this year—produces a 'zoning out' effect through its relaxed repetitions. Start with a problem on your mind, and by the time you're finished, it's either gone or it's far easier to solve.

A recent scientific study went even further and suggested that such feel-good effects are actually physiological, and that soil contains beneficial 'happy chemicals' that are absorbed through the skin as you work with it and get your hands dirty. A research team at Bristol University discovered that *mycobacterium vacae* found in soil may help cancer patients by raising serotonin levels.

Growing food is the most therapeutic activity there is according to Restore, an Oxford-based charity that helps people with serious mental health problems and runs allotment schemes to help treat them. In America, allotmenteering is used to help problem city children to learn social responsibility and improve social interaction, while growing food has also been beneficial for those with attention deficit disorder.

Counsellors who treat patients for depression usually quiz them on the quality of their diet. With an allotment you're getting the very best of heart and brain food.

Finally, it's the best treatment ever if you sometimes find you have trouble sleeping. The combined effects of outdoor work and fresh air produce a real, deep and natural tiredness, which will have you out like a light as soon as your head touches the pillow. Zzzzzzzz!

Allotment Diary, Year One

October

It's late October but Plot 34's five-year-old, self-appointed Head of Secret Tunnels (HST) has been planning the minutae of his Hallowe'en festival—on and off as far back as last April I think. When you're five, of course, any day involving loud explosions, being out after dark, dressing up, getting free sweets from every one of your neighbours and then getting high on the E-numbers must head up the year's events calendar, alongside Christmas and your birthday.

Thankfully, our HST finally settled on 'just a vampire' as his Hallowe'en outfit. He had previously dallied with the notion of "building my own real live Frankenstein" to shepherd around the doors with him. Plot 34's key role in our HST's Hallowe'en party plans kicked in back in April when he first proposed growing great big orange pumpkins so he could have Jack O'Lanterns later in the year.

Since then, apart from his master plan for a four-mile underground tunnel linking the hilltop allotment to the house (already excavated to its first 12in thanks to his sterling efforts with a sandcastle spade), his other duty has been to monitor the squash patch—well named given his propensity to squash numerous developing prospects underfoot as he wanders through it again and again.

His use of the term "trick or treating" jars with me because it shows the prevalence of another type of Frankenstein—imported American Hallowe'en. Going round the doors was formerly known in Ireland as, well ... just "going round the doors". Now it's "trick or treating". The holiday has gone full-blown consumer. There's pressure to buy expensive American-style Hallowe'en outfits rather than make your own and pressure on parents to buy elaborate light displays for the house.

Oiche Samhna, the original Celtic festival of our ancestors, was actually a hugely important and genuinely frightening part of the year, when the spirits of the dead were believed to cross over and stalk the earth for one night.

It marked the end of the growing year. By Hallowe'en, whatever you had harvested and stored was your lot to survive on until the first crops again the year following. It marked the death of summer, the onset of cold nights, lean eating and the time when elderly and frailer younger community members were most likely to die. People made candle-lantern faces from turnips and beets, and dressed up to scare away the spiteful spirits who could curse you with bad luck at this pivotal time of year.

Not by coincidence, the vestiges of Hallowe'en were always apples, nuts and turnips—the foods that would best keep through the winter and those which were heavily relied upon. The ubiquitous barm brack was itself made from the last of the dried hedgerow berries.

But Hallowe'en is still for the kids, so, despite reservations, I gave in quite easily to our HST's requests for pumpkins. Back in March, I had picked up a bumper pack of six assorted squash seeds from Johnsons, which included Turk's Turban, a decorative squash which looks, as the name suggests, like a brightly coloured turban; Butternut, a yellow affair; Sweet Dumpling, a small grapefruit-sized pumpkin with green and yellow stripes; Rolet, another grapefruit-sized customer; Table Queen, which resembles a green melon; and finally Jack O'Lantern, the great big orange head of American Hallowe'en.

I meticulously cultivated the seeds indoors until the last frosts had passed, and then sowed the resulting plants into two patches on the allotment in May.

Most died a slow and protracted death in a dreadfully windy and rainy summer. Some gave me false hope by sprawling, vine-like, out of their bed borders and across the ground towards the sun. Big yellow flowers followed, but from then on we were pulling our hair out as one immature fruit after another rotted or simply dropped off.

By Hallowe'en, out of perhaps twenty transplanted vines, we had a miserly four squashes, including two half-green, half-orange Jack O's, about half the size they were supposed to be. One was rounded, the other elongated. From these we sat down and made our lanterns.

We christened the resulting lanterns Bert and Ernie, because their particular Jack O' heads ended up being tall and thin stood up (Bert) and wide and flat on its side (Ernie).

Our little man was happy enough with the results but from a grower's point of view the two squash beds were a complete waste of time and effort.

So following the squandered squashes of this season, next year's Hallowe'en will be a distinctly Irish one. The original Irish reigning head of Hallowe'en is the turnip (or swede as we call the purple and yellow one), a hugely productive root crop that's far more resilient than its fat, vacuous, orange American usurper. It takes a hammering from the local weather, its taste actually improves with the scourge of frost and it stores extremely well in the ground or out. Pulverised with butter, salt and black pepper, it goes heartily with good old spuds and any meat dish you may fancy. At least with neeps, I can be sure next year's yield from those beds won't end up turning into a pumpkin.

By November, our new chest freezer is already half full with some decent surpluses. We have broccoli, peas, berries and even bags of cherry tomatoes which are great for throwing onto the pan whole to fry for breakfast and still somehow retain that magical taste. Up on the allotment there are still sprouts and cabbages to be picked and they should be accessible for another month or two.

Meantime anyone who wonders about the truth of global warming should consider that I'm picking passion fruit, tomatoes and chillies from a patio in Kimmage, in November! And I might have been able to locate a few more passion fruits this year, were it not for the neighbouring grapevine that I bought in the summer, which has put on a late growth spurt and is tangling into the other.

—"Back off, it's November! It's dark at four, for chrissakes!" I snarl, as I hack at the *Vitis vinifera*, a vine more commonly found on the sun-baked slopes of Sicily.

My old man, a veritable spout of all sorts of uninvited wisdom (we've given him the sobriquet EOE—Expert on Everything), looks at the tomatoes, picks his ear and shakes his head before telling me to strip all the leaves off the tomato plants. This, he says, will cause the last growth efforts of the plants to go straight into the remaining fruits. His dad used to do that, so I should.

I tell him that there's nothing wrong with the plants, that they're nowhere near dying. They've survived two licks of the frost brush already, and they're still growing, still flowering, still fruiting, so let's leave them alone and see what happens.

Last year, I left them to their own devices and ended up picking and eating the last of the red tomatoes off the vine on Christmas Day. But in the 1970s and early 1980s, when granddad grew his tomatoes and his grapes, they were ensconced indoors all year in a glasshouse, where the temperature always remained warmer, even in winter.

In those years November meant November: ice, snow, hailstones and whatnot. For us kids, balaclavas, duffel coats and gloves-on-strings weather, Bovril, stew, soaked shoes, smog, 'flu. It was not the "Let's have our fry-up on the patio this morning,"/"Turn off that heating and open those windows,"/ "Did I leave my shades behind?"/ "Wish I hadn't brought this darned coat with me" sort of November we've been having of late—and certainly not, "Let's pick a few tomatoes and chillies and cut back the grapevine in search of passion fruits" weather.

They tell me that at the Botanic Gardens in Glasnevin, some banana trees that were put outside for reasons of space have thrived in the elements. How long before they fruit? Meanwhile global warming means they're in danger in their countries of origin.

For food growers, the last few years have had observable

patterns. January and February produced the coldest weather of the year. But then around Easter in both years we got a mini-heatwave of some length. This was followed in each case by a sudden cold and stormy snap in May. Then summers were humid and overcast, and this year's also brought non-stop rain. And in both years, September to December has been characterised by some unusually balmy and sometimes sunny weather.

What does all this mean on the allotment? First off, it's bad for traditional 'Irish' root vegetables. Parsnips and swedes and other traditionally Irish crops, such as rhubarb, actually benefit from frost and the sort of ice-cold periods we have been missing. Potatoes do not like wet summers and get blight.

The roasting Easter periods have meant that tender plants starting indoors, such as courgettes and tomatoes, will have a growth surge which leaves them even more vulnerable to hardening off in May's storms. But the survivors, like our tomatoes and chillies, will crop right until Christmas.

Chapter Six

Festive Compulsive Disorder

This year for the third in succession, I ventured outside on Christmas morning and picked a crimson, shiny, ripe, homegrown tomato from the, by now, fast-dwindling, patio plantation. I then chopped it up and ate it raw.

Despite a skin slightly thickened by the recent frost, this remaining example of the old year's tomato crop tasted supreme, a globe of edible sunshine in the heart of winter. Because it's the third year I've done this on Christmas morning, I guess it's now become a fully fledged festive time ritual. This year I felt strangely compelled to do it—as if it wouldn't be Christmas proper without picking tomatoes on the patio.

This is how Christmas fads start. Look what happened a single lifetime ago when the Coca Cola Corporation put Father Christmas in a red jump-suit instead of his more usual centuries-old red and green combo; a red sock with a white snowball on the end instead of a knitted green beanie. Long established festive sentimental compulsive disorders for Christmas are usually passed down subconsciously through families rather than corporations. But, like me and the tomatoes, if you're not careful you can accidentally bring new ones upon yourself.

It started out as a little project to see how long they'd last—just to see how far global warming had gone. Those who have grown food over a lifetime or even in the last decade, can see a big difference is what didn't work outdoors years ago and what happily carries on outside today. And this is supposed to be Ireland of the dampen lumpen miserable vegetables—the spud, the cabbage and the swede? Don't be surprised either if the Man from Del Monte is spotted scouring estate agents in West Cork.

After three consecutive years of picking and eating home-grown tomatoes off the patio on Christmas morning, I'll no doubt be compelled to do it every year until I'm an aul' fella. So will my children and their children. And when, in 2050, you ask my descendants why they're passing round bits of Marmande heritage picked from shrivelled plants, on a patio of an icy Christmas morning, they'll give you a strange look and they'll say:

—"Because we ALWAYS do this on Christmas morning!"

Like twins, moles and red hair, Christmas rituals pass down through families like genes and, as people settle down and have children, their genetically programmed rituals are intermingled.

When I asked Her Outdoors last Christmas why it was so vitally essential to eat thickly cut slices of home-boiled ham on coarse brown bread with English mustard, accompanied by a pot of tea—all then to be consumed on the stroke of 11.30 on Christmas Eve night, I got the same answer:

—"Because it's Christmas. We ALWAYS do this at Christmas."

The odd part is that every family believes every other soul in the land does exactly the same on their Christmas holiday.

—"Doesn't everyone go to the pub on St Stephen's Day night at 9 o'clock wearing only green and red, drinking only Advocaat Snowballs with the aim of falling over by 11?" they'll ask.

—"Doesn't your family play Boppit every St Stephen's Day after dinner, with the winner getting to pick the very first chocolate liqueur?"

But the one Christmas ritual we share across the board, and undoubtedly the most vital, is that of Christmas dinner.

For a time I thought sprouts, bread sauce and pieces of roasted pineapple were an essential component for every Christmas Day platter. But I've met others who say you can't have a proper Christmas dinner without a roasted parsnip. Roasted parsnips? That's not Christmas! Where's the pineapple? But it was with even greater shock that I noted this year that our own family's long-passed-on Christmas dinner menu had dropped a vital component.

—"What, no sprouts?" I spouted.

At my mother's on St Stephen's Day—now the replacement Christmas Day with the siblings given that we've nearly all moved out and settled, I learned that a plebiscite had been conducted in my absence by the anti-sprout contingent, whom it emerged, had long been working on my mother over a few Christmases. It had thus been determined that, after many decades, the most Christ-massy of Christmas vegetables, the sprout, was to be ejected from the family plate.

—"Nobody likes them!" intoned my siblings in unison.

—"I like them," I proffered.

Serving Christmas dinner without sprouts is like gin without tonic, Laurel without Hardy or politicians without dig-outs.

The sprouts have done well at Plot 34. They're among the few vegetables that remain to be harvested in winter long after every-thing else is gone and thus they provide a link between the old year's growing season and the new. Latterly I've been leaning towards other winter veg like swedes and celeriac. Much as I love parsnips I keep missing the 'sow by' deadline.

We had our first sprouts in early December and we should be eating them until March by the look of things.

Meantime, on the upside, the boy done good from that other, more widespread Christmas tradition—Santa Claus. The big man in the red and white fluffy jumpsuit brought me plenty of good-ies to enhance the continuing work at Plot 34 and 34A for the new year. Most notably, a 5sq.ft greenhouse and a wormery.

The former comes courtesy of Her Outdoors's parents, who will have no doubt been aware of their daughter's trauma over sharing a house with dozens of trays of seedlings through March, April and May.

Now, at least, the whole lot should be able to go outside. I might also be able to grow some even more exotic exotics. But first I have to find the space—which might demand shifting the raised salad bed down the garden a bit. I will also have to be sure of anchoring the thing properly.

Also welcome is the wormery, a pressie from my brother, which has the advantage, over a compost bin, of digesting cooked food as well as producing liquid plant food. The presen-tation of the wormery was made in my sister's living room and greeted by many murmurs of nervousness from the female con-tingent present.

—"What? Worms? In there? How many?"

There was in fact a voucher inside which you were supposed

to send away to get your worms by return of post. But they didn't know that, and thus, in the interests of fun (for the lads at least) I let on that the bin was brimming to the top with invertebrates, ripped the lid and then let it spill in their general direction. I love Christmas!

Next up for the amateur grower comes the New Year, a time for resolutions, half resolutions to be broken, and forward planning on what you'll grow in the coming year. A time of year for pipe dreams which seldom come to fruition—but it has to be allowed given that there's actually very little to do in the garden or on the allotment at this time of year.

It's also that time of year for another one of my long-standing personal traditions—giving up smoking. Way back when blowing toxic smoke everywhere was compulsory on planes and trains and in hospitals, my teenage self got himself ejected from a college lecture for lighting up a particularly pungent herbal cigarette. Our middle-aged tutor, who believed he was quite 'with it', and 'groovy with the kids' threw an uncharacteristic flap, slapped the still-smoking tab from my mitt and frogmarched me out the door so fast that we left a hole through my classmates' Rothmans haze.

So he began to outline his case: While he personally believed in freedom of choice on the marijuana issue, there were still rules that simply had to be upheld. So he would not—under any circumstances—have someone openly smoking "that stuff" in one of his lectures.

Did he make himself crystal clear?

He did, I assured him.

Had he turfed me out on the basis that it smelt like burning goat faeces (as I first assumed), I'd have wholeheartedly agreed with him. But he wasn't half as 'right on' as he liked to believe. These fags were totally devoid of "that stuff".

These were Honeyrose cigarettes, then a revolutionary new sort of nicotine-free herbal cigarette just launched to help people give up smoking—an early pioneer of today's slick and burgeoning 'give up smoking' nicotine-replacement industry, of which I have long been a loyal devotee. Meaning that I give up every year—buy all the stuff, the inhalers, the gum, the patches, the hypnosis, the books, the mindset, and then go right back on them come February.

Cigarettes are now the guts of a tenner a packet, so it's time to quit (really) this time. Because by the time you're reading this they'll probably be €20.50 and down-at heel-smokers will be robbing handbags to pay for their habits. Money is better spent on seeds and other whatnot.

My other resolutions are for the allotment. All have come about as a result of a year of hands-on learning. Much to my disappointment, I'm still not a grow-it-all know-it-all, even despite writing a weekly column of poised outpourings on the subject. The theme of the newspaper column is a novice's year in charge of an allotment, and I'm just as inept, if not more so, than anybody else. But I'm learning as I go. Hence the resolutions. And so I have resolved the following:

I will not grow any more pumpkins

Last year I devoted an inordinate amount of time to the production of just four pumpkins. Had I known that's all I'd get from sixty seedlings, I wouldn't have bothered. Pumpkins prefer rich American soils to wind-blasted Bohernabreena bog, so I can't really blame them for dying in sequence like some squash-themed version of the ten green bottles song.

I will not buy stuff I don't need—no matter how cheap

After losing the run of myself at various Lidl bargain rushes, I now have blackcurrant bushes in double figures. Apart from throwing them into smoothies, this many blackcurrants is useful only if you plan on becoming a Ribena bootlegger.

I will be ready for a blight

Having been overly smug that I didn't grow potatoes last year, about half my tomatoes later succumbed to the very same spores that historians hold responsible for the potato famine.

I will keep large stocks of copper oxychloride (good old-fashioned blight stop) in reserve.

I will not overcrowd

When you have lovingly nurtured your seedlings, it kills you to throw away the ones you don't need. Those I couldn't give away to my friends were therefore shoehorned in between plants that were correctly spaced in the first place. The results were the lightning spread of blight (see above) and a tangled pea crop.

I will use label sticks

Many different plants look the same until they start fruiting or producing. I now know I can't wait that long to tell them apart, so I will employ proper labelling sticks.

I will not build rocky paths

While everybody else threw the stones from their beds into a heap, I decided on a better plan: to use them to make neat paths between the beds, thus furnishing a grip on the mucky soil and creating drainage between beds, while looking quite natty into the bargain. Great, until I discovered the difficulties associated with hauling supremely anchored weeds from between the stones. And problems shifting the gleeful colonies of pests who boarded in their hordes underneath them, right alongside the crops.

I will plan ahead for harvest time

There is no reason to harvest 600 carrots in one go, or anything else for that matter. While they look great in a big pile, it means entire lost weekends washing, blanching, bagging and freezing.

I will read the instructions...

Beans and peas must be planted directly into the ground, not in yoghurt cartons on the kitchen windowsill, where they get in the way for months before perishing of shock when they go outside.

...and ignore some of them

I have discovered to my chagrin that I should be planting seeds as much as a month later than some seed packets suggest. Many seeds come from abroad, where the growing season starts earlier. Some of my varieties perished from cold as late as May.

I will butter-up a farmer

While the soil at Plot 34 is not half bad, those who stuck a €20 in the top pocket of a local farmer were reimbursed with a truck-load of steaming horse apples and ended up with far more on their plate as a result.

I will break wind

I will buy rolls of windproof gauze. A hilltop allotment, despite its exposed position, does not need to resemble a Tim Burton film set.

Of course New Year's resolutions are made to be broken. My plans to dig the allotment thoroughly in January and February amount to nothing, I'm back smoking again, and me and my boy are out on the patio studying a large box.

My "let's make a greenhouse" game, designed to promote bonding between father and son, is becoming unstuck before it's even started. Plot 34's five-year-old, self-appointed Head of Secret Tunnels (HST) is already singularly disappointed at the blandness of the debris spilling out of the flat-pack box.

Dozens of uniform tubular steel bars and wire-mesh panels jangle out onto the patio, followed by a sea of identikit plastic joints and a big roll of plastic sheeting. When finished it should be a 4ft x 6ft, and 6ft high, self-assembled, portable greenhouse.

—"Hey, that's not a greenhouse!" moans our HST, ruefully prodding the detritus with his toe, hands firmly stuffed in pockets.

After checking the box again, perhaps in the hope of finding a remote control in there (everything came with a remote control this Christmas), he begins to slink off. I'm studying a single sheet of paper with a squidgily printed drawing of what it should look like. The diagram looks like a photocopy of a photocopy of a photocopy. No words, just one big picture. Messy lines seep into one another, making it almost impossible to see what goes where. Underneath are tiny splodged drawings of each component, each with a letter assigned. The components all come with stickers with a letter on.

—"Are those the im-structions?"

—"Yes."

—"Can I see?"

—"Yes."

—"Cool!"

I'd forgotten that his recent enthusiasm for maps (courtesy of the *Pirates of the Caribbean*) had somehow crossed over into a fondness for all official-looking, diagrammatic instructions. It's game on again.

Soon we're kneeling on the grass, surrounded by piles of hollow bars clipped into joints and despite our attempts to follow the "im-structions" closely, we've already got some wrong joints stuck on. Once built, the greenhouse will be perfect for hatching seedlings through March, April and May; hot housing tomatoes, chillies and cucumbers; and starting other crops, such as cabbages and broccoli, from seed. And as Her Outdoors points out, we'll also have our kitchen back for the second three months of the year, unless I can think of still more things to grow in there.

And as HST point out, the greenhouse will also be exceedingly handy for "camping out".

We're assembling it in January to give it a proper all-round wind-testing. We won't start sowing in there until March. And if it remains standing through the gales of January and early spring, nothing will budge it.

For a five-year-old, our HST has a good concentration level but once the construction work goes (literally) over his head, and the support bars are too high for him to slot in, he finds alternative activities. Such as bashing the remaining bars together hard, flattening them in the middle to "stop the greenhouse shelves rolling off" or using the hollow ends of the metal tubes to take soil samples, scientific style by driving them deep into the lawn.

Next he renders Ian (our senior ceramic garden gnome) legless by dropping him on the patio. "I wanted to show him the greenhouse," our HST protests as I pick bits of the pint-sized ceramic patrician off the path. Then I spend the next half-hour jamming a skewer into three of the bars to remove the 8in of mud and grass jam-packed inside. This is part of the fun of working with our HST, who like most boys of his age, prefers to think up his own jobs rather than go along with the established conformist agenda. The sort of stuff which leads to:

—"HEY! What do you think you're doing?"
(a) (chucking a full watering can in the air)
—"Watering the sky."
(b) (wielding a shears on a rose tree)
—"Making the plant so we don't bump into it."
(c) (pulling a cabbage apart)
—"Getting the insects out."

Like any good flat-pack worth its salt, this one finishes with a few mystery bits left over and requires a few partial disassemblies before it's truly sorted. Then the clear plastic skin goes over the whole lot and—ta da! We're done.

Next we sandwich it in flush between the side fence and the foot high raised salad bed in the garden (the council won't allow greenhouses at the allotment). On the box pic, it's standing alone on a neat lawn. Do this only if you want it airborne. This thing stands 6ft high at the apex and 4ft wide, is covered in plastic sheeting and weighs about as much as a kitchen chair.

The Chinese fly similar constructions on strings for sport.

For further insurance, I buy twenty tent pegs to pin it down and lash the whole lot over and around with horticultural wire. We zip it open and step inside. Loads of room. But the HST is already angling a payback for his assistance.

—"I'll have all the bottom shelves, and you can have all the top ones," he announces.

And in the continued absence of allotment things to do, and the need to feel useful, I then got to grips with that other Christmas present of growing significance, the wormery. Indeed if we were sensible, the modern kitchen would come with a wormery by Miele or whomever, fitted as standard alongside the washing machine, cooker, fridge and dishwasher. This ultra efficient waste-processor uses no power and will allow you to dispose of the dinner scraps, eggshells, tea bags and the gone-off food that we regularly dump.

Not only will it save us money on domestic waste disposal, it will also provide us with two by-products—great compost and liquid plant food, both costly luxuries for a food grower.

However, this domestic waste-disposal system might not catch on because people are still a little squeamish about the idea of having a very large can of worms to be opened daily, in the kitchen.

And however you put it or package it or market it, there's just no getting away from the fact that a wormery is a large bin stocked with hundreds and hundreds of worms.

I have just installed the wormery, and I can confirm it is sterile, clean, odourless and, most importantly, the worms don't escape (usually) into the house. Mostly you can't even see them as they tend to stay just under the surface in the bottom of the container.

These are 'tiger' worms, not the subterranean soil-sieving commoner earthworm we're more familiar with. Tiger worms eat rotting vegetation, so they live under rocks or just under the surface. They're thinner, have no 'belt' and are coloured with alternate bands of wine and off-white—hence the name.

You can pay £10 (€13.40) for 150 by post or pay nothing at

all and spend six months peering under rocks. So the voucher was promptly dispatched to somewhere called Uffculme.

It was only then I actually got to thinking about the logistics of 150 worms travelling by post. What about our awful postal delays? What if customs opened the suspicious packages? Were there quarantine issues? What if they were accidentally delivered to the wrong address? Then on my way to work, another horrible thought struck. I rang Her Outdoors immediately.

—"Hi, it's me. If a package arrives, will you, er, not put it on the radiator with the other post? Thanks. What? Er, worms. Yes. I did say worms."

Bless her, a finer woman you'd never meet.

Two-and-a-half weeks later they arrived, sluggish and exhausted from their travels and packed inside an envelope that looked not unlike a full tobacco pouch. In the padded outer envelope was a sealed plastic pack of compressed compost the size of a thin paperback. Despite tiny pinprick holes, the few worms visible didn't seem to be moving. Uh oh. So in the interests of reviving the survivors from their ordeal by mail, I got to work immediately.

You put a few sheets of damp newspaper on the shelf in the bottom of the bin and empty the compost on to this. Then the worms go in on top of that and then you add a small amount of kitchen waste on top of them—to give them a taste for it, you see. Then you shut the lid and leave them to settle for a week. The brochure says you shouldn't open the bin until then as your new housemates are prone to 'exploring their new home' before settling down under the compost.

Give it a stir now and again, throw in a handful of lime mix once a month to maintain a neutral chemical balance, don't overload it and that's pretty much it. Or that's the idea at least.

Then come the benefits. Apart from not having to pay for cooked food waste to be carted away in your bin (the regular compost bin isn't supposed to take it) you can, after a few weeks, start to decant a brown liquid by-product from the tap on the bottom front of the bin. This, the wormery makers assure me, is five-star plant food. Whether you like it or not, you have to decant it or the worms get drowned as the liquid builds up.

These lads will eat you out of house and home waste. They scoff the equivalent of their body weight a day. And you can throw everything at them: raw meat, newspaper, dog food, paper towels, tea bags, mashed potato, hamster muck, organic nappies—lots of stuff the ordinary compost bin can't take. However, I read that they don't like citrus, onions or dairy products—it's bad for the worms and the mix.

The remaining odourless crumbly matter (yes, that's worm poo) is harvested once a year and described in the leaflet from Uffculme as the 'caviar of compost'. I plan to use this and the monthly dose of liquid plant food (dilute to 10 parts water) to give our tomatoes and tray-sown vegetables a head start. And thanks to the wormery, the waste from our allotment veg will also end up being fed back to our newest plants.

But a wormery can cost around €100 and here's where I have a teeny weeny issue.

If the Uffculme contingent walked into Dragon's Den with it, they wouldn't get an investment and the miserable Scottish, long drink of water, who never invests in anything, would sneer, point at it and say: "Correct me if I'm wrong—but that's just a big bin that I can buy anywhere at all, with a shelf and a hole in it...and for that reason, I'm out."

With a regular plastic bin, a home brewer's plastic tap, a grid and a tube of rubber solution sealant, you could make your own for about €25. The worms can be bought separately.

After a day or two, Her Outdoors didn't even notice they were there. So much so that she placed a large plastic bin bag on top of the wormery, covering the air grid which lets them breathe. So when I opened it as instructed, a week later, the would-be helpful invertebrates were all dead—every single one of them. The wormery has been a bin in the side passage ever since.

Allotment Diary, Year Two

New Year

I have good reason to be indebted to red cabbage... or whatever it is. As we began our second year, Plot 34 was forlorn, scattered and splayed except for the red cabbage, big, healthy, proud, colourful and exotic looking, to prove to the other growers that we could run a proper show.

Of course the 'red' cabbage doesn't look red, it's sort of blacky purple. Cabbage can be confusing that way. White cabbage is green, as is 'black' cabbage. We bought the red cabbage plants, along with the rhubarb, sprouts and broccoli, in the Lidl cut-price veg growers' rush last spring. It was labelled simply: 'Cabbage', with no suggestion of variety or type. To make matters even more confusing, the seedlings were bluish-green back then. It was cheap, so we bought loads of it.

With that particular weird colour it has, the red cabbage always stood out even when the broccoli, sprouts, carrots and green cabbage started to come on to fill the gaps in our plot. After a while, they morphed slowly into a PVC-shiny, blackish sort of purply hue. People always asked about them.

—"What's that one up there? The weird-looking plant. It's doing really well."

"Red cabbage," I confided. "Great stuff."

I hadn't a clue. The rest of the plants came and went, and we tended them and harvested the lot but we forgot about the red cabbage.

Last week, amid the sort of high winds (the news reported waves the size of houses on the west coast) and horizontal rain that characterised the start of last year at Plot 34, I, in my infinite wisdom, said to Her Outdoors:

—"I'm writing an allotment column for a leading Sunday

newspaper, and we haven't been up there in over a month. We need to get up there."

So half an hour later (I didn't think she'd agree), I found myself struggling with the keys to get through the gates of our allotment complex. The key wouldn't fit.

—"Some gougers have banjaxed the lock," I shouted in the car window as the wind belted off my parka hood. "I can't get it open. The key won't go in."

I had to go round the side and shimmy over the wall. The adjoining farmer's livestock swarmed over to me. A lot of them had quite big horns which I thought farmers sawed off these days. The city slicker's core suspicion of livestock and their motives came to the fore: "Is that a cow or a bull? Walk tall and confident. Don't let it see fear. Box it in the neck if it attacks... or is that what you do for a pit bull attack?"

The lock on the second gate was also blocked, so I climbed over it as well and shinned up the hill. It was only when I arrived up at Plot 34 that I remembered that the allotment complex was officially closed for a month. Mother Council had turned the locks. If you're reading this, guys, please note I wasn't breaking into council property, it was a genuine mistake. But while I was up there, I might as well have checked the place out and made sure things were okay? (Please don't return my lease!)

The big surprise was that, in this, supposedly the most dead time of year for an allotment, I was greeted by a cornucopia of sprouts, carrots and cabbage. I pulled up a few fresh carrots, bagged a load of sprouts, then struggled to break off a red cabbage. I twisted and turned one particularly big head, but it still wouldn't come out of the ground. Out came the all-purpose mini Swiss army knife/light/ pen/screwdriver/scissors thingy. The blade had been sharpened so it could nick the hairs off the back of your hand. But had I persisted, like Andy Dufresne, the patient prisoner in *The Shawshank Redemption*, it would have taken me the entire duration of his two and a half hour feature movie to harvest a single cabbage. So I grabbed the head tight in both hands, braced my feet on the ground and heaved. It came up on the third attempt.

Now while I was always grateful for its allotment show-manship, I've also been a tad suspicious about the red/black/purple (whatever it is) cabbage. Because unlike everything else we've grown this year, the red cabbage hasn't been touched by pests. At some stage, everything we've grown has been at least nibbled at—the green cabbage was derooted by cabbage fly to the extent that we haven't managed to eat even one; the carrots have had the odd squiggled indenture courtesy of some grub or other; and even the onions have suffered break-in attempts, leaving a porthole or two to show for it. But nothing had touched the red/black/purple whatever cabbage. Not one attempt at an infringement.

So what did the grubs know?

We found out just weeks from Christmas when we decided to cook a nice dinner of juicy steaks, split spuds (our own), salt and butter, carrots (ours too), red cabbage (the subject of the conversation), sprouts (ours as well) and wine.

And so the black/red/purple PVC was spliced and placed in a pot. Despite being turned up to gas mark six for a half hour, the cabbage water stubbornly refused to boil. Not only that, it transmogrified into a purple sort of soup. I couldn't even see the cabbage in there, so I tipped the deep purple water out and threw in the still boiling carrot and sprout water. Now the mixed water wasn't boiling either.

Despite the stringent attempts at boiling, under the sort of heat and for a duration that makes peas transparent and turns even the toughest turnips to sludge, the cabbage remained the consistency of industrial-strength rubber. I took a bite. It tasted like industrial-strength rubber. But the East Europeans love it, apparently. A quick check on the internet shows that some people add vinegar to the water to help to break it down. I administered lashings of the stuff. The water was bright purple soup again but still those leaves didn't seem cooked.

Could it be one of those 'acquired taste' things? Nasty stuff that you convince yourself is actually nice if you listen to enough people saying so? Time for the litmus test. I doled it out onto the plate along with the steak, sprouts, et al.

Munching away, Her Outdoors proclaimed the carrots supreme, and that the sprouts were also top dollar (grubs and all).

—"I wouldn't be mad on that red cabbage, though."

She was being diplomatic. The whole inedible lot went in the compost. We found it three months later...still intact. I'm thinking of contacting NASA. I heard they need something new to replace those re-entry tiles on the shuttle.

Chapter Seven

Standing Your Ground

"Who's interested in growing vegetables these days?" was the question I was most often asked when I started 'Plot 34' in *The Sunday Times*—Ireland's first national newspaper column devoted to the the practice of growing your own food. People were genuinely puzzled as to why I was writing gardening pieces that dealt only with growing fruit and veg—and not a delphinium or rhododendron in sight.

Today, three years later, the question I'm most commonly asked is:

—"How can I get an allotment?"

So what has changed? Back in 2006 when the column started to take shape, the then economic boom was reaching its pinnacle and the 'foodie' craze had reached its high tide mark. Expensive farmers' markets became the 'in' places for well-off trendies to pick up fresh organic produce for their dinner parties. More than anything else it was this 'foodie' surge and the resulting quest for the best tasting and freshest veg—rather than any allusion to thrift—that started the first new wave of people putting their names down for allotments.

This trend was paralleled in the burgeoning environmental movement by the newly green-minded. The latter began to realise that growing their own food was a natural extension of their efforts to promote a sustainable lifestyle. From both directions, growing your own had become a lifestyle choice, mostly pursued by the middle classes.

The original motive for many of those 'old-fashioned' allotment veterans of pensionable age who have been at it for forty years or more, was a somewhat different one. Sometimes we forget how tough things were for previous generations. I have talked to older people who recall walking through Dublin city and witnessing the type of scenes on the streets which today we can only relate to the Third World. In the 1950s, it was common to see city slum children showing signs of malnourishment, or worse. One retired newspaper reporter told me of his daily walk to work through the north inner city slums and how he usually saw terminally ill children in their bare feet.

—"You knew which ones had TB and each day you saw them getting smaller and frailer until one day, they weren't there anymore."

While we've a long way to go before we match the poverty levels of the 1950s, it's not surprising that it was only when the recession hit with a vengeance that interest in urban food growing exploded. Because, as in the 1950s, saving money has become so much more important as joblessness returns on a large scale alongside slashed wages, cut hours and forced early retirement. In such times, a pastime which saves money is always more popular.

—"Where are they all coming from?" I wondered aloud in front of an old hand one sunny afternoon as we looked down over the complex, which was buzzing with the biggest turnout we'd ever seen.

—"I'd say it has something to do with people having a lot more ... em, time on their hands, wouldn't you?" he replied.

In an instant food growing has become the dinner-party conversation subject of choice, stealing the march from property prices—the pet favourite topic of the boom era. A number of national newspapers now feature regular allotment columns alongside mine in *The Sunday Times*, while RTE's television series, 'Corrigan's City Farm', Ireland's first food-growing programme, has proven hugely popular. His project was so successful that Cork City Council, in whose jurisdiction the project is based, is now adding an extra sixty allotments.

Michael Fox, of the South Dublin Allotments Association, has seen his organisation's membership double in size since I first contacted him, three years previously. Such is the demand for learning how to grow food that Fox, as with many other enthusiasts, is himself now offering classes in growing skills to the public.

—"It's great to see so many people interested again, no matter what the reason," he says.

In response to the surge of interest, the city councils have genuinely tried hard to create more complexes—a far easier option for them in times when land prices have collapsed.

South Dublin Council provided a lead for others to follow by opening the first new Dublin allotment complexes in decades, at Tymon Park and at Friarstown in Bohernabreena. The latter, which is home to Plot 34, has trebled in size in three years. The staff in South Dublin should be congratulated for the enthusiasm with which they have taken on and administered this expansion of allotments on their turf. Officials from its development department, which has steered allotment creation and allocation, were always at the end of the phone to give their help, time and advice.

However, despite the best efforts of many Irish councils to provide more allotments, the explosion of interest in food growing means that Dublin and Cork, in common with most European cities, are experiencing allotment waiting lists which are longer than ever; so much so that at the time of writing, some councils here had ceased taking new names altogether.

As I write, Fingal Council has completely closed its waiting list even despite having 225 new plots coming on-stream with plans to develop more at Turvey in Donabate and plans to examine ground for suitability at Baldoyle, Malahide, Skerries and Balbriggan. But while the property slump has made land readily available, it has also cut right back on council finances from development fees and has left most councils pretty broke. Many will have to rein in their allotment expansion programmes as a result.

For his part, Michael Fox believes a solution may be found in the greatest financial crisis this country has experienced. The National Asset Management Agency, or NAMA, created to deal with the land and property held by bankrupt developers, offers a chance, he says, to create many more complexes.

—"We're looking at a situation where there are now vast amounts of land that is not commercially viable to develop and won't be of any use for building for some time to come. It would

129

be a natural progression to use these sites as temporary allotment complexes. In that way, they'll at least generate a small income for the Government," he says.

Indeed from the state's point of view, having such surplus land occupied and looked after by rent-paying allotmenteers certainly seems to be a far better option than paying out for expensive boundary fences and for security and maintenance crews to keep such land in reasonable and safe condition.

Not surprisingly in such a climate there has been a huge rise in the number of private entrepreneurs offering their lands to rent out for allotment purposes, and often at quite prohibitive rents. Amounts of €400 are being sought annually and achieved for fairly small plots, often too far from population centres to be of any practical use.

This has generated a fear among existing allotment holders that cash-strapped councils will move towards treating allotments as a moneymaking business, thus abandoning their obligation under the 1926 Allotment Act to provide allotments as an amenity (in the same way they provide parks, football pitches and tennis courts).

At the time of writing, South Dublin, along with most councils across the country, has just levied huge increases in their annual allotment rents. Mine rose from €48 to €120. Worse still, they wouldn't rule out further increases for the years ahead. Following negotiations with the South Dublin Allotments Association, our own council eventually agreed to stall the increases for another year. But it seems that a steep hike in annual rent now looks sadly inevitable. In truth, anything over €200 for 100sq.m renders the exercise hardly worthwhile on a financial basis. I have worked out that our council is probably taking €15,000 a year in rent from ten acres of scrap ground which, because of its former history as a municipal dump, cannot be used for anything else but sheep grazing.

But even given the huge waiting lists and the problems being experienced in new allotment creation, it's always worth putting your name down with any council that has complexes located within a reasonable distance of your home. I have talked to hopefuls who have put their names simultaneously on the waiting lists of a number of councils and then got their brothers, sisters and even their mothers-in-law to put their names down as well—all to increase their chances of success. In truth, you never know what might happen and if you're not in you can't win.

Then, of course, there's your own back garden if you have one. A whole lot of good healthy food can be produced from surprisingly little ground. Most allotments stand at around 100 sq.m, which is about the size of a medium rear garden. Even a small section of the average urban back garden will make a dent in your fresh food needs, the only drawback being that due to restrictive light conditions and space, you might need to be a bit more choosy in what you grow.

My herbaceous borders have already been cleared away to grow cabbages, chives and herbs with soft fruit and tomatoes stretching upwards on the fence behind. Those who don't want to turn their borders entirely into a vegetable patch can instead mix the vegetables in among the flowers in the French potager style. Indeed plenty of food plants like courgettes, chives, beans and even cabbages produce colourful displays and attractive foliage which put the most colourful flowers and shrubs to shame.

There are few more breathtaking sights than that of a runner bean teepee erupting in scarlet butterfly-like blooms. Some varieties, like Painted Lady, have red and white blooms which look even more exotic than the most richly coloured sweet pea. Indeed sweet peas themselves are a variety of pea. Garden peas feature exactly the same type of blooms, only in uniform white. Tomatillos flower in yellow and black pansy-like bloom cascades, while tomatoes flower in bright yellow spills and chillies come with delicate little white cups.

The patio is another prime space for food growing, and bamboo supports or poles can be used to support tall plants against sunny walls where they do best. It's here against the patio wall where most of my annual tomato crop grows, in a ground space against the wall measuring about 1ftx6ft. The patio and path areas running alongside the house contain a long chain of planters, mainly large white plastic buckets obtained from commercial catering refuse. Restaurants and kitchens buy in their mayonnaise and cooking oil in these types of 2ft-deep lidded buckets. Mine hold herbs, tomatoes, and other food plants.

The front garden can also provide plenty of food growing space, and it has to be said that the habit of maintaining an immaculately groomed lawn is a bit ridiculous unless you need soft ground for children to play on. Don't be afraid to dig all or some of it up to make room to grow. Small front lawns in particular are useless, good only for spending electricity or petrol trimming them through the summer months. If you want growing space and you don't need the grass, then bite the bullet and dig the whole lot up. Just make sure the ground you need gets a minimum of six hours of direct sunlight each day.

And if you've no ground at all, or otherwise don't want to give up your garden, there's more than one way to skin a cat, as my late grandfather demonstrated through his successful procurement of various plots in different locations through his food-growing years. None of these, incidentally, was at a formal allotment complex.

What most would-be allotmenteers fail to realise is that there are plenty of people out there who have a good deal of ground, the maintenance of which they are neither willing nor able to keep up with, particularly older homeowners. So if you keep an eye out for overgrown areas, or take the trouble to knock on doors or advertise your need on shop noticeboards, you should be able to broker a 'crops-for-space' deal with somebody in your area who has land or a garden that is surplus to their needs. This is also how food growing can help bring back a sense of community to our city estates.

Another good source of borrowed ground is from landlords of rented homes, particularly those who own the sort of multi-unit buildings which come with large gardens. With these buildings, tenants don't usually bother with the upkeep and it's down to the landlord to come over every week and cut the grass and prune the hedges. As a result many of the 100ft-long gardens which typically come with these types of buildings have been either let go fallow completely, or subdivided to make maintenance easier. Often landlords will maintain only the areas close to the house itself and fence up substantial end tracts of garden which are let go wild.

An old developer's trick was to travel by double-decker bus to check out land, so why not try it around the area you'd like to get an allotment in. Sitting upstairs on the window side, or at the very front, you have the position and height necessary to spot these disused sites over high garden walls.

Another consideration is to identify a piece of ground where there is surplus public space in your estate. Often there are widowed strips of land here and there which do not provide any great amenity value, but must nonetheless be maintained by the council. You and a group of neighbours can then approach the council and seek permission to garden there in what's known as a community garden. This is in essence a shared allotment. An example of a community garden is the Sitric Garden in Dublin's Stoneybatter. Utilising two end to end patches of ground which were nothing more than grass verges, the locals produce salads, tomatoes and herbs for their tables in this tiny communal garden in the heart of the built-up city centre. Each year the Sitric Garden has its own street party where much of the food is eaten. They've called this the Sitric Picnic.

For apartment dwellers, unless the sun is completely offside, you can grow plenty of food in containers on your balcony. Balcony growing has achieved remarkable results for the improvising citizens of Havana in Cuba. They were forced to grow huge amounts of food in all sorts of hitherto implausible places from within their urban midst. This occurred from the early 1990s after the former Soviet Union broke its trade links with the island and ceased the substantial subsidy support scheme for the Cuban economy. Today Havana is a city which pretty much feeds itself and its 2.5 million population from its balconies, patios and even food grown in old paint tins arrayed along the street.

Indeed apartment dwellers who live in modern buildings will often find a communal roof garden on the top of their building, usually containing nothing more than a few cheap benches and a widespread bed of gravel. With an array of containers and planters, these too can produce substantial food crops, once you get the permission of the management company, of course.

A number of my apartment-dwelling colleagues bemoan the fact that they don't have gardens in which to grow food, but I have assured them that a balcony and some windowsills is all you need for a good larder load. And so, following a request by one apartment-dwelling work colleague, I came up with a practical combo for the standard modern apartment or flat with its French doors and tiny balcony area which will produce a hell of a lot of food indeed.

The secret of good crops is in the soil and this is especially true of containers. A mix of four parts loam to two parts manure and one part agricultural sand is about right. Make sure all your pots have deep water trays underneath so the water does not dribble down to the balcony below. Ballast your pots with a few inches of broken crockery or stones in the bottom. This keeps them on the ground when they're dried out and provides drainage when they're wet. Mix your potting compost with water-retentive crystals and, after you've planted, top them with mulch to further lock in moisture. Terracotta pots are out—nothing dries out faster in summer—so use plastic. Here's your apartment garden:

- **Courgettes**

Plant about ten seeds indoors in April or May, and when they germinate keep them indoors in a warm, bright space by the window or in the greenhouse, taking care not to let them get intertangled. Transplant them outside in late May, each plant in a pot, planter or bucket at least a foot and a half deep and the same in diameter. With healthy full-grown plants, you should get at least two or three courgettes a week.

- **Cherry tomatoes**

Get two deep planters and place them indoors close to the French doors. Buy a packet of thick, 6ft-high bamboo canes and peg them into the planters, placing them in a quadrant. Wrap twine or training wire around them to provide a frame for your tomatoes to climb. At peak growth, eight vines should give you half a punnet to a punnet of tomatoes a week. The sunnier the position, the better the crops. Once the plants get off the ground, pluck the leaves off the lower regions and fill the space in the planters with basil or salad seeds.

- **Chillies**

Start chilli seeds off in the hot press and discard all but six of the healthiest plants. Plant three in a row in a long window box container about 1ft deep. Place them indoors either side of the tomatoes. Without bees to pollinate them, use a paintbrush to do as the bees do.

- **Salads**

Lettuce and rocket will grow in any window box, can be snipped on demand and sown in two-weekly relays to keep them coming.

- **Strawberries**

Plant strawberries in hanging baskets or vertical grow bags attached to the sides of the balcony. The advantage of being high up is that slugs and snails won't get them. They do need sunlight, however, and plastic netting to keep off the birds.

- **Beans and peas**

Take two large square containers and make two 5ft teepees from the bamboos (one foot sunken in the container). Plant one with pea seeds, the other with beans. If required, attach your teepees to the balcony above. Beans and peas are vines and will grow upwards.

- **Herbs**

Grow your herbs in separate pots. Parsley needs moist soil that could put paid to thyme or sage.

- **Spuds**

Buy a plastic bin about the size of a small wheelie bin or old-fashioned rubbish bin. Put in some compost into the bottom, plant the seed potatoes at intervals facing up. Cover them and build up the inside with more compost and then plant another circle of spuds with a few scattered inside and repeat—building it up in layers. This old gardener's trick produces a bin full of spuds from a tiny space.

- **Carrots**

Take a wide-topped pot about 2ft deep and cover the top with a sprinkling of carrot seeds. If successful, you could harvest close to fifty small carrots in a 1ftx1ft wide planter. The tops do in fact look like houseplant ferns.

Fruit bushes like gooseberries and redcurrants could also do well on balconies as could those grape vines more suited to Irish climes which can be properly trained along a wall, taking up only the space where the container stands. There are also a range of miniature and heavy-cropping fruit trees now available, like the Irish-developed Coronet apple, which will live happily in a container. And if you keep your plants indoors on windowsills, there's no reason you can't make edibles of your indoor pot plants.

And for those rare wretches who have no outdoor space at all, you can still grow food indoors on your sunnier windowsills. Replace your useless cheese plants and decorative potted ferns with food plants instead. In the cult comedy film *Withnail and I*, the plummy and gay former thespian, Uncle Monty—as portrayed to overblown perfection by Richard Griffiths—keeps vegetables as the decorative pot plants in his home. There's no reason at all why we shouldn't imitate the tweedy middle-aged queen by adorning our living rooms with pots of his beloved carrots the tops of which resemble lush green ferns in any case ("There's a certain je ne sais quoi about a firm carrot," he minces), or else grow chillies or tomatoes instead of useless cheese plants.

While we haven't yet tended indoor root crops, myself and Her Outdoors regularly have half a dozen pepper plants fruiting in the ensuite bathroom. They flower in delicate cream-coloured blooms and are just as attractive as any of the more popular flowering house plants, especially when dripping with fire-engine-red chillies. We also grow them on the kitchen window and we keep basil in pots on the floor by the glass sliding doors.

So there's no excuse not to grow your own, unless you don't really want to. But if you do have your heart set on an allotment, get busy and mobilise your neighbours, get canvassing and take names. There's never been so much land lying idle and never as much enthusiasm from the councils, Government and politicians towards setting up allotments. It's up to us all to make the best of this golden window of opportunity. Unless that is, the only vegging you really want to do is on your sofa and in front of the gogglebox.

Allotment Diary, Year Two

March

It's always something. Last year we didn't get the keys to the allotment complex until late in the growing year. This left us behind with the digging. This year we have the keys but it's been raining steadily for weeks. I popped up the other day to Plot 34 to note that the soil is still pretty waterlogged. Too wet to dig.

I'm planting up my seeds in the new, soft, plastic-coated greenhouse, which Her Outdoors seems worried that I've turned into some sort of a private office because of all the time I'm spending in it. Today I've got *The Sunday Times* in here, a beer, a pen, labels and a comfy chair. It's spitting rain outside. Nice and relaxing and quiet. Thanks to the greenhouse, we won't be sharing our home with two dozen trays of seedlings this year. I'm planting the finer seeds in shallow trays into a seed compost commonly available at the local garden centre. I've gotten into a sort of routine with the seeds by now. The tray gets a few sheets of newspaper pressed into the bottom and then I sprinkle some water on it to get it to mould into place. I discovered last year that seed trays dry out really quickly. The paper not only helps keep the moisture in, but it also makes for some protection from the pests which crawl in via the drainage holes. Best of all, it helps keep the roots together when I take seedlings out to plant them. You can press the whole lot out of the tray and tease the seedlings out with the roots intact, one plant at a time.

I throw the compost into the tray, level it off and then sprinkle more water on to make sure there's plenty of moisture for the plants. The seeds are sprinkled into the tray rows—

the difficult bit is preventing too many falling in the same spot. If they fall in clumps I go back and pick them out again.

Then a thin topping of compost is sprinkled over the seeds. I tamp it down. Sprinkle it lightly again—water too heavily and the whole lot gets mixed around. Next comes sticking in a marking label, which is hugely important because most plants look the same in their early development. It's virtually impossible to distinguish between not only different varieties of the same plant, but between different types of plants overall.

I buy the sort of flat-pointed white plastic stick labels from the garden centre for about two quid for fifty of them. I also bought an indelible pen for writing on them. I write the name of the plant, tomato; then the variety; Gardener's Delight. Then underneath I write the date, useful if you are staggering your planting to stop them cropping all at once. I stick the labels in and then I cover the whole lot with a layer of Clingfilm. I seal the sides with Sellotape to keep the moisture in and to stop the soil getting cold. When the water in the compost evaporates, it hits the Clingfilm, condenses and drops back down again. It means I only have to water them once until they get tall enough to hit the Clingfilm cover. At this point I remove the film. Using the same tray sizes allows you to stack them neatly on top of one another criss-cross style until they germinate.

Some seeds, however, need the hot press to get going. Chillies and peppers simply won't sprout in the temperatures in this part of the world. This year I've decided to ditch the sweet peppers. Last year's chillies are still in use, dried and put into grinders. Larger seeds like courgettes, I tend to plant individually in yoghurt cartons. These also get a wrapping of Clingfilm. This year I'm experimenting with tomatillos, a South American tomato-like thing which comes in its own little paper case. I've planted a tray of basil and I've six types of tomato, which came in one pack courtesy of Her Outdoors' sister-in-law, Her Overseas.

Chapter Eight

What's It All Got to Do
with the Price of Potatoes?

And so I ascend the steps to the Dragon's Den, lugging a green-grocery display on wheels laden down with rustic baskets of fresh produce. The seated figures remain impassive as I pass around the baskets along with plates of raw chopped carrots, celery and onions for them to taste. Lots of sniffing and then crunching. The sour Scot holds up a carrot and sneers to the Matron:

—"It's a carrot!"

I clear my throat and start my pitch, outlining a plan to make money by saving it. I am going to do this by working on an allot-ment one day a week for two years and, with the help of a quite small investment, I will produce most of my own fresh food instead of having to buy it. The Scot laughs.

—"This… is a carrot, I buy these at the shops for next to noth-ing. Why should I be interested?"

I tell him he should be interested because it's a different sort of carrot. It's organic, it has many times more nutrients and min-erals, it is healthier for his children than the ones he normally buys.

—"Well I eat the cheap ones and as you can see, there's noth-ing wrong with me. I think it's idiotic!"

The pernickety blonde matron asks me about my profit record over my first two years. About three grand after costs are deduct-ed, I tell her.

—"And… what were your costs?"

About a grand and a half, I tell her, and also make the point that the big start-up expenses for the more costly equipment like the petrol strimmer and the chest freezer are now out of the way and so I can expect costs to be 50 per cent less each year from now on. I'm also expecting to increase my profit margins as I learn more and make fewer mistakes.

The tanned Australian seated on the end introduces himself and asks his first question:

—"What level of mark-up have you made on your higher-yielding lines?"

I explain that on some items, profit can be as high as 1000 per cent. The Scot openly guffaws.

—"There is no product out there that can earn you a profit of 1000 per cent! Completely nuts. Are you Irish? He's come in here with the fairy tales of Ireland!"

The Scot smells blood and is grinning. I hold up a packet of tomato seeds, variety: Tigerella.

—"Last year I bought this raw material, this packet of seeds, for two quid. By the end of the year, I had turned it into two hundred quid's worth of tomatoes. And I can prove that." Suddenly there's a stony silence. Eyebrows are raised. They're all interested now.

But inevitably, by the end of my imaginary Dragon's Den pitch, the tables have turned again on me, this time irreversibly. The dour Scot:

—"As a businessman, I just don't get it. I can buy all of this stuff very cheaply in any local supermarket. I eat it all the time, and as I also said, there's nothing wrong with me as you can see. The cheap carrots do the job for me and I don't see any point at all in all this mindless effort. And I think you're mad. And for those reasons, I'm out."

The matron concludes:

—"I like the basic concept and I can appreciate the level of returns on some lines, but I really don't understand why you don't go 100 per cent with the same idea but reapply it to much higher-earning lines. I can't understand why you don't grow gourmet truffles, for example. But you've come in with this idea and the carrots and the celery and so on, and for that reason I'm out."

The tanned Australian beams generously:

—"This food is absolutely gorgeous. So I have to say that I

What's It All Got to Do with the Price of Potatoes?

DO understand completely what you're doing. I think it's a truly great idea and I really do sincerely wish you the best with it. But to me this Plot 34 concept is just simply not a business in the true sense, and for that reason, I'm out."

That's where pitching the allotment and food growing concept as a business would get me—at least on Dragon's Den, the popular show where budding entrepreneurs pitch business ideas to millionaires in the hope of generating an investment.

Because Plot 34 is certainly not a business. It's about far more than that. But saving money, particularly in the recession, has become at least one of my motives for continuing my allotment.

And when I first set out on my food-growing project, one of my aims was to discover whether growing food myself would save me any money at all, and if so, just how much?

But businessmen and women aren't always right because sometimes they too just miss the point. Growing food doesn't work as a business or for profit because that has to mean not only selling some of your produce but selling it on at a profit. That takes you into the realm of commercial farming. The benefit to you—both the supplier and the consumer—from your own allotment should be a negation of the need to buy at least some of your food at the supermarket, preferably most of it. But also and most importantly, the food you eat is completely fresh, and much better for you. If you will compare your homegrown carrots to bought carrots, then you need to at least match them with the most expensive organically grown carrots you can find.

But let's look at the money question on its own for a minute. The value of our harvest was about two grand in both years. We estimated our start-up costs at about a grand and a half. Ongoing costs, for seeds, compost, manure and so forth, run at around €200 a year—€100 for manure and compost, €60 for seeds, and €40 for sundry.

So if Plot 34 were a start-up business, it would be performing far better than most and its balance sheet sits healthily in the black for both of its first two years. If I was running a business though, and wanted to stand a chance of making an impression on the Matron from Dragon's Den, I would have grown only those crops which are most expensive in the shops and thus those that saved me the most money.

Calabrese, tomatoes, chillies, berries and salads were the

crops which served us best financially on Plot 34 because these were the items we grew in large numbers which were also the most expensive to buy.

A tray of young calabrese plants bought in Lidl for three or four quid gave us a harvest that would have cost us a few hundred to buy in the supermarket. God knows what in an organic farmers' market. But we didn't grow expensive crops only. The carrots and onions, despite the vast numbers in which we harvested them, are not particularly expensive to buy. We grew them because we eat a lot of them. So even though we were self-sufficient in both for most of either year, that fact didn't save us a whole lot of money because they're so cheap in the first place. The carrots probably saved us thirty quid, the onions fifty quid in all. I grow large amounts of crops which aren't expensive to buy simply because I far prefer the taste of the homegrown versions and know they've got far more nutrients because they're cut fresh from the ground and are eaten within hours. This I can't buy.

Cabbages, swedes, carrots and sometimes—depending on the price—potatoes can all be cheap as chips in the shops. But once again, the value to us is the extra taste and quality of what we're eating. At the moment, even in the best organic farmers' market, we can't buy better quality carrots, onions, swedes and spuds.

Similarly our entire pea harvest, if you valued it by supermarket prices, has earned us just €4, a pittance for the time and effort expended. Ridiculous too given that the two packets of peas we planted in our second season cost exactly that. Plant €4 to earn €4? The dour Scot would be apoplectic! When we shelled the half-sack of harvested pods (and this took an entire evening in itself), the amount of peas they yielded comprised about the equivalent of just two large standard bags of frozen supermarket peas. But there's more to it. Shelling peas is something everyone should do once a year. Kids love it. And those homegrown peas were treated like beluga caviar by us. Because of the sheer pleasure they provided our taste buds, the most beautiful tender and sweet tasting peas we ever tasted, every single little one was worth all the bother.

On the other hand, the cabbage harvest actually lost us money with the cost of protecting them with netting and ground covering material, determining that we actually spent far more money than we recouped. Cabbage costs about €1 a head in the shops while our total cost of producing them amounted to about €1.30 apiece. We had heavy losses in our first year in particular to cabbage fly and birds.

Where we lost out most dearly with our spend was where we bought dud seeds; or plants which didn't actually sprout in the first place; or seeds which didn't take; or those which died totally in the ground in their early stages of development. This was the case with our squashes, grapes, sweetcorn, most of our strawberries, our cucumbers in the first year and melons in the second. Seeds cost between €1.50 and €4 a packet. It sounds cheap enough until you're buying thirty packets in a season and that's a whole lot of money. And there are far fewer seeds in the packet when it comes to slightly more exotic plants like cucumbers (fifteen seeds), squashes (about ten) and worst of all, in Year One when I got just nine in a packet of strawberry seeds.

The next problem with saving money through an allotment is that food only benefits you financially if you do actually eat it. Tomatillos (we grew perhaps two hundred of them) can cost €1 a piece in the few specialist grocery shops which stock them. This should have made them a phenomenal money saver/earner. But because tomatillos are only really useful for making salsa verde and we don't eat much Mexican food, they're still in the freezer and will most likely end up on the compost heap after they expire. So while they might have saved us €200 if we were big fans of tacos and guacamole, because we didn't think about how to use them in our cooking before we bought the seeds and spent time tending them, they've ended up costing us money. This is particularly true given that we could have put the same effort into another more worthwhile crop instead. But we also thought tomatillos might be nice to eat fresh off the vine as fruit, just like tomatoes. Neither of us had ever tasted a ripe tomatillo and in the absence of finding any in the shops near us, we had to grow them to find out. They tasted awful. But hey, nothing ventured, nothing gained.

The runner beans, grown only because Her Indoors put in a special request for them, were rendered useless in one foul sweep when she looked at the picked crop of beans and said:
—"They're not beans?"
—"Yes they are!"

She paused for a second and then said:

—"Ohhh! It must have been Mange Tout that I was thinking of!"

I don't eat runner beans myself, in fact I can't stand the sight of them. It turns out neither can Her Outdoors stand the sight of them, so these too have cost us money—again via the opportunity cost. The seeds only cost €2 but the days spent digging the bed, building the bamboo support teepee, watering them and weeding them could have produced perhaps €100 worth of something else that we might indeed have eaten.

Mistakes due to our inexperience also cost us. Our leeks in Year Two mostly went to seed because I didn't know enough about their growth cycles and left them too long in the ground. Those which didn't go to seed were far too tough to eat. Again more waste and loss of money. In the case of last year's carrots, about a quarter went rotten because we had too much of them and we harvested too many at once instead of taking them as they were needed from the ground. The celery we grew from small plants tasted sour all along until it went to seed. Again we let it run too late before harvesting. Another large deposit for the compost bin!

However, your losses do shrink as you gain experience. We don't grow any of those crops which have previously proven too difficult. After a few seasons under our belt, we now know roughly how many seeds make for how much food. We understand processing better, we understand timing better and so we won't waste as much. But expect, when you're new to food growing, to make a whole raft of similar mistakes.

Blueberries, at a fiver for a tiny cigarette-box-sized punnet in the shops, are the single most expensive item we grow. The one blueberry bush I bought in Year One has only produced about three such punnets because it's still a relatively young plant. Thus as a moneymaker/saver, it has just about broken even—we paid fifteen quid for the plant in the first place. However, it should double that annual payback in its third year and double it again the year following. It truly is a worthwhile investment.

The fruit bushes, particularly the blackcurrants, redcurrants and gooseberries, were the first investments we made and probably the most lucrative of all from a money saving/making point of view. We got them small at about a quid a piece from Lidl, a bargain in the first place. They need hardly any attention and they grow larger every year, the crop increasing by perhaps 40 per cent from each plant in every new season. Berries are a super-food and they're also expensive to buy—about €4.50 for a frozen punnet of mixed berries. In our second year, Lidl repeated the offer. We repeated our purchases and doubled the number of fruit trees. The blackcurrants, gooseberries and redcurrants, all supremely high in vitamin C, were frozen and used to make early morning smoothies over a six-month period. They go in the blender with natural yoghurt, honey and milk.

But if I wanted to go all out to make money on an allotment, it would be best not to grow any veg at all. I'd follow the example of a grower on our complex who actually turned his allotment almost completely over to cut flowers in Year One. Now I'm not saying he sold them to make a profit, because that's illegal at an allotment complex. But if he had been of the mindset to do so, I believe he could have achieved a fiver for every large bunch from a shop (they were very impressive), which in turn could then sell them on for a tenner. At those rates he would certainly be looking at profits of at least ten grand on an allotment which cost forty quid a year to rent. That much money could in turn buy his family's fresh food groceries for two years or more—if, that is, the making or saving of money was all that the urban food growing exercise was about. But it's not.

Before the allotment we bought almost of all our fresh produce. These days, in the few months when we have none of our own produce to eat, we spend about €500 a month on groceries, and about 20 per cent of that goes on fruit and veg. Which would indicate that our bill for shop-bought fresh food or frozen produce before we took our allotment was somewhere in the order of €1,200 a year.

The fact that we generated two grand worth of fresh produce not only means that we got value for money from what we produced, but it also means that we actually ate more fresh fruit and vegetables than usual, simply because it was there to eat. We had meat and three veg instead of meat and two. That has to be good. This is perhaps what the true, hard-boiled businessman or woman doesn't understand about food-growing and why, for so many years, anyone who does it is regarded as a daft hippie.

But we're talking about money now, so back to costs. Our start-up costs in the first two years included two strimmers (one faulty version which couldn't be returned) at about €250. The chest freezer to enable us to store our harvests cost just over €100 and the raised salad bed with its timber surround cost in the order of €120 to install, which also includes the necessary compost and manure to fill it. We got the plastic greenhouse as a present in Year Two. It's a necessary piece of kit and would have cost us at least a hundred.

Ongoing costs which we'll have every year include seeds, as I've already mentioned (between sixty and a hundred euros a year), and sacks of compost and manure (around a hundred euros a year). The latter can be acquired cheaply if you know a farmer or a riding school willing to sell it cheap or give it away. After looking into it, we didn't bother because any manure we sourced was not rotted and mature enough to use. We would have had to store it for a year or two and we couldn't be sure it hadn't come from animals which had been treated with chemicals or allowed to gorge on weed plants. Much of the manure used around our allotment carried weed seeds the animals had ingested.

We do make our own compost in the garden but our composter seems to be a never-ending pit which, despite getting a big bucket of kitchen waste a week, never seems to fill up. So while composting properly is good for the environment, it doesn't actually provide you with a whole lot of compost.

Finally we spend around fifty quid a year on young plants like fruit bushes and strawberries (which are difficult to grow from seed) or slightly larger investments like the blueberry bush and our grape vine.

The lease on the allotment began at forty quid a year (although it has since increased). Then there are the costs you don't take into account such as the price of the petrol used in getting there and back and petrol used in our strimmer, which consumes about a tenner's worth over the entire season. It might seem petty to include these outgoings, but if we were running a business, it would all have to be taken into account.

Once these costs are deducted then our clear profits probably stand in the order of €800 to €1,000 a year.

This sounds pretty good. A car insurance firm which could save you this much on an annual premium would have customers swarming to their door. But then comes the killer blow—that which knocks Plot 34 as a business idea right out of the window. The labour cost of the whole enterprise. If you had to employ someone to work one weekend day a week to maintain your allotment, you'd probably need to pay them at the very least fifty quid a day for the service at a casual rate.

So it is time and effort which is the biggest cost of an allotment. Just think how much you might charge your boss for giving the company one of your Saturdays or Sundays? It's probably going to be a good bit more than fifty quid? Around forty eight-hour days are required through the year, so that's around €2,000 for labour. The reality is that it's likely to cost nearer to €3,000 or €4,000. This is where the profitability argument falls right down on its face with an allotment.

Grow calabrese or blueberries only and then find a way to sell them to the shops and you're in with a shout of running a good business. Better still, take the matron's advice, go swot up on the husbandry of rare subterranean fungi. As I write this, a big international businessman has just paid €90,000 (a new world record) for a particularly tasty truffle at an auction where he was chased all the way by a rash of other big businessmen. And if it wasn't for that pesky 'good food' motive that spurs most of us allotment holders along, who knows, I might have already been on my way to my first million.

Meantime, at Plot 34 the answer to the 'money only' question I raised at the start of the chapter is: I save €800–€1,000 a year.

But the point of it is: I grow food for the exact same reason that guy dropped almost 100k on a single truffle.

Allotment Diary, Year Two

April to May

It's mid April and I'm blaming Hugh Fearnley-Whittingstall for the fricking tomatillos. And whatever they say about never meeting your heroes, sometimes if you did you might just know that they're crazy from the get-go.

I had vowed before not to waste any more time with stupid crops that were either (a) not practical or (b) didn't pay their way. Then I find myself sitting inside my plastic greenhouse in the misery of April rain, painstakingly pricking out the spindliest, stupidest seedlings I've ever had the misfortune to handle: tomatillo. Variety: Toma Verde.

Germinated in the hot press, they shot up almost overnight, and are themselves now behaving like green wusses. If they could talk, these South Americans would be whining: "Wee don't like eet in this countree...too cold...wee don't wanna stand up straight...wee just wanna corkscrew our long fragile stalks around one another a trillion times until getting us apart requires tweezers, the nerve of a bomb disposal offeecer and half of ze Sunday afternoon." All because Smartarse-Wussingthrall made them look so bloody exotic on one of his endlessly repeated River Cottage instalments.

—"Tomatillos!" he whistled enthusiastically, holding up a freshly picked sample of something that looked like nothing I'd ever seen before—a sort of light green tomato wrapped in its own little delicate Chinese paper lantern—and sniffing it with the relish of a Vicks-prepped porcine with his nose in the truffles.

—"Lemony apple in taste, they're hugely popular in South America, where they make up the core ingredient for salsa verde," he adds...or something like that.

—"Also perfect for a more exotic sort of chutney," he whitters on.

The chutney is so good, in fact, that Hugh wins a great big rosette at the local yokel fair in Devon.

So when I happened across a packet of tomatillo seeds at the garden centre, straight into the basket they went. I, too, would have a trophy curio from South America among my crops, to be transformed into sensational salsa verde and gong-winning chutney.

After sowing them, I looked on the internet to see what else I could use them for. The answer, apparently, is absolutely nothing. No use for anything else but salsa verde...and chutney. And in the past twelve months how many times have we cooked Mexican or eaten chutney of any sort? Not once.

The relationship between the hobby food-grower and horticultural exotics is an odd one. Although we're growing veg for the table, we can't resist keeping a bit of ground aside for exploration and experimentation, for forays into the great unknown. Last year, for example, I tried to grow the squash Turk's Turban. I should have known what to expect when the text on the seed packet—that which normally states its use ('ideal in salads' or 'great for stews') said nothing more than 'ideal as an ornament'. The only use in fact for a Turk's Turban fruit is as a dried-out version of itself for the mantelpiece.

When it comes to the watermelons, I accept sole blame. At 59 cents a packet, the seeds were too cheap to ignore—just like that batch of inedible black cabbage I bought last year.

And to top it off, I also bought three honeydew melon plants at the garden centre, for three quid each, thanks to the nice pictures on the label that inspired thoughts of sitting barefoot on the patio on a sunny summer's evening, feasting on cool sweet melon flesh, twisting my shoeless, sockless toes and spitting pips at the skeeters.

All the melon seeds and the three plants are currently in the plastic greenhouse. Only problem is, having surfed the net to gauge my chances of producing fruit, I have discovered that each plant will sprawl out over a huge area and is only likely to produce one or two melons, maximum, of any good edible size. This means it would have been cheaper buying two melons in the shops for each plant I bought. On top of this, if they're grown upright, the melons will need 'hammocks'—netting to support the weight of the fruit. And there's only so far you're prepared to go. It's a greenhouse not rehab.

And now there are the tomatillos to tend to as well.

Bad choices perhaps. But then again I wouldn't be growing chillies, grapes and blueberries again this spring had I not experimented last year and reaped the rewards.

Like HFW, who'll eat anything from calf's testicles to a road-killed squirrel's arse, I'll try anything once. Twice, if it doesn't leave me feeling like a pillock.

As we get to the end of April, I know I'm a proper allotment holder because I'm feeling proud of my cabbages. Rewind twenty-five years to short pants and I lived in fear of the stuff. Even Roald Dahl, that fiendishly clever enthraller of young children, realised and applied to full effect the universal fear of cabbage among young mites everywhere when he made it the sole food of poor Charlie from the Chocolate Factory. In Tim Burton's 2005 film of the book *Willy Wonka and the Chocolate Factory*, Helena Bonham Carter, as Mrs Bucket, sends a cleaver through a cabbage head and a chill through the heart of every dinner-fearing child in the land, with the immortal line:

—"Oh well ... nothing goes better with cabbage than cabbage." The Dahl guy really knew how to frighten children.

Cabbage, you see, could traditionally be harvested in winter when the cupboard was bare, and it stores and pickles well. Therefore it was a shoo-in to become the national dish of all countries with a long pedigree in abject peasant misery, from the sauerkraut (fermented in a bucket) of eastern and middle Europe to bacon and cabbage, our own national dish—more often eaten through the centuries Charlie Bucket-style, i.e. minus the bacon.

Cooked to the traditional Irish method, it must be stewed for approximately three weeks until completely reduced to green goo with transparent floating slivers. This hard-boiling method is necessary to generate a retch-inducing smell strong enough to cling to the innards of a house for weeks on end.

It was served tepid and accompanied by a strong character-building lecture on why they had to eat it when they were kids, so now you do too. That and the one about how children in some miserable country would happily trade their parents, Bob Geldof and all their wind-up radios for a lick of it.

At least that's how I viewed cabbage until early last year, when Her Outdoors served her special par-fried cabbage. Crunchy, sweet and almost raw, it was absolutely gorgeous and I was immediately converted.

After I had planted a load of it, I found I wasn't the only one who thought so. You know those cute little creamy white butterflies everybody loves—the ones that flutter aimlessly into your garden on the first true sunny day? Well, I don't love the little gits any more. I've learned there's nothing aimless about them at all. They're on a mission to get into your heads. Cabbage heads.

From dawn until dusk, they're constantly flouncing about, looking for your cabbages. And when they find them they lay a million eggs which hatch into a fast-moving, caterpillar, cabbage-killing demolition crew. Worse again is the underground terrorist, the cabbage fly maggot. As I've probably told you at least four times already, last year, my entire crop of green cabbage was murdered by this savage beastlet within weeks of planting.

The cabbage root fly lays its eggs in the soil at the base of the cabbage, and little white maggots hatch and burrow down until they find the roots and start to munch. When they've properly killed your cabbage, they pupate. Each year brings no fewer than three generations of them.

So this year I'm hoping to beat the bug squad. First, the cabbages have gone into last year's onion patch in an effort at crop rotation. It's not a perfect switch, but it does at least mean the soil isn't already festering with a prepacked colony.

Of course the root fly, which looks pretty much like an ordinary house fly, has wings and will travel. So sticking this year's cabbages 20ft from last year's murder scene might not actually prove so effective. Having acquired three trays of baby cabbage plants (about thirty in all) for under a tenner, I also invested twelve quid in a roll of weed-proof carpeting material. This lets the water in and keeps weeds down. I'm also hoping it will protect the cabbages from their nemesis. Planting the cabbages through holes cut in this wasn't the easiest thing in the world, however, and I was left with sizable gaps, which could still admit the crawling marauders.

The cabbage plants cost a tenner, the protective carpet costs twelve—that's €21—the cost of 21 supermarket cabbages already. And I've got thirty? And I'll probably lose eight to ten of them anyways.

Bugger.

Meantime the plot is playing a stormer. The carrots are up and the onions are adding height. We're getting into that time of year when everything indeed looks rosy at the plot. But back home in the garden there's trouble afoot, or rather, underfoot. This time last year, we were eating copious amounts of salad from the raised bed in the back garden. The crops of lollo rosso, butterhead lettuce, rocket and mixed spicy leaves were growing faster than we could swallow them. Well, nearly.

This year, though, our salad patch is almost bare. Despite our having sown the same lines of seeds, only the mixed-leaf salad has come up with any degree of success. There are no butterheads. Three icebergs were floating alone in a vast open space, until they were joined recently by a reluctant row of lollo rossos, now standing 3in-5in in height. Then last week one of my lacklustre lollo rossos looked as though someone had let the air out.

I gave it a flick and it fell over. The root was gone, and munching at the stub was a long, thin, yellow worm, an inch long, with leg-like stubs at one end. This little git had just robbed me of the prospect of one decent head of lollo rosso—recommended retail price two quid—just the same as if he he had eaten it out of my pocket. For that, he would die—in this case, stunned, drawn and quartered with the business end of a suitably blunt trowel.

The next day, two more lettuces had deflated. Once again, the remaining roots were girdled by nasties. It turned out the soil was infested with them. My salad days were over until I dealt with this devastation. But I didn't know what sort of maggot I had. Even the internet didn't sort it. (Much later I discovered it was a wire worm, larva of the click beetle which can live as a salad-eating maggot for five years in your soil and is almost impossible to remove.)

Meantime the seductive strawberry is the most demanding plant in the garden, but we just keep falling for it—red, ripe and dangerously alluring; usually delicious, but all too often lacking in taste—strawberries are the shallow seducers of the garden centre. A strawberry's good looks can carry it further than it deserves. While it oozes sexy indulgence, the strawberry's high-maintenance will break your heart.

The siren-hued Fragaria, the most likely fruit to get an eat-on part in a porno flick, is in many ways like so many of those actresses who feature in the same movies. The supermarket strawberry has been augmented to exaggerate its good looks. It has been artificially pumped up, its shape has been genetically massaged and it has had its skin colour enhanced—not to mention the numerous tinkerings carried out artificially to elongate its shelf life.

Be warned: if you're seduced like I have been by such a high-maintenence and showy fruit plant, they'll bleed you dry and underperform miserably. First, there's the battle to fight off an army of would-be suitors—slugs, snails, beetles, vine weevils, birds and millipedes, for a start. Because everyone loves strawberries.

After the plants have fruited, they have no qualms about doing a runner. Runners are the reproductive shoots that strawberry plants start throwing out about now. This time last year I vowed never to be seduced again by these good-looking wasters. Now I must eat my words, if not the strawberries.

I bumped into them again on the garden centre shelves.

Much of my grief was forgotten. The plants were looking great—all bushy-topped and adorned with pictures of promised juicy fruit.

I loaded up my shopping trolley with two varieties—Elsanta, a Dutch-born variety, and Symphony, a Scottish strawberry. This time, though, I had a plan B. I would put them on the floor of my plastic-skinned greenhouse, where birds, weevils and mites would not get them. No pests, no worries?

They thrived. They bushed up all over the place and were soon three times the size of last year's plants and flowering at pace. I congratulated myself on having found a way to keep them productive.

All the Elsantas delivered fruit—about two dessert bowls full from six plants. It was beautiful fruit, but hardly enough to justify their €6 purchase price. A punnet costs €3. The Symphonies were complete duds, producing just one or two warped fruit: four quid's worth of fruit from plants which cost three times that. After the fruit stopped, the plants kept growing and growing. Now they're crowding both the chillies and the tomatoes in the greenhouse and they're sending out runners all over the shop for new plants which I don't have the space for.

If you do want to avail of these offshoots, you should pin the runners where they kink into pre-prepared pots. They will root in these and then you can move them where you want for the following year. Let the parent plant break its own link to the new runner plant, don't cut the umbilicals yourself.

The trouble is, while you might get lucky with herb pots, planters, hanging baskets and rockeries, strawberries need plenty of space and a richly fertilised loam soil to do their thing properly. Professional growers tend their strawberries on metres and metres of raised table beds covered with protective plastic. A big strawberry plant will need about a 2ft-diameter of growing room. And all for a handful of fruit per plant.

Whatever you do, you'll need protective netting to keep the birds off, drenches for weevils if they're in planters and

protective mulches against frost. Even then they are susceptible to a rash of crown rots, moulds and mildews.

If you do manage to keep them happy and are blessed
with a bumper crop, you can freeze the strawberries. First,
flash-freeze them by placing them apart on a tray. Then bag
them up and return them to the freezer. Don't throw them
straight into cold storage or you'll pay for it with one great big
heart of strawberry ice that you'll need a lump hammer to
break. But if you want my best advice, next time you're at the
garden centre, ignore the promise of romance—walk right
past the seductive strawberry...and opt for a gooseberry
instead.

Another better option are blackcurrants and ours are
going great guns at the allotment complex. Some online
research reveals a little about their excellent nutritional
value. Were you one of those children who regularly stran-
gled their siblings in the tussle for the sought-after black Fruit
Pastille? If you were, look away now.

Fresh blackcurrants are not possessed of that gooey,
warm, feel good flavour we're all so familiar with. In fact
that's a processed blackcurrant taste that is created only after
they have been cooked and sugared. In contrast, the freshly
picked berry, which is ready to harvest at the moment, deliv-
ers a sharp, greeny, sappy, off-kilter tang, which continues to
trigger involuntary facial shuddering long after you have gri-
maced and swallowed. In short, it certainly doesn't taste like
anything we should be busy stuffing into children. Indeed,
the hugely popular Ribena cordial has its origins in a wily
wartime solution to the stuffing of blackcurrants into children
problem.

During the Second World War, the British government
encouraged widespread blackcurrant growing to compensate
for the shortage of vitamin C as a result of the difficulties and
expense of importing fruit. Given how they taste, it's not surprising that even the hungriest of war-starved, blitz urchins
wouldn't eat them fresh.

So a solution became the solution. The cordial idea was
concocted to sweeten up the blackcurrants. Once perfected,

the entire British blackcurrant crop went into the cordial process. The drink was distributed free to Britain's children from 1942. It later became known as Ribena after the Latin name for the berry.

Around the same time, thousands of Irish families were growing their own blackcurrants alongside gooseberries, redcurrants, raspberries, loganberries and tayberries. These were used primarily to make jam, but also stewed for desserts, baked in tarts and fermented into wine. The trouble is that these old-fashioned domestic skills don't always sit well with modern living, so far fewer people grow blackcurrants, redcurrants and gooseberries today. Jam, for example, isn't considered particularly healthy any more, because of the amount of sugar that goes into it. It also takes a lot of time, which modern families don't usually have.

Each blackcurrant has to be 'topped and tailed' before you start, and it takes thousands of them to make a reasonable quantity of jam. You also need outsized cooking pots.

Other berries are slightly more practical. I find redcurrants tasty and enjoy their bitter flavour, but many people find them too tart. I use them, along with blueberries and raspberries, in stuffing for game. Gooseberries and blueberries, on the other hand, are tasty to eat fresh. They are also easily made into pies. The same goes for tayberries and raspberries. I have all of the above growing in my allotment but not yet in large enough numbers to worry about until the bushes mature. Blackcurrants, along with the blueberry, can be considered a 'super food'. They are extremely high in vitamin C and bursting with antioxidants.

Recent research claims that blackcurrants can help prevent Alzheimer's and MRSA, fight cancer, and protect against cardiovascular disease, thanks to substances called anthocyanins that are found mainly in their skins. Also, unlike fruit imported from abroad, berries tend to thrive in an Irish climate.

While my fruit bushes are only two years old and still maturing, next year or the year after I expect them to crop heavily enough to raise the question of storage. The solution to storing berries (if you're not going to make jam or wine) is—like the strawberries—to flash-freeze them.

Berries have been coming back into vogue for a number of years because of their nutritional turbo charge; we have witnessed the surge in popularity of the imported goji berries and, of course, the blueberry. Blueberries can be grown in Irish soil but they need slightly acidic soils to thrive.

Chapter Nine

What You Need: The Stuff and the Shops

So you've got your allotment from the council, you've cleared a large stretch of your garden or have somehow managed to blag a long-term loan of some land from a friend or acquaintance. Next you're going to have to spend some money on stuff—namely seeds, plants, tools, compost and manure. Back when we first decided to get an allotment, we planned to buy fruit bushes which could yield year-after-year and perhaps also lay down a windbreak to the side of the allotment to protect us from the exposed conditions. I heard from my dad, the Expert on Everything (EOE), that they were selling them cheap at Lidl. Cheap! cheap! in fact because to buy them you need to tangle with a flock of rather strange old birds—the greater spotted Lidl magpie—of which my dad is one.

These are to be found hovering in vast numbers at daybreak outside any Lidl outlet set to open for one of their special offer days. Identify them by a silver crest and their distinctive call: Cheap, cheap...shit! Like the common magpie, they will compulsively pick up just about anything shiny, new, obscure and useless for their nests—in this case, so long as it's half price.

Dad and indeed all his sixty-something mates are hardcore Lidl magpies. They fly in and raid the place with the planning and execution of the discount SAS.

First comes mission research. They peruse those advance Lidl brochures which come free with the newspapers. Constantly in mobile phone contact, each operative purchases on behalf of the flock so they don't all have to flutter down at once to the same shop.

—"Taiwanese shooting sticks, four left, fiver each... three left... put you down for two. Roger."

I noted some time ago the old man's growing stockpile of useless new stuff including a large presentation case of assorted chef's fish knives (you never know when you might need one) and a second recently purchased chainsaw (that one's electric, this one's petrol). His garden is the size of two bedrooms.

Just as I was considering which fruit trees to get for the allotment, my old man eagerly pressed into my hands a Lidl catalogue which announced a forthcoming offer at three for three quid. They're usually a tenner each or thereabouts. I needed raspberry canes and perhaps some tayberries and gooseberries. So why not?

But there was more in the brochure: rhubarb at four quid for three plants; strawberries at a quid a plant; ten cabbage seedlings for two quid. Wahey! Cheap, cheap!

And so Her Outdoors and I found ourselves wandering our local Lidl outlet, locking trolleys with steely-looking punters, all in a hurry, and none taking prisoners. The first clue that we were out of our depth was the theft of our still empty trolley, for which we had paid a one quid deposit. This does NOT happen at Tesco!

Although the offer had been launched just that morning, we arrived at the fruit tree area to find the display stripped except for batches of blackcurrants, blackberries and redcurrants. There were no raspberries, tayberries or gooseberries.

And therein lies the catch at Lidl; you'll always buy stuff you don't need. Lots of it.

After a second or two of head scratching, I decided blackcurrants would provide excellent windbreaks for one side of the allotment. But because they each came attached to a blackberry and redcurrant bush, we'd have to take them, too. Three quid was still cheap for a blackcurrant bush. Great value.

Cheap! cheap! When Her Outdoors began questioning this logic, I muttered something about how pheasant tastes lovely stuffed with redcurrants—cheap, cheap!—and you could do something or other with apples if you had blackberries—cheap, cheap!

I felt utter jubilation at grabbing the last two trays of cabbages. And I caught myself zealously guarding the trolley's contents against cabbageless types who were peering into our basket to see what we'd got.

Oh and I'd also bought a 'world-receiver' radio to pick up channels from all over the world. This, by the way, turned out to be just a radio, which just about picked up channels from beyond the county area.

And there you had it.

I'd been stricken with the virus. We returned home with a car full of stuff we didn't need, apart that is from two trays of cabbages. I'd bought nine fruit bushes I didn't want, two trays of brussels sprouts I didn't really need and two trays of calabrese. Worse still, word had got out on the Lidl magpie network that I was after fruit trees and the old man had mobilised his own special forces who had somehow managed to buy me another three packs of bushes—with two raspberries and two tayberries in there somewhere.

"Aha, you have to get up early in the morning," he boomed smugly as he handed them over and I dispensed yet more cash into the Lidl registers, this time by proxy. Their loyal adherents even fix it so you're still buying even after you've left the store.

Okay, so I wanted raspberries and maybe the odd gooseberry, but now I had eighteen bushes, including two blackberries, two redcurrants, and nine blackcurrants. Out of eighteen bushes, about five that I actually wanted in the first place.

Don't believe those Ribena people when they tell you they buy up all of Ireland's blackcurrants. Me and hundreds of other Lidl magpies now have private plantations. Unless I start making jam, they might just be getting a call from me come autumn.

Cheap! cheap! cheap! shit!

The DIY/Garden Centre can also be quite a harrowing experience for the uninitiated and it doesn't help that the companies who run them are generally unwilling to pay much more than the minimum wage to their staff. It means that many (not all) of the floor staff know even less than you do about what's what in food growing.

Not so long ago, if I needed, let's say, a chemical cure for blight, I could have taken my problem to the all-knowing Browncoat at the local hardware or garden shop. Despite his cranky countenance, he knew his stuff. On description of your problem, Mr Browncoat would have "Hmmmmed" in an authoritative tone, before wandering down along some shelves and picking out a bottle of cure-all from a dusty box.

These days, the big chains have put him out of business, his shop replaced with a retail barn stuffed with semi-comatose teenagers whose chief skills are grunting and running away from customers. As a couple who have spent a lot of time of late trawling the local DIY/garden hangars, we have become accustomed to the sort of terse, monosyllabic zombettes and lobotomised walking pimples who seem to staff these places. When finally cornered at the end of a joinery aisle, these 'assistants' emit a low guttural distress call, something like: "Ivids norron deshelffs we don hav ih!"

Trek then to the 'information' counter to where the more confident former assistants have been promoted. Usually female, bottle blonde with black roots, and of orange complexion, these devote their days to popping bubble gum intermittently while punching OMG!!! repeatedly into a candy pink mobile phone with a twinkly tassel attached. You will need to embark on some throat clearing, coughing, waving, throwing stuff, setting off flares and such before they even notice you're there.

Expect them to look surprised, then annoyed.

—"Hang on." ...OMG!! GTG.. CSTMR : (LATR HGGLES

—"Yeh can I help you?"

—"Do you stock a cure for blight?"

—"Wha?"

—"Potato blight?"

—"Em (pop!) have yer looked dowan by the da potatizz? (pop!) Ya mite foynd it dayre."

You will at this point look to the centre of the panda mascara for any degree of irony. Blank. None.

—"It's more likely to be in with the chemicals."

—"Oh. Well yell hafter ask horr overdere, cos I'm just gowan-on-meebreak." (pop!)

Having spent significant tranches of my non-working and non-sleeping life confronting the retail undead and unsuccessfully seeking the answers to such impenetrable riddles as: "How much is this?" I am personally embracing the recession—if only because it will shepherd these poor unfortunates back to their proper place—at the end of a dole queue where they can do nobody, least of all themselves, any harm.

The usually enthusiastic and bright, foreign contingent among the staff could probably run the place single-handedly and in their sleep, if only they had any English. Any at all.

—"I'm looking for a potato blight cure?"

—"Yes thank you," (smiles) "please come this way."

At the end of a long journey you are looking at a barbeque accessories display.

—"Skewer Yes? You can put potatoes on! Yes?"

If it wasn't for the tall African security guy in the Ray Bans who quite possibly has real war zone experience against peace keepers, you could probably walk in and load up a van and they wouldn't notice. Perhaps the information desk might send a text to the cops: DEER PLEECE :) DIS GY HAS JST OMG!! ROBD DE SHP : O !!!! CUM QUIK!!!

Certainly do try and find out exactly what you want before you get there by using the internet, which is excellent for researching various garden products and equipment. Otherwise you take your chances with Kylie, the self-harming, black-finger-nailed goth at garden equipment who has been filching Stanley blades of late, to explain the relative values of swatch-top and cord-strung strimmers.

And while those plants can look verdantly healthy in the garden centre, remember that they've been shocked into life in a hot-house somewhere in Holland and that there's some sort of serum they inject into the air in garden centres to keep these plants preserved, healthy looking and alive on the premises. Because once you get them home, they've already died.

And it sounds obvious, but when you're buying plants, always keep cost versus yield in mind—there's no point in paying a tenner for ten young cabbage plants when a cabbage costs a quid each in the shops, or paying three quid for a strawberry plant which will give you a quid's worth of strawberries.

Seeds are perhaps, above all, the most important product you will buy for your allotment. And there's usually plenty to be had in the displays of leading garden centres and indeed supermarkets. But you do have to bear in mind that some varieties are better than others. Garden centres offer a rash of varieties, many of which are only on the shelves because the head buyer, based in another country, has got himself a great deal on them wholesale. Many of these varieties produce vegetables or fruits of a tasteless sort. Moneymaker tomatoes for example will crop heavily but the resulting fruits taste like attic tank water. Others are just not suited for your local climate and soil conditions, a factor which does not interest the big chain purchaser who has bought them for his firm. If he can offload them to unwary customers, he gets a big bonus for Christmas.

Marrying seed stock to outlets based in countries in which they can actually grow is not something that buyers lose much sleep over. The best tactic is to take notes of what varieties are available and then go home, research the reaction to that variety from other growers online (as local as you can) and then decide.

When it comes to plants, big-chain garden centres also sell a lot of more exotic stuff that doesn't gel with local conditions. Among my costly failures (a fiver each) were four aubergines that probably should have been sunning themselves somewhere in Sicily rather than crawling inside themselves with cold on a damp patio in Kimmage where they found the sandstone's hue a sunlight-sucking, snot green instead of a reflective peach pastel they might otherwise have been used to.

What you should also know is that seeds, just the same as with strimmers or garden tools, have brand names which vary in quality. And some brands do deals with big garden-centre chains which help their profits but compromise your food-growing success. As a result, the best seed brands may not be available down at your local appliance/gazebo barn.

In my first year on the allotment I came across an invaluable report from the Which? consumer organisation in Britain. Which? tested brands of leading seeds and discovered that just six out of fifteen leading seed distributors actually managed to achieve the minimum in British industry standards for their sector. The tests were carried out on the wares of fifteen big seed companies, who, among them, account for about 90 per cent of the seeds that tend to be bought here. To any gardener they're familiar names—Mr Fothergill's, Thompson & Morgan, Unwins, Johnsons, Suttons and so on.

In the case of Edwin Tucker & Sons, the worst performer in the Which? tests, just 15 per cent of its Little Gem lettuce seeds went on to produce normal seedlings which germinated. In another category of plant seed from the firm, 99 per cent were found to be dead. More disheartening is the fact that the vegetable categories generally performed far worse than the garden flower categories in almost every seed company's case. So here's your checklist—this is how the vegetable seed germination fared with those other well-known firms whose seeds are most commonly bought here:

- Mr Fothergill's: — poor
- Johnsons: — acceptable
- Unwins: — acceptable
- Suttons: — good
- Marshalls: — acceptable
- Thompson & Morgan: — very good
- Chiltern: — excellent
- Plants of Distinction: — excellent

Now this is a pretty sorry state of affairs: it emerges that the standard of 'very good' as set by Which? means, in the case of Thompson & Morgan at least, that 83 per cent of that company's veg seeds germinated. This does not mean they matured or produced any vegetables, only that they sprouted—clearing just the first hurdle to a successful crop. It also means 17 per cent of the packet's contents, almost one in five seeds, were dead before the packet was even opened. In Plot 34's rating system, that falls into the category of 'not very good at all'. Which? also surveyed the quality of seed catalogues and packet information, vital if you are to choose seeds that are best suited to your soil and to understand how to treat them regarding sunlight, temperature, how deep they should be planted and how big the plants grow.

The better scorers in the germination tests actually fared poorly in the 'quality of information' category, including Chiltern and Plants of Distinction.

After seeds you'll need to buy tools. Because while the average household already tends to be in possession of many of the tools and accoutrements necessary for a spot of light gardening, most are usually not up to the intensity of use which will be required on an allotment or in a vegetable garden. They're fine for a bit of light drilling in back garden flower patches, but not for trawling, thrashing and gouging in rock-studded spud furrows. Within a few weeks on my allotment I had completely bent what I had thought was a perfectly good spade and the head had fallen off my trowel.

There are spades and there are spades, and there are trowels and there are trowels. And so on it goes. So here are a few tips I picked up through our first two years experience.

When it comes to tools you should generally ignore the cheapest and the most expensive. The metal components of tools should be made in one piece, with no welds.

To start with you will need a spade, a fork and a trowel, the three implements that will get the most punishment on your food-growing endeavours, and also the ones that you will take the most punishment with. If you're taller, get longer-shafted implements.

For bigger items like spades you should go for steel heads for strength. Stainless steel makes the best cutting edge. Go for wooden shafts, because they're more forgiving than anything else on your bones (which are also prone to wear and breakage if you're not careful). A T-shaped handle is supposed to better suit bigger hands. Mine are big and I prefer a wide D-shaped handle.

It might be stating the obvious but the spade is primarily for slice digging of sods, turning sods, prising out rocks and digging holes. Despite what you might think, it's not good to have the spade end too wide. The wider it is, the more weight you have to lift or turn each time. My grandfather's favourite spade was only five or six inches wide at the business end, mine is perhaps eight.

In the case of a fork, a four-pronged version is the ideal. You will use it for busting endless sods. Prise, turn, bash, lift and shake. Then bash again. You will also use it for carrying large heaps of trimmings and waste. So it needs to be sturdy but light. Once again, a wooden shaft is best and ideally with a dividing D-shaped handle. Both your spade and fork should come to your hip. The business end should be light but sturdy so the prongs don't get beaten inwards too easily when bashing frantically, or at the end of the day, in slo-mo, at the ground.

More dreadfully useless trowels are sold than anything else so it's worthwhile, above all, to invest in a good trowel. The trowel is your right hand on the ground, and it should turn and rotate as an extension of your wrist. You use it for digging holes, scooping, planting, weeding, bashing smaller sods and levelling. It's also for poking, investigating and minor prisings. And you will use it to deal with pests you come across while working. You will also find yourself crouched on the ground attempting to lever up a large stone, but being too lazy to get up, go over there and get the spade. So it too needs to be tough. Once again a steel-headed, one-piece version is best and preferably tempered. This is a reheating process which strengthens metal. The trowel doesn't need to have a cutting edge, but it needs to be strong and durable. Get a good ergonomic handle which fits your grip as comfortably as possible and if you can, don't buy painted versions because the paint comes off and then they rust. Too heavy is bad too because it will tire your wrist. Like a fisherman who swears by a particular make of rod, so too will you drift towards the right trowel. Personally I have found that narrower, longer trowels by the True Temper company suit me best.

And unless you've worked down a coalmine all your life, any amount of heavy digging or weeding will blister your hands. So you're going to need some gloves. I use a heavy leather pair which have, over time, sort of moulded into the shape of my hands. The disadvantage is that they're a bit like oven gloves—they're useless for anything which requires dexterity and sensitivity. Rubber gloves are better for lighter tasks but don't last terribly long.

Once you've got the main three tools, as a newbie you can skimp a bit on the rest. A rake is needed on every allotment to level off soil and to slough off stones and weed roots. Get a T-headed version, not the claw variety which is designed only for gathering leaves. The hoe is used for running through the top of the soil to snuff out young weeds before they can get established. Buy a sharp one with a heavy metal head. If you do manage to stick at your allotment you'll quickly find you will spend more on a sharper version.

You'll also find that you drift towards certain types of clothes. A big heavy coat is no use on an allotment even in colder weather, because once you start digging or weeding, you'll work up a sweat and have to remove it fairly quickly, possibly revealing clothes underneath which are far too light. For suitable rain attire, another hobby of mine, fly-fishing, presents novice allotmenteers with the best example of how to keep dry while working without restriction or overheating. We fishermen also have to faff around a lot in mud and foliage, and an old fisherman's saying goes: "There is no such thing as bad weather, just bad attire." The fishing fraternity can teach the rest of us a bit about rain. If it's dry, they go fishing. If it's raining they go fishing. The secret, as I've said, is having the right gear.

Garments of an extremely high quality which are perfect for

movement in all weather can be picked up in angling shops for half the price charged in those specialist outdoors shops, if you don't mind olive green or camouflage patterns. They are, in essence, pretty much the same items except priced (and coloured) for no-nonsense, middle-aged, crabby, penny-pinching fishermen instead of for young, enthusiastic, hell-may-care, fashion-conscious adrenalin-junkies.

Normal rain gear keeps rain off. But you'll need something which breathes, blocks the wind well and also lets you work freely without overheating. For practicality's sake, you'll also need, like the fisherman, something which cleans easily without too much fuss.

My lightweight fishing jacket cost just over a hundred quid and it's festooned with deep, robust, wide pockets, perfect for string, measuring tape and secateurs. It's 100 per cent waterproof and comes with a detachable hood because most anglers prefer hats. It's light, warm and fully breathable. It gets covered in mud and gunk when I go fishing and the rain cleans it to pristine.

Fly fishermen also wear hats rather than hoods for the same reasons experienced allotmenteers do. Turn your head inside a hood and you're looking at the lining. You've got tunnel vision and Kenny from 'South Park' syndrome, so get a wide-brimmed hat with enough grip in the lining to stay pinned to your head in a squall. My first cost about €15, again from a fishing/hunting supplier. More recently I spent €35 at a country fair for a felt-lined wide-brim hat which has on the outside a high-tech synthetic material which repels rain without ever soaking it up. And its best kept secret—felt ear flaps which fold down for a squall. Look for hats designed for 'beaters'—people who wander through the foliage, making noise and driving pheasants into the air so that posh people can shoot them. You can buy a beater's hat from a fishing/hunting supplier.

Wellies are a tenner anywhere. They're all you need for outer footwear. Extra thick or thermal shooting or hiker's socks are also a good buy to keep your feet warm—it's surprising how feet go cold and icy so quickly on cold damp ground. If your feet get cold, you'll soon be heading home. An old-fashioned thermal vest will ensure the main bits of the rest of you don't freeze.

With machinery like strimmers, go for a petrol rather than an electric version, the latter just doesn't have the necessary oomph.

And do keep the receipts, especially if you're a man buying anything mechanical. The innate failure to read instructions combined with the natural exuberance to grab things mechanical without research means you could end up with a dud.

Because it's not just rock musicians who feel the urge to smash up their equipment.

During an interview filmed shortly before his death in 2002, John Entwistle, the late, bass guitarist of 'The Who', was asked to explain the presence of the debris of a very expensive but thoroughly totalled bass guitar, broken bits of which were strewn about his home. By way of justification, Entwistle said (and not without some menace): "I did warn it—several times."

And he's right; sometimes errant equipment needs to be taught a lesson, even if it achieves nothing but mindless damage.

In my case, my electric strimmer had also been warned—several times. I bought the Trabant of electric, cordless rechargeables for €90 and it gave me nothing but trouble. It was strimmer world's version of a circus-clown car. A different bit fell off every time I used it. One day it just jolted with a sharp 'whack!' and the dahlia bush to my right shook suddenly; the motor surged to a high-pitched mocking squall. I cut the power and looked at the disc spinning slower and slower until I was peering into a neat hole where the swatch-holder fitting should have been.

That's when I should have done an Entwistle. Right then and there I should have lifted the accursed thing over my head and smashed it repeatedly against the wall until its miserable head was hanging off by a single piece of flex. Preferably to the accompaniment of high-volume bass licks turned up to 11.

With manufacturing standards hitting the deck harder than Amy Winehouse's front row, it's no wonder that—as the line from the spoof rock film *Spinal Tap* goes—so many drummers meet their demise in "bizarre gardening accidents".

First, the slot-on plastic guard that prevents your shoes becoming sandals wouldn't stay on, so I threw it away and worked a step ahead to avoid a toe-trimming. By the way, do follow this procedure if you have a penchant for green trousers. There's no better way of making your strides permanently verdant than by spraying them with minute particles of freshly cut, wet grass pulp.

Then came the flyaway swatches. This strimmer used solid-plastic swatches which slot onto a holder sprigot rather than the usual wrap-around cord. Sixty plastic swatches came with it, so I thought they should last—maybe forever. Not if they fly off into the undergrowth at the rate of one every four minutes they don't. Within three weeks I had two left and the DIY store was out of stock. So, I went back to the shears.

Being strimmer-less in July and August is a problem because we have grass walkways between the beds on the allotment, and in the summer monsoon season, the grass, thistles, docks and buttercups on the walkways are the fastest growing crops of all.

Thankfully a neighbour lent me a petrol strimmer with an engine big enough for a motorbike. Revving and wielding this with some degree of satisfaction and watching the grass, and ground, blast away before me, I thought: "Now this is strimming!"

My neighbour made me put on sunglasses to protect my eyes—the blasting deflected more than a few flying chips. While Entwistle's life, spent using high-powered bass amps, rendered him deaf, those wielding high-powered strimmers will end up reaching for white sticks if they don't use eye protection.

The following week, I turned up triumphant with my own petrol-powered strimmer, albeit half the cc strength of my neighbour's. With a 25cc engine it was no Harley Davidson, but I wielded at least half a Honda 50 against the forces of rapid growth.

Petrol strimmers are more complicated than their electrical counterparts. I might have ruined mine altogether had my uncle not pointed out that I'd have to mix the fuel for it myself. Not being one who understands engines I was surprised. Mixing fuels? Surely it just takes petrol plain and simple? Nope. This baby, along with most petrol strimmers and mowers, takes unleaded petrol mixed with one twelfth two-stroke engine oil. A fact not made obvious in the instruction manual.

Then it took me three days of rip cording just to get it started. I flooded the engine again and again. The starting instructions are complicated. Here they are reproduced word for word:

"Turn switch to 'on' position. Press fuel-feed plunger six times. Move choke to 'full choke' position. Squeeze and hold throttle through all remaining steps. Pull ripcord not more than six times (while still holding throttle down). As soon as engine sounds as if it is trying to start, move choke to 'half-choke' position (while still holding throttle down). Pull ripcord again not more than six times. When engine starts, let run for 10 seconds. Move choke to 'run' position. Allow engine to run for 30 seconds more, before releasing throttle."

And so on ...

Finally, on the fourth day, the monster was stirred into life. It buzzed and snarled in my hands. Jubilant, sunglasses on, and now fully armed, I was ready to let rip. I began to attack the buttercups and thistles. They disappeared into oblivion. My power had been restored.

The only drawback is that this monster uses half a tank of petrol at a time. That and the fact that Stg£240 spent on strimmers chews up a quarter of the money we'll save this year by growing our own food. But hey, I've just christened him—John 'Endthistle'.

Allotment Diary, Year Two

July to Early August

Into July and my cabbage patch kids—twenty-four perfectly formed football-shaped heads with sound hearts—have just been murdered. The star performers of the allotment are now coleslaw, slashed to ribbons like they've gone ten rounds with Freddy Krueger.

As I survey the scene of the brassica massacre, a couple of old hands drop by to empathise and to aid in the post-mortem analysis—although the plants are still rooted and there's a chance they'll come right again by growing new heads as damaged cabbages sometimes do.

Both my visitors are convinced my cabbages have gone to the birds.

—"How can you tell?" I ask one.

He points to the white streaks down the netting fence our neighbours had just put up. One day there was a bit of picking evident, the next day the cabbages had been shredded wholesale.

—"They must have just turned ripe for them," mused a neighbour.

There it was: as I concentrated on the ground forces of pestdom by laying minefields of slug pellets, hoeing out weed cover and planting through pest-proof ground cloth, I was caught napping by the massed airborne. Crows most likely. As a temporary protective measure, I cover the patch solemnly with some thick windbreak netting. Someone else said they saw masses of caterpillars on the cabbages. But surely they couldn't do that much damage in a week?

Either way, it has all been for nothing—the digging, the root clearing, the laying of the cloth barrier, measuring out and cutting the holes, then planting through them and watering through six rainless weeks. When you grow your own food, there are always days like this, when you just want to throw your sun hat at the whole thing and walk away.

Everything is way behind this year, perhaps by a month to six weeks. The cabbages were to have been the first big crop of the year. So far, all we've eaten are a few jalapeño chillies, four red peppers, a handful of blackcurrants, two bowls of strawberries, chives, a few gooseberries and one courgette. We're also back to combined rain and heat. As a result, the blight warnings are coming in fast for spuds and tomatoes.

In times like this, you need to take stock. So I got a notebook and did a head count to try to get some perspective on this year's growing efforts. Apart from the 1,200sq.ft allotment—about 65 per cent planted up—I use my back garden (30ftx25ft), my patio (10ftx8ft) and my plastic greenhouse (5ftx4ft).

Planted in the garden and on the patio, I have:
15 healthy courgette plants, starting to produce
25 tomato plants
30 young leeks
2 bell pepper plants from last year
3 jalapeños, also from last year
5 tomatillo plants, flowering and starting to fruit
24 outdoor chillies, small but heading towards flower
12 celeriac coming on well
10 slow-growing celeries
and a 6ft-high grape vine that is already covered in tiny green grapes.

In the raised bed are the salads: the spicy leaf mix and rocket are ready to eat, but the lollo rosso, butterhead lettuce and icebergs are growing slowly. The herbs are all ready to use and we have mint, lemon mint, chives, oregano, thyme, rosemary, dill, fennel and basil, although some of the latter's leaves are looking a bit tatty and the blight weather will probably put paid to them.

In the greenhouse are twenty-two full-sized tomato

plants, a dozen strawberries that have been fruiting as well as can be expected, one sprawling but impotent watermelon plant that can't cross-pollinate because the other two died, and sixteen more chilli plants, bushy, healthy and heading into flower.

Up at the allotment we now have:

50sq.ft of coleslaw (see above)
50sq.ft of broccoli (doing well)
40sq.ft of King Edward potatoes (about to flower)
50sq.ft of peas (almost ready to start picking)
10sq.ft of runner beans (flowering)
30sq.ft of carrots (still tiny and miserable)
80sq.ft of onions (behind schedule but looking healthy)
10sq.ft of rhubarb (limp)
6 blackcurrant bushes (fruiting well)
3 raspberry bushes (fruiting so-so)
3 gooseberries (fruiting well)
2 tayberries (with mould-covered fruit)
1 blueberry bush (looking a bit ropey but fruiting well).

All in all, about forty varieties of food plants. In the weeks ahead, we'll plant spinach, swedes, parsnips and winter cabbage.

By rights I should have put up a scarecrow to chaperone the cabbages (if I only had a brain) and keep the birds off. But when I see the overall progress on paper, it doesn't seem quite so bad. So there's no need to eat crow just yet.

Although if I wanted to, it's nice to know I can.

A cathartic check online reveals recipes for crow and mushroom soup, twice-baked crow in cranberry glaze, crow loaf in puff pastry and potted crow with bacon. One recipe provider asserts: 'Crow, like revenge, is a dish best served cold.' Even better, I would imagine, when stuffed with cabbage.

Meantime the peas in their pods are safe at least from birds and although we vowed not to grow them again after last year's small yield for a whole lot of effort, we have since learned that peas and other legumes are useful nitrogen providers in the soil. They take it from the air and store it in their roots. So given this bonus feature, we decided to go again, this time planting many times more peas while at the same time opting for a variety with a far larger pea (we grew petits pois last time out). The crop was looking a good deal better this year. Picking peas, like deadheading roses, encourages new growth and the new pods will keep coming until the end of the season. Then the plants shrivel up and die. To benefit from all that nitrogen stored up in their root nodes, it's important to cut the plants at ground level but leave the roots intact. Then when it comes to spring, and they've rotted for a while, you can dig the nitrogen accumulation back into the soil.

The beans are also looking good, covered in pods and the most beautiful scarlet flowers. These plants were first brought to these islands not for food primarily, but as a spectacular decorative flower. The other day I noted that the breathtaking red and white flowers which customers were admiring so much in the courtyard of a city centre café were in fact runner beans; variety Painted Lady.

Throughout July I've also noticed that our complex is filling with 4ft-high steaming piles of horse manure, delivered on request by our entrepreneurial local farmer who sells small trailer-loads for twenty quid. Unfortunately, his marketing technique may just get him a stiff phone call from the council. As you drive into the complex, you see scrawled in thick black marker on the white wall of a council building: 'Manure for sale' and his mobile phone number.

The fact that my fellow allotmenteers and I are delighted to pay for a trailer-load of the stuff shows just how much times have changed—or rather, reverted. The green movement and the rise in popularity of food-growing have made horse dung valuable once again. It was a prized commodity in granddad's day—a colleague of mine recalls his grandfather hitting the brakes on his car at the sight of any pile of 'horse apples' on the street, keeping a small shovel and a bag in the boot for such an opportunity, and bagging the manure for his roses. There were far more horses around then of course.

Horse manure isn't just good for roses. It packs your soil full of nutrients that feed your veg, particularly vital if you grow 'hungry' crops such as courgettes or potatoes which take a lot of nutrients from the soil. The big mistake people make, however, is that they chuck the manure on top in big clumps without working it into the ground, or they use it before it has fully rotted. Too fresh, and some of its acids are just too much for the plants to take. It should be applied in a dry crumbly state when the familiar farmyard hum has disappeared. By the look (and whiff) of some piles of horse muck delivered to our allotment, it will be winter before it is ready.

Composting and traditional fertilising techniques are gradually replacing the bought bags of compost gardeners have become reliant on for a generation. Apart from being ridiculously expensive, they are often laced with peat and other environmentally questionable substances. Some, in fact, do very little for your soil at all.

Homemade compost is, of course, free and has the advantage that you know what went into it. It takes surprisingly long to make, though, and there is a knack to getting the balance right between the nitrogens found in green leaves and most fresh kitchen waste and the carbons derived from paper, dead leaves and woodier materials.

Muck and compost have been on my mind of late because some of my food-growing areas on the allotment are showing signs of nutrient depletion. A number of the fruit bushes, which love a good dose of manure, have not done as well as they should. The rhubarb, another manure lover, has been a disaster with the stalks thin and wilty. In the garden at home, the raised salad bed is also underperforming. When I set it up three years ago, it was brimful with homemade compost from our garden composter—or 'the Dalek' as my dad likes to call it because of its distinctive shape not unlike the 'Doctor Who' villains. A recent tray of lettuce seedlings went two-thirds into the raised bed and one-third into some planters with soil taken from another bed in the garden.

Two weeks on, the planter lettuces are ready to pick, while the ones in the raised bed are stunted—so that's my previous diagnosis confirmed. Usually in a situation such as this, I'd simply raid the Dalek but at the moment ours has digestion problems. The crumbly black compost usually found at the base has been replaced by a soppy mush.

This problem has in turn generated a family-wide dispute over whether Daleks should be fed cooked food or not. Dad says not. I say yes. But I'm the one with the sick Dalek.

He suggests I dose the Dalek with a powdered accelerant, available in most garden centres, and stop feeding my Dalek cooked veg and mashed potato. In the kitchen, I also have another composting casualty—a large plastic bin also full of food guck. This is the wormery I was given last Christmas—the vent of which was unwittingly covered by Her Outdoors. By the time I'd discovered the problem, the tiger worms had all died. Perhaps if I pretend I don't have a binful of undigested food muck in my kitchen, it will go away. The alternative is just too much to deal with.

What I am still getting from the wormery, though, is a superb liquid feed for the tomatoes, which is decanted from a hollow space in the base of the bin via a plastic tap. Had it been working properly, I would also get fine compost. The strange thing is that I'd been making fine compost for two years, quite by instinct, without properly learning about the process. Now, a glance through a book on the subject shows it can be rather complicated. But I'm swotting up.

Meantime it's middle August and the tomatillos on the back patio are 6ft tall and crowding out the outdoor tomatoes on one side, while out-climbing a particularly gregarious (although relatively grape-less) vine on the other.

It has to be said that the tomatillos, like runner beans, are quite an attractive plant to look at when in flower—in their case middle-sized blooms that don't look unlike little black-and-yellow pansies. The bees love them, and the foliage, with its large spade-like leaves, is a pleasing lush green. And in recent weeks the fruits have been developing in droves.

They are like nothing you've ever seen. First a little green paper lantern starts to grow until it's about the size of a plum. Inside this grows a fruit that doesn't look unlike a green tomato. It swells and swells until it cracks its outer wrapper and then it's time to pick them.

For the purposes of writing about them, I decided I'd better taste one—but the shops don't stock them here. Even the specialist, stock-it-all greengrocer around the corner from where I work didn't have them.

—"We did get them once, but they work out far too expensive after they have been imported. Last time they were pushing €1.65 each," he said.

So in the interests of Plot 34 research, I cut down the largest tomatillo fruit and unwrapped it. The skin was gooey.

As a small child, I had a simple test to determine what was and wasn't safe to eat. I handed it to my younger brother. If he vomited, I didn't eat it. And so I cut the unripe tomatillo in half and offered a piece to Her Outdoors. She eats it. I watch. Her face immediately screws up.

—"Yeuch!"

Not good.

Risks aside, I decided I'd better taste it myself. As a fan of tart redcurrants, my palate might appreciate them more. I wasn't too sure about the taste myself—a sort of kiwi crossed with a pear, but with a heavy sappy tang dominating. Maybe they're not ripe yet.

But if they do turn out to be tasty and can be eaten fresh, I've hit pay dirt with the tomatillos. Any plum-sized fresh fruit which grows vigorously in the Irish monsoon season, is inexpensive to produce and turns in a bumper crop of expensive fruits/veg in rainy conditions is a most welcome addition to any garden. And they are also high in potassium, vitamins C and A and folic acid it seems. So what are the chances an unknown South American exotic could catch on here? Ask Sir Walter Raleigh. Nobody had heard of his 'patatas' either.

As we get towards the end of August, I'm learning fast that there are few reliables in this allotments racket. The broccoli which served us so well last year and cropped so heavily that we had to buy a freezer, has done very little this time around. Apart from a small bag of heads harvested, we've had little since. Maybe it's the wettest summer for years that's to blame. Maybe it was a massive caterpillar attack. Who knows? Meantime we've had almost no tomatoes forming on the Gardener's Delight cherry tomato plant which also did so well last year. In the raised bed, the salads are a bit wet as well. I'm suspecting the soil might need more humus. We're getting perhaps 40 per cent of the rocket, spicy leaves and lettuces we had this time last year. On the positive side, the Tigerella tomatoes we put in for the first time this year are doing well, as are the San Marzano plum tomatoes which also have plenty of fruit on the way. The onions are cracking along and it'll soon be time to bend the tops down, the precursor to harvesting them. But the continuous rain coupled with warm temperatures means more pests and more disease. Blight has hit the tomatoes and the potatoes but we've treated the tomatoes—losing only a few plants—and we cut down the potatoes to stop the blight going into the tubers.

Chapter Ten

Processing and Storage
from Frigidaire to Natural Fake Tan

My grandmother's fridge looked like no-one else's. Expansive, curvy and chunky, it was like a great big snowman standing guard at one end of her 1940s-style kitchen. It seemed to fit in flush with the squat enamelled stove/oven, and the similarly rounded pedestal budgie cage beside it—all snug together and matey by design in the same big kitchen of apple pie aromas and morning breakfast fried in lard from a big earthenware pot. Other people's fridges were square, pinched and sort of mean looking compared to Frigidaire, whose name was spelled out on his door in confident, squat chrome letters instead of the nasty stuck-on aluminium stickers banged up in the corner of everyone else's.

Frigidaire had an assuringly heavy door with a thickset chrome handle the size of a chair armrest which offered a firm handshake and a well-engineered, clasp-clip mechanism. You couldn't sneak his door ajar to whip something on the quiet because he announced his opening each time with a great deep Klunk-Klick! And if you managed to climb inside—I'm sure two people could have got in there—you could be sure if that great heavy door clicked shut behind you that you weren't coming back without outside help. If they could hear you that is, because Frigidaire also came with a rubber seal akin to the whitewall tyre on a 1950s Cadillac.

Frigidaire's Klunk-Klick! was the defining characteristic and assuring sound of that kitchen.

Until only a few years before she passed away, my grand-mother kept Frigidaire standing guard despite the fact that he was obviously, like herself, quite ancient and unable to do some things, but still solid and reliable. While he had acres of white space inside, his one big drawback was that he didn't have much in the way of freezing capacity. The extent of this was one tiny metal freeze box which could maintain a single block of HB ice cream and a lone tray of ice cubes.

I learned later that Frigidaire was the American brand which produced the first stand-alone domestic fridge ever sold and thus gave the mod-con its generic name. It was taken over almost immediately by General Motors, makers of the mighty chromed, streamlined and finned Cadillacs and Chevrolets of the 1950s, the luxury liners of the road with which Gran's fridge shared classical design touches alongside its legendary solidity. She and Frigidaire were a team from the 1940s or '50s right through to the late 1980s.

No doubt my grandmother was pressed many times to update Frigidaire, who was actually looking quite classically retro and chic round the time he finally died—to be replaced by a fussy little Japanese rectangle with all the solidity of an origami biscuit box.

When it came to food storage, Frigidaire had big help from another equally important feature of Gran's house, the pantry. This was a 'food room', a single narrow room jutting from the outside end of the house filled with plates of bones covered in white gauze, pheasants and rabbits hanging by their necks or feet and any cooked meats that needed to be kept cool. The room was, with its tiled floor, tiny window and fly-excluding screen, always cool inside.

In the pantry at Gran's you always found glass jars of the big 1lb-pot size required for preserving food in the days she first tied on an apron. Today you can pull something from the bottom of your freezer, thaw it and eat it whenever you please. You might even find a woolly mammoth in ours, it's been so long since we've seen the bottom of it. But back in Gran's day, preserves like jams were an important part of the family meal precisely because they provided a way of locking in vital vitamin C in a form which would store for a year or more. She made loads of it from Grand-dad's fruit garden. Loganberry, gooseberry, blackcurrant and even rhubarb jam, usually sweetened with the addition of some sultanas or raisins.

If you want to grow food in an amount that will actually make a real impression on your life, you will quickly discover that the average modern home is not equipped for the unexpected arrival of big harvests, as older homes were with their pantries and larders.

The two sacks of calabrese heads we took from Plot 34 last year come to mind—this is a vegetable which often needs to be harvested all at once but also one that loses most of its nutrition within a few days. Although it sounds obvious, we never gave a thought to how we'd store our food when the time came to harvest it.

Because the novice is used to shop-bought foods, bred for longevity, the speed at which homegrown produce goes off can take you by surprise. Homegrown varieties are popular on the basis of taste and texture difference but they don't do mummification.

This means you have to get your head around the home processing and storage end of things as much as around the growing of the food. Otherwise all your efforts will have been for nothing.

On a recent visit to a largely self-sufficient farm, the owner/operator told me that one of the biggest single misconceptions about the self-sufficient lifestyle was the idea that almost all of the work is done outdoors. In fact, he asserted, about 40 per cent of the effort is food processing and preparation for storage, the sort of activities generally conducted indoors and often late into the night. The sorts of activities which require a one-man, mind-numbing production line for hours, sometimes days—podding peas, top and tailing blackcurrants, blanching carrots. In his case, preserves and bottling also played an important role—the old-fashioned way of keeping fruit and veg through pickling them in brine or vinegar in airtight jars.

As soon as the crops started coming in during the first year of our allotment, we had to go out and purchase a chest freezer. The next thing I learned was that freezing crops wasn't a simple matter of banging them into the freezer. Most needed preparation before freezing.

My first properly dealt with surplus came with Year One's great big carrot crop and the following efforts to process them.

—"Do you smoke many these days?" enquired Her Outdoors's mum across the table one day.

Her folks don't approve of tobacco consumption, you see, and there is a rather heavy brown-orange stain running conspicuously between all my fingers. Not that of a 20-Benson-a-day man like me, more the deep-set finger tan of the talons more commonly found attached to the sort of unsnuffable nicotine pickled octogenarian smokers which unrepentant puffers are so fond of citing as their champions:

—"Smokes 80 Players Navy Cut unfiltered a day, since he was six, and still climbs the mountain every morning with three sheep strapped to his back!"

When Her Outdoors's mum visited, my own paws were a lurid hue of tangerine thanks to two days and nights spent slaving in a carrot-processing sweatshop of my own making. Exposure to vast amounts of that root's carotene, the substance that gives the vegetable its name, makes you go orange. It goes into dyes and those artificial suntan creams that have turned so many self-conscious young ladies in recent years into tangerine-skinned Oompa-Loompas. Just one unexpected result of dealing with a vast crop surplus.

When you start growing your own food, it takes a few years to gauge exactly how much of what you are likely to consume. Then comes understanding which quantity of seed translates into how much food and finally comes the establishment of how much of that produce you're likely to eat. Only after a few years of undershooting and overshooting do you get the balance right for each crop you stick with.

At Plot 34, the carrots came in spades in Year One. At first I'd estimated that we had got about 400 large ones out of our 40sq.ft plot. In the end, once I started digging them, it became apparent it was closer to twice that number.

That April we sowed two packets of Nantes, a popular variety known for its large rounded roots and extra-sweet taste. And when harvest time came at the end of September, I stupidly dug half of them up in one go. Straight away I realised I had made a grave mistake because, unlike the shop-bought carrots I'd been used to, the Nantes lads started to go soft after just twenty-four hours, largely I later learned, because I had washed and scrubbed them, a process that starts the rot early.

So a master production plan to process them was called for. We had already bought the chest freezer with our surpluses in mind and it was already half-full with calabrese, peas and what-nots. Since the bumper calabrese crop I had learned that frozen veg has to be blanched before freezing to help kill off the natural bacteria that may spoil them in the freezer. Blanching is a process of parboiling and then cooling. Each vegetable takes a different amount of time, depending on cut and size and these can be checked on the internet. For carrot slices, as I was doing, it takes two minutes of boiling. Then the carrots are transferred to a pot of ice water for two more minutes. Boiled vegetables stay cooking in their own heat for a time even after being taken off the cooker. The ice-water treatment stops that internal cooking process. Next they go into freezer bags, the thick Ziploc bags are best because they prevent 'freezer burn'. Finally the air needs to be squeezed out of the bags before they are sealed. I later learned a tip from an internet board which suggested closing the bags until there's a tiny gap into which you insert a straw and suck in all the air from the bag before zipping it shut. Reducing air-contained microbes will also prevent the food from turning and helps it to last even longer.

Done right, you should have the nearest thing to a ready supply of fresh vegetables from your freezer for up to a year. And believe me it's worth it, they do taste so good.

We went into action with the intention of processing the whole lot—four bin liner sacks full in one go. The other half were left in the ground, which is another suitable way of storing them up to a point, although they get tougher and stringier with age if you do this. Most root crops indeed can be left over winter in the ground and in the case of swedes and parsnips, a good winter's frost improves the taste.

And so that evening, the whole lot was cast out on the kitchen floor—muck, carrots, insects, green tops, the whole lot. The roots ranged in size from four inches long and the thickness of a finger to 1ft long and the shape of a large parsnip. Luckily, the 'That's Life' selection of multi-legged and sexually suggestive mutants accounted for only 5 per cent.

Pretty soon I realised that, just like in a regular commercial processing plant, these carrots would have to be graded. In the end we had twelve piles of differently sized carrots on the kitchen floor. I then spent six hours up to my elbows in mucky water, scrubbing off each and every one. When the washing was done, it was time to cut the tops off them, then shave them, top and tail them and chop them into pieces for blanching.

—"Are we not doing any batons?" probed Her Outdoors, halfway through Day Two as I sliced the ten millionth button-shaped slice off the end of yet another root. Then seeing my face, she backtracked:

—"Er, I guess they're all the same in the pot anyways" and off she tiptoed to embrace Simon Cowell.

The next thing you need to remember when blanching is to store your produce in suitably sized amounts. There's no use opening a freezer pack which feeds ten if there's only two of you. And if the bits all stick together (and they do often) you might end up with a large carrot football which needs a hammer and chisel to break it into usable parts.

From midnight, the production line ground on until near 3am, when the processor-in-chief retired to bed thoroughly knackered and appearing to wear shrivelled lady's evening gloves, in orange.

The following day the production line resumed—washing, grading, topping, tailing, shaving, boiling, cooling, bagging, freezing. By the end of the next day 80 per cent had been done, leaving just the massive stewing carrots and the 'That's Lifers'.

By Day Three, however, I didn't want to see another carrot again.

That night, reading John Seymour's excellent *The New Complete Book of Self Sufficiency*, I learnt from the man himself (Seymour inspired TV's 'The Good Life') that our carrots, like many root crops, would have stored for months in wet sand provided I didn't wash them. "Wash them and they won't keep no matter what," he writes. The last batch were left overnight in water and the next morning I found the whole lot scummy and stinking. So I dumped the whole stinking mess in the compost bin and washed my hands of them. The hands stayed orange for days, though.

We don't have a garage and the shed is full of the usual rubbish, so where do we keep our big boxes of wet sand? Mr Seymour would tell you to build your own from orange boxes.

Processing and Storage

The only question now is, with enough carrots for two dinners a week for the next year, what would I do with the other half of the crop still in the ground? The only certainty was, that as far as our dinners were concerned, the future was most definitely orange.

And unless allotment holders happen to have an empty shed, greenhouse, outbuilding or garage, they'll always have to sacrifice space at home for nursery plants early in the year and large amounts (if they're lucky) for produce at the end of the season.

This is why older homes had larger kitchens and larger spaces like larders which were designed for such storage needs. If you don't have this space then for certain times of the year, expect to donate your regular living spaces temporarily to accommodate a harvest—space which you will have to tolerate being dirty, hopping with insects or smelling like the back end of a dustbin.

If you or your partner (I'm talking particularly about ladies) won't accept your home being compromised in this manner, then it might be wiser to stick to small-time pick-as-you-eat-growing.

The mind-numbing production lines I mentioned also include (for variation): topping and tailing a thousand blackcurrants— they need the top (the nipple) and tail (the stalk) pulled off each berry before eating; podding peas—you get about eight peas to every five seconds if you get good at it; then washing, scraping and chopping root crops for freezing.

Some produce needs special treatment for storage. Onions and chillies are dried out and left to hang on strings. The former need to spend a time outdoors on sheets to dry out properly, though wet weather means this sometimes has to be done inside. Some crops, like courgettes, tomatoes, cucumbers and onions, don't freeze well. These we process into sauces which can in turn be frozen. Tomatoes can be skinned with the help of a splash of boiling water and the resulting pulp will keep in the freezer, invaluable for bolognese long after they are out of season.

After being tangoed by the carrots I was thiosulphinated by the onions. You see, thiosulphinates are the chemicals in onions that produce that distinctively cheesy, socky whiff. In our onion harvest week, multiply that by about four hundred, the rough number which ended up drying out (and apparently farting) on our kitchen table in Year One when it was too wet for weeks on end to dry them outdoors in the more usual way, by lying them on sheets or hanging them on a fence.

Here's a little chemistry lesson: when you slice or bruise onions, the cells are broken open and produce sulfenic acids. These are highly unstable and decompose very quickly into syn-propanethial-S-oxide (SPSO), a volatile lighter-than-air gas, and also thiosulfinates, SPSO's whiffy companions.

The SPSO gas is what makes you cry when you chop onions because it reacts with the water in your eye, the two combining to produce sulphuric acid, albeit in a mild form.

On the other hand, the thiosulphinates are the stinkbombs of the equation. They break out every time onions are bruised, cut, or in our case it seems, glanced at. And our latest cornucopia is certainly not to be sniffed at.

We had to harvest the lot at once because they had been ready for a number of weeks, but persistent rain meant we couldn't dry them off outdoors. The exact same thing happened in Year Two. In both years, some were showing the early signs of rot so they had to come up and be dried indoors, en masse. The only other option was to lose the lot and after putting two days into digging and preparing the beds and then planting them, and hours more bending over to weed them, that just wasn't an option. The first year's harvest filled three bin liner bags and a large cloth shopping bag. Chuffed with our haul, we parked them in the car and returned to work on the plot. It was only at going-home time that we first discovered the joys of thiosulfinates, and as we got into the car we were thoroughly socked by the hum.

Her Outdoors, into whose pride-of-place automobile said onions were stuffed, was not the least bit amused by this fascinating but whiffy scientific phenomenon.

Indeed, as we proceeded home, she stated baldly, with more than a hint of retaliatory consequence, that she wouldn't be at all happy if said profusion of thiosulfinates turned out to be a less-than-temporary fixture inside her automobile.

I was about to make light of the matter and quip "now your car's a Hummer, yuk, yuk", but a cursory sideways glance quickly told me that keeping schtum would be a far safer policy.

Alarmingly, the next morning, after the bags were removed and put in the back garden, the car still smelt of BO (bloody onions, as they were now being termed).

Worse still was that the rain was still belting down outside and fast filling the onion bags outside with water.

Processing and Storage

In years when you do get a dry summer/autumn, it's supposed to be done thus: First bend the stalks over about a week or two before harvest to send the growth back into the bulb, a step which also helps prevent them going to seed. They say you know when to harvest your onions when most of the tops fall over. Most of ours had already taken their final bows.

You're supposed to harvest onions in dry weather to help storage, but on that summer, and the next, we just didn't have dry conditions at all for a six-week period.

If you do get them in dry weather you spread them out on the ground for a week or so to let them dry in the sun, on a sheet of plastic or sack material if the ground is less than dry. This makes the tops shrivel and the skins dry out so they can be stored without sprouting any further. The sheeting also stops them killing spots on your lawn as you can move them daily.

In Year One, the rain continued, so with Her Outdoors out at the shops, I retrieved the whole sodden mess of mud, bugs, water and onions from the garden and spread them out on a sheet covering the kitchen table, removing as many of the creepy-crawlies as I could before she got back.

But it wasn't long before the all-too-familiar pong of thio-sulfinates was mooching around the kitchen, albeit considerably less virulent than before. The onions weren't cut or bruised, but the green tops had been broken in all directions and presumably they were the source of the odour.

Ten days on, and they still hadn't dried out properly. Some of the tops started to rot to mush and the bulbs needed to be moved around to stop this. And each little shunt lets off more thiosulfi-nates.

Now house-proud ladies are not generally amenable to their men filling the domestic abode with dirt-encrusted, insect-infested matter and 400 farting bulbs, but Her Outdoors was remarkably patient.

Despite her understandable narkiness about her car smelling like a sack of socks, she's been generally quite amenable about the house being full of plants and compost. But losing the dining table for two weeks to 400 mud and heebie jeebie infested flatulent onions might be another matter altogether.

And therefore, so as not to add to her angst, I didn't feel the urge to inform her of the accompanying crop of mobile-phone-sized slugs (they're absolutely huge on the allotment), which appear to have hitched a lift in the bags and by now have gone slimeabout in the house.

So far, I've intercepted them as far afield as the living-room carpet.

Anyway, my policy to ensure the onions got the continued benefit of indoor drying for as long as possible was to behave as if they weren't there at all.

Until my dad called round, that is.

Knowing the likely brouhaha he'd make, I decided a warning to Her Outdoors was in order.

—"My dad's coming over. He'll probably make a big fuss over the onions. He'll probably laugh out loud, shake his head and say something like: 'For God's sake. That's ridiculous. Where are ya goin' with all the onions?' You know how he kicks up a fuss."

And so nothing but light was made of the matter when, twenty minutes later, he burst into the kitchen, stopped in his tracks at the covered table, and bellowed:

—"FOR GOD'S SAKE, THAT'S RIDICULOUS. WHERE ARE YA GOIN' WITH ALL THE ONIONS?"

And once they were dry the next step to preserve them was to string them up and hang them—the time-honoured method of storage. The twenty or so strings could hang in the shed.

In Year Two the weather was wetter still; the onions had absorbed such moisture and the shed was so warm inside that they actually began to develop a mould. They had to be cut down and each one had its outer skins stripped. We lost a third of the crop, but the rest still lasted us for six months.

For some plants like chillies, it's a matter of drying them out all the way through. Again we hang them in strings. Berries and tomatoes can also be dried out, although in a wet country this can also be tricky. Unlike many types of veg, fruit can suffer from being frozen as it breaks down the cells completely within their skins. This isn't a problem if you can consume them in this manner. Tomatoes can be fried in the pan or processed into sauce after being frozen while frozen berries are great in smoothies, baking and desserts. Unlike veg, fruit is not blanched when being frozen. We flash-freeze berries.

Why do we growers suffer it all? For the same reason

Norwegians like to ferment a raw fish for two months before eating it; the French use hundred-years-old, wood shelves to inflict blue mould into cheese: the Chinese will putrefy a duck egg over months before eating it; and the Scots store their malts in oaken casts only for twenty years—for a subtle and unique one in a million taste that makes you feel thoroughly alive!

And what you can't store or reasonably expect to keep of your harvest, you'd be best advised to just give away free. When you do this, you'll discover that people are far more appreciative than you think. Because a bag of homegrown, heritage-strain tomatoes can be something really special to a foodie who pays big money for them at the farmers' market and hasn't yet become as immune to their charms as you the grower who eats them until they come out of your ears. You'll also likely discover that these people will later surprise you and weeks after you dropped in the bag of Marmandes, they'll come around and give you something back.

—"The wife works in a bakery and she brought home this box of pastries for you."

People feel honoured to get an unexpected pressie and might want to honour you back. Go there and you'll find yourself sucked into the world of *meitheal* or whatever else it's called in other countries.

Meitheal is the old Gaelic term for a labour system whereby farmers pool labour and resources to help one another out. When one farmer's field needed harvesting, all the local farmers came to assist. On another day they all harvest someone else's and so on.

It also extends to goods. The farmer who owns a harvesting machine might lend it to all the other farmers while another who owns a threshing machine might do the same. In this way, the farmers don't all need to buy a machine each because at least one of the group owns one and you know he'll lend it to you because you've got the only hay-baler.

In the wider sense, I have been lucky enough to see the principles of *meitheal* applied in city life, largely by rural-born elders who carry it out instinctively and without intention. This usually involves giving stuff away, such as a surplus of homegrown food, which is shared around to their friends, neighbours and colleagues.

It is the loosest form of barter—so loose that it's almost sub-conscious and if you ask the giver whether they expect anything in return, they'll be genuinely indignant that you asked in the first place.

—"It's just nice to be nice," they'll sniff.

And while nothing is ever formally expected in return, it is no coincidence either that these surpluses tend to be doled out specifically to those who have either (a) already recently done a favour or given something to the giver or (b) have, from time to time, access to surpluses which the giver might reasonably expect to benefit from.

I've picked it up myself. It's not intentional or worked out, it just happens. My brother is an ardent shooting man and I'm a passionate fly fisherman. The end result of our hobbies is that from time to time I end up with more fish than I need and he ends up with more pheasants. While I don't doubt that I'd get pheasants from him even if I didn't give him any fish, I'd also be quite sure that he wouldn't be inclined to give me quite so many birds if his freezer didn't also happen to contain one of my fish.

A long-time fishing companion of mine of rural birth catches far more fish than me largely thanks to his natural fishing skills and long years of experience, but despite going fishing perhaps even three times a week, he seldom eats the fish himself. Instead he hands them all around, in work, to neighbours, to friends and acquaintances. Even acquaintances of acquaintances he's never even met. One of his classic catchphrases is: "I gave him a fish… and you know it was like giving him a million dollars."

Because to most people, a fresh, wild brown trout is something quite special and not commonly available in the shops. In this manner, my good friend has generated an endless amount of returned favours which most usually include (among many other things), free tickets to race meetings, free cuts of prime meat, dog sitting services, homemade pies and cakes, free cases of wines, bottles of whiskey and free use of holiday homes. His *meitheal* instincts have become so finely honed that in certain weeks pre-ceding particular sporting events, he puts himself under pressure to catch a certain number of fish. If he doesn't get them, he unashamedly pinches mine. But he's right.

These *meitheal*-type relationships also lead to what used to be old-fashioned community. Because handing over a fish, or a surplus bag of carrots, or potatoes, or celeriacs, isn't a matter of posting them in the letter box, it's also a social affair usually accompanied by a bit of an auld chat.

In this way, homegrown food surpluses can be like karma, and come back to you in unexpected and surprising ways. *Meitheal* rocks.

Allotment Diary, Year Two

August to Early September

When it came to horror in the fruit and veg department, I thought I'd seen it all. But here, before me, was...an incontinent pineapple!

Listing to one side in a pool of its own ooze and sporting a spiky haircut of bluish white penicillin, the ailing creature before me was quite an achievement, even by the standards of our local convenience store.

Its fruit and veg shelves are the stuff of legend round our way, and it could probably provide enough material for one of those sensational, clip-based reality cable shows that run around the clock on the Bravo and Dave channels. Not so much 'When Good Food Goes Bad' as 'When Bad Food Gets Worse'. All that was missing was the gravel-hard male voiceover rasping across a metal-guitar soundtrack: "Shopperzzz...got more than they bargained for...when they encountered (drum roll)...delinquent onions squirting their own acidic innards."

Our minimarket is bog standard. It has the usual automatic doors, an 'out of order' screen display that looks like a cash machine and a brace of orange-skinned checkout bunnies.

It is on their shelves that I found the blackened carrots so past it that you can bend them end-to-end without breaking them, mushrooms so shrivelled that they could have come up with Tutankhamun, and celery so brown I thought it was ginger root. Before starting our allotment, we'd already stopped buying large sacks of potatoes altogether—both there and at the supermarket—because half of them were usually off.

Of course our convenience store with its corrupted

grocery for even stinkier prices was, as I said earlier, much of the inspiration behind my taking on an allotment. So personally I'd like to thank the guy with the pencil behind his ear who comes out from the back when the OMG!!! girls' tills go "Weeeeeee...," for setting us on the road to growing our own. Meanwhile, since we started our allotment, fresh-food prices have sprung up faster than mould on the convenience shop's tomatoes.

This is the time of year when we realise all our work has been worthwhile and we can relax a bit. It's a time when the sum total of the work our allotment requires is a bit of light weeding, occasional strimming and plenty of harvesting. We're currently completely self-sufficient in vegetables, a state that should continue in various degrees until the early new year.

From the patio and plastic greenhouse I'm picking four types of tomatoes, taking in an average of seven a day. Also in the garden, we're harvesting courgettes at the rate of three or four a week. There are chillies outdoors and in the greenhouse (four types in all), tomatillos on the patio, and some lettuce and all the herbs we need in the salad bed.

Up at the allotment, our King Edward potatoes have been saved from blight and we're digging them up as we need them. There should be a few months' worth there. It took a bit of getting used to them because they cook far more quickly than shop-bought potatoes. Unlike those bought in shops, none of them is rotten. The peas have just finished but we've still got string beans which, regrettably, we probably won't eat. The last of the broccoli and calabrese is still on the go and there are enough onions to do us until well after Christmas. Last weekend, we bent the stalks over to redirect growth from them into the onion instead, and this weekend we'll be hanging them to dry on the fence around the allotment.

We've got fresh cabbages, too. On their way to going to seed, the caterpillar- and bird-shredded heads we were left with earlier in the year produced yet another round of smaller but nonetheless tasty heads. And although they did go in late and it will be a month before they're full-sized, we've been thinning out the carrots. The baby-sized Nantes variety are delicious to eat, raw or lightly boiled. We've been using the tops off harvested onions to keep the carrot flies off them.

Still to come, we have sprouts and swedes, which should be ready around Christmas and early in the new year. The back garden will also hopefully be giving us celery, celeriac, chard and enough leeks for stews for many, many months.

And Plot 34's six-year-old self-appointed Head of Secret Tunnels (HST) is eating his vegetables a little easier, realising where they come from. Our ten-month-old little princess is also eating vast amounts of fresh veg mushed up.

—"No, I'm not interested in growing my own veg," sniffs my not-long-ago-retired dad in early September when I suggest he think about taking on an allotment or perhaps even share mine as a healthy new hobby for his retirement regime. By now, as you've guessed, I've starting turning evangelist for the grow-your-own league. My dad is proving tough as a convert, however.

Unlike many who take up pastimes when they get the golden fob, my dad appears to have dropped all his but still insists he's too busy to do anything.

—"Why should I bother growing vegetables when I can get huge bags of them for next to nothing down at...?"

And then he rattles off the names of his favourite local discount stores, which he and his mate prowl in their eternal quest for anything cut-price—be it groceries, a carp weighing kit or a wall-mounted chocolate fountain.

—"To get you out in the open air!" I say, although it's raining outside. "To get some exercise. To help you eat properly. To have access to a supply of fresh food that's not dosed with chemicals, that hasn't been harvested weeks or months ago and that isn't inbred and cloned for longevity. Food that tastes better."

He's still laughing at me.

But perhaps the best example for his 'value' argument is the humble swede. You'll get a whopping great big one in any expensive supermarket for about 70c. A swede is nutritious, delicious, substantial and cheaper than cheap. And it seems to keep forever.

Use half of it and then leave the other half in the fridge for two weeks and you can still use it again. At least with homegrown broccoli and tomatoes you can use the economy argument, because they're so expensive to purchase. But swedes are cheap as could be.

So, the reason I'm growing swedes this year is partly for a bit of interest on the allotment at a time of year when I'm left with very little else I've yet to pull from the ground. I'm also keen to see whether allotment-grown versions are, like our carrots, a million times more delicious than shop-bought equivalents.

After May's great rush at Plot 34, they were pretty much the last crop to go in. I think I even sowed them in June, six weeks after you're supposed to. Then I forgot about them. Like spuds and carrots, you sow them in situ—they're not brought up in containers and then transplanted.

By the middle of last month I'd been overdue in thinning them out. You plant the seeds and then, months later, you need to remove enough juveniles so they don't crowd themselves and they have enough space to grow. With autumnal rain keeping me off the plot for almost a month, I returned three weeks ago in order to harvest the last of the spuds.

Then I noticed that the juvenile swedes I'd pulled out and thrown onto the grass were, thanks to the rain, still alive. So I had a brainwave. After extracting the last of the spuds (it's a bit like a treasure hunt), I decided to plant the uprooted 'neeps' into the potato patch to see if they would take. They did. Unfortunately, in the end they turned out to be too small and hard to eat. So swedes don't transplant—another lesson learned.

Most people I know seem to have hated swedes as youngsters but developed a real taste for them in adulthood. They're one of my favourite vegetables and I like to mash them up with butter and black pepper or mix them in with mashed carrots.

September finds me musing that if our allotment was a

country, it'd be a lot like Ireland; after a solid period of sustained growth, it looks like Plot 34's salad days have come to a temporary halt. With the change in the season, this geographically small and exposed area is now poised to take a battering from the foul winds starting to blow as another winter looms. We stand exposed because, despite all our opportunities to make contingency plans for the inevitable storms ahead, we were far too busy enjoying the cornucopia to care.

Like Ireland Inc, we're suffering from dreadful infrastructure but it's time for emergency measures. We have drawn a development plan, although recent purse-string-tightening means some key projects will surely have to be dropped. As the harvest clears, I'm hoping to make some big structural changes on the allotment.

First there's the state of the roads—or walkways in our case. Our allotment has about eight rectangular plots with walkways between them ranging from 1ft to 3ft wide. In the sodden months (most of this year) these walkways have turned muddy and slippery. This isn't helped by the site's slope.

When I first dug out our beds, I thought it would be clever to throw the stones, sticks, weeds and roots onto the walkways to keep grass growth down and provide a modicum of grip.

It worked well for a while but I hadn't counted on some of those weeds getting walked into the ground and resprouting, although this time the stones made it difficult to extract them. The plan is to get ourselves grounded by getting a trailer-load of bark mulch. My brother, who's in the large-scale landscaping sector, predicts it will end up costing €120 to €220 depending on how and in what form it is delivered.

Mulch will bury those weeds like bad loans, insulate the ground and provide non-mucky grip, but only for a time. Perhaps we'll get a few years out of it. He says it will keep bigger weeds down, but perennials such as dandelions will eventually get to seed on it. Mulch is a temporary solution, but I can't afford tiles or paving stones for such a large area.

When ordering mulch, you'll need to plan ahead. First, measure the area you need to cover—in our case it's about

30sq.m. You'll also have to consider access for your delivery. The issue for us is the steep, uphill, narrow track leading to our plot. We need to make sure that the delivery vehicle is wide enough to fit by informing the supplier of the track's measurements. A trailer delivery may be a problem because, with nowhere to turn around, any vehicle that goes up our steep track will have to reverse back down again.

You need to know exactly how much mulch you need. This means measuring the ground you intend to cover. My brother reckons 30 or 40sq.m equates to about a skip load of 3sq.m. It might seem obvious, but you need to select a site to set down the mulch. You can't tip a huge pile of it onto a public footpath and it needs to be within reach of the track.

Raised beds were planned for this year but I don't think I'll have the money for the timber. Plan A—harvest the timber from skips around town—backfired, because people always use them as reserve siding to let them overload the things. As with the banks, remove one set of planks and the whole lot falls apart. We reap what we sow.

Chapter Eleven

The Interweb Thingy

On a lazy September day in 2005, JMaxx was eating his lunch at his desk in an office somewhere in North America. Not finding a bin close by, he dumped his leftovers in a plant pot on the desk in front of him. After a few weeks, a little plant sprouted. Curious to find out what it was, JMaxx did some online research, and discovered it was a chilli—most likely sprung from a stray seed from his lunch of all those weeks previous.

Soon it began sprouting flowers. Unfortunately they fell off almost as soon as they opened. JMaxx figured, again perhaps by consulting the internet, that they required pollination; and because there were no 'bugs', as he calls them, flying round his office; he deducted that he might have to help nature's process along by becoming a surrogate bee. So JMaxx picked up a paper clip, straightened it and prodded it into one flower, then the next. Months later, the plant is still growing, and JMaxx is eating his own desk-grown chillies, picked right off his plant, in turn sprung from his lunch.

I know all this because I came across the internet chat forum in which he related the experience.

As it turned out, not only did JMaxx use the internet to first identify and then pollinate the mystery plant which sprouted in his office, but thanks to JMaxx, his discarded lunch and his random missive on the internet, I myself now have a healthy crop of chilli plants fruiting on my windowsill. And without JMaxx, his discarded lunch and the internet, I wouldn't have had them at all and would certainly have given up the chillies a long time ago. Today they're one of my most productive and pleasing food plants.

Forget the spade, the trowel or the hoe, the internet is by far the most useful tool available to the modern allotmenteer. In days of old, the experienced grower next door or down the road provided you with advice, knowledge and solutions to your problems. Or else you went down to the library and looked up what you could in specialist books. Today though, the most knowledgeable sage you can have is the eminent Dr Interweb with his myriad split personalities and a brain which includes every word put down by internet users from all over the world, right through the past decade. He is the all-knowing, talking computer of science fiction made real. And if you know how to ask, you shall always be answered.

I choose chillies to illustrate the usefulness of the internet because in my first year growing them, they caused me endless trouble. For Northern Europe's drab climate they're a fun plant which can present a challenge to grow and thus a real sense of satisfaction when you end up harvesting your first fire-engine-red, homegrown chillies. But because chillies are not a gardener's crop typical of the northern hemisphere, there's little information to be found on how to treat them when you're growing them here. The internet is the answer. With its help, newbie allotmenteers can educate themselves in a short time with the level of knowledge that it would have taken growers of past generations a lifetime to accumulate.

I started my chillies in the hot press, something the seed packet did not instruct me to do, but it turns out that this step was entirely necessary for germination to take place at all. I learned this from an online contributor's forum where someone pointed out the temperatures chilli seeds need to get started. When they did eventually sprout I moved them to the upstairs bathroom window. By surfing the internet for random chilli plant facts, I also learned how to add improvements in their environment. And always, almost without exception, I discovered that the most vital tips came from random punters like JMaxx posting their seemingly bland daily experiences online in forums, bulletin boards or groups—often in response to queries by other internet users.

One of the criticisms most often levelled at the internet today is its excess of 'useless' knowledge. But as a learning food grower with quite specific problems to research and solve on an almost weekly basis, I would argue that within stories like JMaxx's random account of what happened to his discarded lunch you will often find the most valuable nuggets you can glean from the vastness of the netscape.

From another random posting I learned that chilli plants like to be in touching proximity to one another. This allowed me to house more plants on the limited windowsill space than I otherwise would have attempted and in turn, more plants for me meant a bigger chilli harvest. For some reason, just as my chillies were beginning to get out of the seedling phase, a plant would simply droop over and die for no obvious reason. But looking through messages posted by other growers, particularly in northern Europe, I saw that this was a common trait in countries with less light and something that growers in that part of the world just needed to accept. It was assuring to discover that it wasn't anything I was doing wrong. That's another thing about the internet—safety and assurance in numbers. When you learn other people are experiencing the same problems, you don't feel so bad. Indeed such solidarity encourages you to persist.

The first plague to visit my surviving chillies was a film of transparent web-type gunk which seemed to completely envelop the stems and the new leaves which were only then developing. Before long the leaves were shrinking back and it was fast becoming evident they were in serious trouble.

So I went back to the all-knowing Dr Interweb and his worldwide community for help. I keyed in the terms 'chilli' and 'web' and, within minutes, I was perusing messages posted from all over the world, all telling similar stories. It seemed that web gunk had been enveloping chilli plants on windowsills from Montana to Hamburg. Some people, just like me, were asking for help on relevant forums while others, who thought they knew what was wrong, were offering prognosis and diagnosis. One contributor with the sobriquet 'Grease Monkey' posted a question on a forum in 2006 about exactly such a web choking his chillies. There was a clamour to help him out and among the suggested solutions was a simple spray of soap and water. I loaded a sprayer with water and mild green Fairy Liquid and doused the lot. The problem quickly cleared up. Other solutions for mites had included washing the leaves with water which had been used previously to wash rice, and one chilli grower even suggested covering them in chicken soup!

If there is a big failing with internet information, it is that it's totally random and sometimes hard to tell which is misleading and possibly downright wrong. But once you keep this in mind, using the net properly is just the same as putting a problem to a group of friends in the pub. Three say one thing, one says another, one doesn't know and someone else suggests something else entirely. You draw your own conclusions, discard what sounds ridiculous and go with what seems like the sensible majority. It's just like using the 'Ask the Audience' option in *Who Wants To Be A Millionaire?*

My chillies recovered for a time. But then, not long after the spider-mite infestation, the leaves began to curl and soon thereafter Swiss-cheese-type holes started appearing in them. Once again they seemed to be at death's door. So once again I went back to the online community and I discovered a post dating from 2005 by a Mike Mascio which suggested that this new problem was caused either by overwatering, over-fertilisation or root restriction. I cut back the watering and repotted the plants. Once again my chilli plants recovered as new, whole and healthy leaves formed to replace the tattered ones.

Soon after, the plants flowered but these delicate little blooms immediately fell off almost as soon as they had formed. Without flowers there would be no fruit. Back to the good Doctor who allows me as many consultations as I like, at any time of day or night and all for a small monthly broadband fee.

This time I key in 'chillies' and 'flowers falling', and once again the all-knowing one has my answers. I am taken to a chat room where I first read JMaxx's experience. I had missed the obvious. Although I knew already that fruiting plants needed pollination, and that this process required bees, the thought simply never occurred to me that they couldn't pollinate indoors without them. So instead of JMaxx's straightened paper clip for his bugless environment, I began using a spayed paintbrush to cross-pollinate the flowers—the nearest household object that might replicate how I imagined a bee might ... be.

The chilli fruits soon started to develop well and in their dozens. I got great value from them, using them in all sorts of cooking but most regularly to give my winter stews more zing. I dried out my surplus and still have a big bag of them which I feed into a grinder whenever my food needs pep. Of all the food plants I've grown, the chillies must have given me the most satisfaction not least because their success involved confronting, teasing out and overcoming a whole succession of problems.

I couldn't have succeeded with them, or with many other crops, were it not for the net, which has helped me identify various bugs and grubs, diseases and strange behaviour in almost all my plants. It's help save my entire tomato crop in the second year by helping me to identify and catch in time, the blight that would have killed the lot. What I found most interesting as a grower was the fact that the most useful information didn't come from 'authority' sites like the Royal Horticultural Society or the seed suppliers themselves, but from ordinary punters telling of their own experiences growing on balconies, windowsills and in back gardens.

So when searching the net, I'd recommend starting your search by selecting the 'web search' option, but when you've exhausted that route, you should always go back again and this time search the 'groups' option and then the blogs where random punters tend to voice their views.

The real gems of knowledge came from people like Frazer Pearce in the UK on whose workwhiledrunk.com blog he writes about various aspects of his life in Welwyn Garden City in the UK, including his own efforts to grow chillies—in a climate similar to ours. Like me, Pearce had tried a selection of chilli types, and of the varieties tried, only some were successful. Invaluable to me was his list of those varieties that did prove successful on his cloud-exposed windowsills. Similar information supplied by people like Pearce across northern Europe and then tallied with my own experiences taught me that many of the really hot and exotic chillies on sale in the shops just don't work in a European climate. More importantly, it taught me that the two varieties I had been successful with—jalapeños and cayennes—were also the ones which others in my climate were most happy with. Without Pearce and co., I might have spent years ploughing through more varieties and wasting my time completely in the process.

Universities, newspapers, seed companies, hobby forums, group messages and random personal outpourings—not only do they come from every corner of the planet, but as I've said, most of it gets stored like little time-capsules for years on end.

While by now most of us take Dr Interweb for granted, to me he's the single greatest technological marvel of our generation. Surfing the internet makes me feel like my grandparents must have felt when they watched planes fly overhead for the first time.

How does it work? I still don't understand the sheer brilliance of it all, even despite looking up a number of simplified online explanations on how the internet functions. Perhaps one of the most interesting aspects of the internet is that, unlike the plane, the car or the light bulb, it wasn't 'invented' as such. Like so much in nature itself, the internet evolved organically. It was there before people knew what it was or what to call it. Before its advent, learning something as specific as how to rid chillies of spider mites in a northern European climate just wasn't possible and you went without. The knowledge existed somewhere, possibly in the thesis vault of an agri-university abroad—but it wasn't accessible to someone like me or you. Thus I'd compare its importance in the field of knowledge and education to the arrival of the printing press.

But the internet is also the reason why we growers should learn from those old gardeners who don't use it. Why we should learn from them and and stick everything we learn out there, no matter how trivial it might seem. Some of the things I've learned from the 'old network' of crusty allotmenteers are just as valuable as the nuggets unearthed online, albeit only available at times when these guys are in the mood to chat. From them I've learned things like how to do things like make fertiliser from nettles and a bucket of water (soak them for weeks in a covered bucket) or how to catch a veg-thieving rat with poison without killing birds (put it in the end of a sealed pipe). And if everyone takes the trouble to do the same, their knowledge, passed to them and acquired by a lifetime of growing, has then been saved and preserved and passed on, not just to their friends and family, but for everyone who can use a computer all over the world.

Then there's YouTube. The site, which allows people to post up snatches of video, is a wealth of growers' knowledge. It's like having the very gardening programme you need to watch at any given time. Although still reaching its potential for allotment knowledge, YouTube is particularly excellent at showing you how to do something, on video. Some things aren't easily explained by writing. See someone else do it though, and it's more easily picked up.

When I was trying to learn how to prune apple trees, I searched 'apples' and 'pruning' on YouTube and found a step-by-step film made by Fruit Wise Heritage Apples in the UK who keep an orchard with 800 different trees. One of its growers, Stephen Hayes, takes you through the process, demonstrating clearly and easily. An American gent named Frank Cook took me on a tour of some woodlands to show me blackcurrants in the wild. He revealed to me a rash of facts I hadn't already known, such as the fact that blackcurrants can grow very well in the shade.

This is particularly useful to me because I have a dark spot in the corner of the garden in which I can grow nothing but ivy, slug-attracting hostas and leylandii. Cook also revealed to me that the small leaves of the blackcurrant bush are also edible in salads and are medicinally good for the digestion.

But YouTube can equally expose you to bouts of allotment envy and inadequacy after seeing some of the masterpieces that other urban farmers have managed to create. After taking a virtual tour of George's allotment in Liverpool ('raised bed allotment summer 2008') I felt pangs of jealousy over his meticulously structured food-garden, which is only a year older than mine. While I wouldn't go as far as housing my food plants in such a rigid series of wooden compartments and cages, Liverpool George does demonstrate, as you accompany him by camera around his patch, just how many varieties of food plants you can grow in relatively small spaces.

But perhaps it is the blog which is the communications comfort blanket of the internet. Blogs mean you can follow the progress of back garden growers from all over the world, and interact with them if you so wish by email, assuming that you can actually contribute to their food garden, be it in Bali or in Boston, and they to yours. It helps, you see, that disaster doesn't single you out for its attention, that these things simply happen.

One of my own recommended regular stops would be 'Claire's Allotment' blog by Claire Moriarty of BBC Hampshire; the 'Nearly Good Life BlogSpot' from Yorkshire (Webdreamer.co.uk); or, for those in harsher conditions, 'Urban Bumpkin BlogSpot' from Glasgow (Urban-bumpkin.blogspot.com).

The Interweb Thingy

Claire recently taught me how to make use of the dandelions which plague my garden by placing a bin lid over them to blanch them, to make them useful in salads. That's the sort of knowledge the net throws at you simply by 'surfing'.

And while my namesake Margaret Keenan of BBC Wales seems to have ceased her blog, her old contributions are still online for us to peruse.

There's the Food Urbanism BlogSpot (Foodurbanism.blogspot .com) which follows the growing experiences of a green-minded Canadian living in Dublin and then there's Fluffy Muppet who runs a diary (Fluffymuppet.blogspot.com) of her own attempts to grow food in an urban environment and whose online friends and contributors include Bifurcated Carrots and Beansprouts. It could be in New Zealand for all I know. In this way, you can build up a bank of contacts and tap the knowledge and experience of people you don't even know. And if you want to, you can ask them your own questions via the email addresses they provide.

The internet is also very local. It is the parish notice board of the 21st century. The website for the South Dublin Allotments Association is a regular stop of mine not only for its strong advice sections, but also for its news of such local events as the regular seed days which are held now and then in the Dublin area.

Pest identification is one of the most relevant uses of the internet for me as a novice grower. It tells me within minutes not only how to get rid of them, but perhaps more importantly, how to identify them in the first place. Using the 'images' search on Google or any other search engine, you can sometimes (not always) identify the unknown maggot that's been eating your cabbage roots by keying in relevant search words into the same search panel. It might take a few combinations of different words (white, maggot, root, cabbage) before a pic of your unidentified beastie comes up on your screen, named and shamed, but it works. The same process can be used to identify plant diseases and weeds.

Another aspect of the internet is that it has greatly increased my appreciation and enjoyment of food plants via its stock of endless trivia about plant origins, history, science and nutritional qualities.

Surfing, the random following of one link to another, can wrap a person up for hours and this is how research on soil conditions for carrots led me to discover that they are actually good for your eyes, albeit not as a means to see in the dark as the popular myth suggests. Surfing took me to the story of John Cunningham, a World War Two fighter ace who, in 1940, became the first person to shoot down an enemy plane in the dark. 'Cat's Eyes Cunningham', as he was popularly known, was one of the best-known air aces of the war, having shot down at least twenty enemy planes. During the early war years, the British press was fascinated by him and those other British pilots who seemed to have an uncanny ability to see their enemies in the skies at night.

What the RAF didn't want the Germans, or anyone else to know, was that the real secret of their success was the greatest weapon of the war, radar. To put the newspapers off the scent and to mislead the Germans, the RAF deliberately spread the story in the papers that their pilots were encouraged to eat large amounts of carrots, which improved their night vision. Hence the myth that carrots help you see in the dark.

The same surfing session also led me to discover aspects of the nutritional science of carrots, including the fact that they are one of the few plants containing carotene. This is converted by the liver to the equivalent of vitamin A, which in turn travels to the eyes in the blood where it is then transformed into a substance called retinol, which is essential for the working of the human retina. Without vitamin A the eyesight starts to deteriorate. And while vitamin A might well have been in short supply through the dietary restrictions of the war years, carrots were readily available in Britain. Therefore it's possible that those pilots eating carrots would indeed ensure their eyesight was always maintained at its optimum level. So the RAF story wasn't entirely without foundation. On top of that, it's also useful, as it has been since the war, to get reluctant children to eat their carrots on the premise that they might end up being able to see in the dark.

Of course one of the big failings about using the internet for plant research, or indeed any kind of research, is that some 'facts' posted are either skewed or simply untrue. There are hoaxers, cranks and idiots among those who post information.

And successful use of the net for growing food plants means always bearing these drawbacks in mind. Information that might be correct to the person who posts it might not be right for you, given regional variation. The net may make the world smaller but it doesn't change the weather differences between your allotment in northern Europe and Bob B's in Salinas, California.

Usually it's easy enough if you can decipher where the advice you're reading comes from geographically. If the people who post the information don't say so, then the clues are in the content, the language they use, or in the website URL address itself. Ireland is a small country so its internet presence isn't huge, which in turn means there's far less relevant food growing advice out there. The best source of online information is therefore from the UK, our nearest neighbour, which does have plenty of strong content online. Even so, bear in mind that important differences still exist. The UK's climate is generally a bit warmer, producing a longer growing season, and the soil conditions there tend to be more alkaline and chalky.

Finally, the internet is also for entertainment, for fun, for light relief, for the strange, the odd, the side-splitting and the startling. As well as the information and empathy, there's the oddballs like Uncle Wilco, who runs readersheds.co.uk, where gardeners and allotmenteers send in pictures of their own customised sheds for others to look at. These devotees of shed voyeurism call themselves Sheddies.

For entertainment on the food-growing subject, the internet's content leaves PT Barnum in the ha'penny place. Take the circus that is the world of competitive outsize vegetable-growing. One of the big champions is Irishman John Evans, originally from Dungarvan but who lived for decades in Alaska, where he swept the board at country fairs annually with his array of monster vegetables. Evans's outsized veg has held no less than seven Guinness world records. Look him up on YouTube and you get the full internet experience, as the infectious Evans takes you, via your computer screen, through a tour of his former garden in Alaska and shows you his 35lb cabbages, his 60lb chards, sprouts the size of apples, his potato plants which produce forty tubers from one plant, his 45lb celeries and his 68lb leeks. Evans says the secret to his success is a special compost tea he invented by running an aquarium aerator through a mix of specially selected compost and water. Evans shows us how he brews this magic mixture and thus you can try and make your own, or if you're not up to it, just buy his because he sells it online.

And that's the next great use of the internet, the ability to purchase items necessary for your allotment from all around the world—items that you simply wouldn't find in your local shops. Because our local garden centres certainly don't stock John Evans's compost-tea-brewing kits.

Seeds are probably the best example. The very best brands of seeds can be bought online (some of them can only be bought online) and it is considerably easier to browse at home at your computer in the winter months, perusing through online catalogues, than having to hit five or six different shops in March to ensure you can get what you need. The shops often stock different varieties in different years and if you want a particular type of tomato which the shops no longer sell in your area, it can be in your hands in two weeks by ordering it online.

Online purchases are also usually cheaper because the stockists don't have to pay rent or a mortgage on a big expensive premises; they can operate from anywhere and with minimal overheads.

The internet has also become particularly important in its role in saving heritage varieties of plants, which would certainly have died out otherwise. The Irish Seed Savers Association, an organisation which has spent years hunting down the last varieties of old apples and other pre-F1 vegetable varieties from all corners of this island, dispenses most of its seeds via online orders.

The internet is also indispensable when it comes to choosing new varieties of plants which you're not sure about. Grower-based boards, forums and groups regularly offer independent and fair reviews about the performance of different seeds from different suppliers along with other qualities of certain varieties such as taste, resistance to pests and so forth. There are literally hundreds of varieties of tomatoes, for example, each offering different tastes, yields, sizes and colours.

It was through these sorts of reviews posted from online growers that I learned, for example, that Moneymaker, despite being a popularly purchased tomato variety whose seeds were stocked in most of my local shops, was not in favour with experienced growers because of the poor flavour of the fruit ('dishwater' is how one reviewer colourfully describes the taste). Moneymaker is one of the three most available tomatoes on the seed racks where I regularly shop. I would certainly have tried it were it not for the unanimous views of gardeners from all over who took the trouble to let the rest of us know how poor it was. In contrast, rave reviews made me buy Tigerella, a pleasingly green and red striped tomato which cropped heavily and tasted supreme. Job done!

Finally, Wikipedia is incredibly useful, like an old-fashioned encyclopaedia dusted off and brought to us online—with the key difference being that anyone is welcome to contribute. But because it's open to all contributors, you will need to cross-reference and double-check the information that you get elsewhere to ensure that it's accurate.

The most reliable information, but also generally the last you'd look for, comes from government, semi-state or university websites, the latter of which will even offer access to a range of college theses and texts which are relevant to growing.

The main television channels also post online where relevant programmes can be found and viewed outside of screening schedules. The BBC in particular, with more critically praised gardening coverage than any other television network in the world, is particularly excellent. There's also our own Government website at bordbia.ie.

And it gives me plenty of information to trade over the fences with the older holders thanks to to JMaxx, Fluffy Muppet et al.

Allotment Diary, Year Two

September to December

We've had to take the onions up in the rain which was a disappointment. It's a bad idea to take them in if they're wet but it's been raining endlessly and elsewhere on the allotment complex, onions are starting to show signs of rot. I'd like to have draped them over the fence to dry as the early birds did, but it's just too wet for it now. I'm not savouring the job of tying them for storage. And this year they might have to dry out indoors which is a problem when you've no more room in your house. Nonetheless there's a huge haul of them, enough to keep us going until February at least. Despite salads coming along late in the garden, we don't actually have the stomach for them. No one wants to eat crispy greens when it's been raining constantly outside. Stews are your only man and the carrots are great for them. Once again the carrots have done well and we've grown the right amount this year so none will go to waste. We're going to leave them in the ground and take them as we need them.

The potatoes are great. Despite us having a blight and cutting down the stalks, the tubers are still fine, solid and tasty. We're digging them up at the rate of two to three plants per week. Each one is producing enough for two dinners for a small family (that's us). We get a couple of really big ones, a lot of middling sized versions and lots and lots of tiny ones which are great for boiling whole with the skins on.

The blackcurrants didn't fare too well this year, but nonetheless we got two bags for the freezer. With the disease-inducing weather, the raspberries were hit with perishing white mould, but we salvaged some. We got some gooseberries too off the two surviving bushes which are still that bit too immature to give a decent crop. But they'll get there next year hopefully. All in all though, we've got bags of berries in the freezer to keep us in daily morning smoothies until Christmas and beyond.

Redcurrants, with the clusters of healthy scarlet berries glistening on the branch, really encapsulate what's best about having an allotment. Unmatched thirst-quenchers, you pick off a strand of a dozen and pull them through your teeth. A dozen tiny tart explosions in your mouth. The blueberry bush was pretty sparse though—probably due to the soil in its vicinity becoming too neutral; it likes acidic ground, something I'll fix in the new year.

In the garden, the celeriac is coming on brilliantly. We couldn't fault the herbs either, handfuls of which have gone into most of what we've cooked. We haven't had to buy any sage, oregano, parsley, thyme, mint, chives, dill, fennel or rosemary. We've been making our own mint sauce which is particularly delicious with lamb. Sometimes we feel like gourmets with tastebuds in all the right places.

In fact having fresh ingredients around is prodding me into learning more about cooking. On the advice of a colleague who knows his good food, I've bought the Prue Leith book *Leith's Cookery Bible*. It's one of the most useful things I've ever acquired and would recommend it to anyone growing their own fresh food who's not quite sure what to do with it.

And after lending me his strimmer for a few months, the gent next door has just given me reams of fencing wire and green plastic mesh to form windbreaks round our turf. I hope to follow him with timber-framed raised beds in the new year.

The swedes we sowed in September are coming along nicely and the cabbages, which sustained a heavy bird and/or caterpillar attack, have new heads on the old stalks. There will also be plenty of sprouts for Christmas.

Meantime out in the greenhouse and scattered around the patio and on the outside kitchen windowsill, we've got the chillies. Again with the wet weather, they didn't crop as heavily but thanks to last year's bumper harvest we've got tonnes of them dried and bagged in storage.

I'm trying to build up my fruit harvest for next year at Plot 34. My last trip involved planting seven or eight raspberry canes and three gooseberry bushes. Not everybody's back garden can take fruit trees but today many varieties at garden centres are manageable miniature breeds. Some, like the Coronet apple tree, can be grown in a container. An apple tree in a container, developed in Ireland by a long persisting genius from Wexford. Buy some. Pears can be grown fanned out along a wall—you can learn how on YouTube.

If you're looking for a hedgerow, what's wrong with growing a few gooseberry bushes, raspberries or hazels running through it? You can pick and choose when they fruit and they won't take up much extra space. Perhaps it will take a few more years of recession before homegrown fruit and forage make a comeback.

As we get into November, the news is all about 'ugly' fruit and vegetables. But club-footed carrots, snaggletoothed swedes, carbunkle-like cabbages and cack-eyed peas—we've had the whole freak show up here on Plot 34. The EU has finally relented on its inane twenty-year quest to force growers to manufacture vegetables to fit in a box. Rules which ban misshaped and non-uniform produce are to be dropped. Therefore 'ugly' veg is being allowed back in supermarkets from next July.

A celebration of vegetable mutation was long overdue. Not just because it's wrong for a country to throw away 30 per cent of its perfectly edible produce for an entire generation, but also because of freak chic. Not since PT Barnum first rolled into town have we had such a desire to gawp at nature's uglies and oddities. Cable television is stuffed with the world's smallest siblings, most-overweight mums, hairiest children and fattest dogs, while magazines are fat on picture exclusives of the cellulite craters on Jennifer Aniston's behind (for the airbrushed version, see *Hello!*).

It was inevitable that mangled marrows and palsied parsnips would be dug up sooner or later. If we at Plot 34 had known the 'Zeitgeist' for ugly veg was coming, we'd have taken ours on the road rather than banged them up in the freezer. ("Roll up! Roll up! You'll be shocked and amazed! See the carrot that looks like a couple fornicating! Your children will be frightened witless by the dreadful tentacles of the crazed celeriac!")

But what happens when the fuss dies down? Will shelves really be overrun with three-legged carrots? Probably not. Despite the landmark ruling, they still don't machine-wash, fit in boxes for transport and storage or, most importantly, impress the supermarket bosses.

I talked to three commercial growers—of cabbages, onions and carrots—for their views on the new-found ugliness. Cabbage guy was delighted. He hopes someone will now eat the 30 per cent of his crop which he has been ploughing into the ground for years.

—"Supermarkets only want cabbages that weigh 500g," he says. "Although the bad weather this year means nobody has them as everyone is just under, those supermarkets still want their 500g cabbages. The growers have been trying to put a deal together whereby you can get two slightly undersized heads in a pack for a lesser price. The supermarkets said: 'Okay, but we want to see one of our competitors do it first and see if it works.' Meantime, I've got thousands of otherwise perfect cabbages I can't sell."

Onion guy says it won't make a difference.

—"It's the supermarkets who really decide what they sell, not the EU. They're all competing to sell perfect onions. The law might have changed, but they won't and I'll still be throwing away thousands of onions next year."

Carrot guy, in contrast, was outraged.

—"I've invested a fortune in classification. To get the product looking uniform. Nobody hand-picks and cleans food anymore because it doesn't pay. You'd go out of business. So now it's all done with machines. The machines can't process deformed produce and if the market is flooded with substandard goods, the price will collapse and we'll end up going out of business."

In truth, 'ugly' vegetables are a comical distraction from a bigger monster that's being growing this past generation:

the supermarket-promoted "perfect" vegetable. It's like the supermarket chicken. They'll look bigger and better than twenty years ago, but when you actually get into the level of nutrition you'll see there's less and less goodness in them, less nutrition as time goes on.

"The supermarkets paid 30 per cent less for their carrots this year—but you have to understand they're not the same carrots. Growers who have to keep their businesses alive on fast-depleting margins simply have got to cut costs. They might not be rotating (crops) as often as they should, or replenishing the soil properly and that reduces the nutritional value of the food."

And so the growers believe supermarket bosses are behaving like boom-era bankers, so engrossed in short-term profiteering that they don't realise the future impact of their actions—a continual fall in the nutritional value of fresh produce.

The growers want the EU to get tough, rather than deregulate.

—"I'd like a nutritional content limit for sold produce," carrot guy told me. "We really can grow good food in Ireland and if supermarkets are forced to sell food with a decent nutritional limit, they'll have to buy it. The end price to the consumer won't be much different. Currently, families are feeding their children on produce which they believe to be as nutritional as ever, and this is not the case. If we keep going the way we are, we are building a huge problem for the future. Why eat vegetables? To provide nutrition. So, do you want to give your kids a bag of water?"

All of which suggests that for the truly ugly side of veg, look to the actions of the supermarkets. For them we need the stick, not the ugly carrot.

In the middle of November, I fall ill as does Her Outdoors and our year-old-girl, Evie Margaret, otherwise known as Waterer of Everything (WOE). At first we thought it was a bug. Quite troublesome nausea, vomiting and a bit of flu-type weakness. I think I have traced it to our potato crop, some of which has turned green on account of it being left out on the patio.

We forget that gardens sometimes produce their own poisons. It's only after thousands of years of evolution that we humans know what's safe and what's not safe to eat. Ever eaten tapioca pudding? The roots of the cassava plant from which it's made contain a substance that, when eaten, can trigger the production of cyanide. In Africa, tribes who rely on it for food have learnt to crush the root and place it in wicker sieves in rivers to strain out the toxins.

The pity is that so much inherited knowledge is being lost today—and most of it through these past three generations. And vegetable gardens harbour toxins of which we need to be aware, especially when children are around. I just poisoned my family—with potatoes. Nobody told me you couldn't eat green potatoes. And spud bags don't come with health warnings. How could I have known?

Having harvested our own grand crop of King Edwards, we stored some in a transparent plastic drawer unit kept outside. What I didn't know is the golden rule that potatoes must be kept in the dark. When exposed to daylight, a chemical change occurs in them. To protect itself from insects and birds, the exposed spud starts producing solanine, a poison, the presence of which is denoted by another change—the production of chlorophyll. Her Outdoors doesn't read my newspaper column and probably won't read this book (that's loved ones for you) but if you're a friend of hers reading this...don't tell her or she'll kill me.

So I cooked green potatoes for dinner and we became ill. It was only after doing some research online that I found out about solanine. A straw poll of my friends and family determined that few knew anything about the dangers of green potatoes. About 20 per cent knew something vague about them being bad for you, but couldn't say why. And solanine is dangerous stuff.

In 1979, 78 south London schoolboys were taken ill with symptoms including disorientation, nausea, neurological disorders, confusion and hallucinations. The source of the illness was a single bag of green potatoes in the school kitchen.

It takes only 2mg of solanine per kilo of bodyweight to make you ill, but between 3mg and 6mg is likely to kill. The smaller you are, the more dangerous it is. While you would need to consume a great deal of solanine to kill you, a huge feed of very green tubers might just do it.

The incident—we got ill and vomited, but are okay now—shocked me and made me research. I learned that care is needed when teaching young children about edible plants. When Plot 34's self-appointed Head of Secret Tunnels (HST) was two years old, I would pick off a lettuce leaf or a tomato for him to eat. I thought it was a good idea to start him young. Then I caught him trying to feed a poisonous berry to a little two-year-old friend. He didn't know the difference between a lettuce and a rhubarb leaf at that age. Nor the difference between picking and eating a cherry tomato or a rowanberry.

Most poisonings occur in children under the age of five, the peak age being two years, and boys are more likely to be poisoned than girls. So what should they steer clear of? Green tomatoes, as with green potatoes, also contain high levels of solanine which, because children are smaller and lighter, is more dangerous to them. Potato and tomato leaves contain even higher levels.

Rhubarb leaves contain high levels of oxalates. During the First World War, the leaves were misguidedly recommended as a substitute for other veggies. This resulted in illness and in fact, some deaths.

Apple seeds and cherry pits contain amygdalin, which, when introduced to the human digestive system, degrades into hydrogen cyanide. The seeds have to be broken to release the poison. While it is estimated that it would take half a cup of broken apple seeds to make someone seriously ill, it takes fewer to get them sick.

Then there are the unnatural poisons we expose ourselves to in the vegetable garden. According to one commercial grower: —"There are chemicals available in shops that people use on allotments which should never, ever, be used without proper procedure and protection. We use gloves and masks with them, but in gardens we see people spraying these substances around liberally with no protection whatsoever."

Recently, my dad gave me the highly toxic weedkiller Roundup, which he had decanted into a plastic mineral bottle. A stick-on label showed that it was weedkiller, but young children can't read. HST, then five, picked it up, even though it was hidden by being shoved down the back of the next-door allotment's compost heap, and asked if he could have some "lemonade". Luckily, he asked.

Finally, anybody who grows in built-up areas should think about lead in the soil. Lead gets into the ground via petrol from busy roads. It also gets into the ground near buildings that have had lead-based paint used on them. Most plants don't absorb it, but some, such as lettuce and carrots, are known to take it in. For those living in old houses or close to heavy traffic, it might be advisable to replace your soil.

Growing your own is still the best way to provide children with the most nutritious and pure food. But if you want to play Russian roulette with nature, there's always a fugu fondue—look up 'fugu' to find out how crazy the Japanese really are.

As December rolls in, as a small—very small—farmer of 120sq.m, I have come to the end of my tenure on my second growing season on Plot 34 and now it's time to renew the lease for a third. The rent is the best forty quid I have spent this year.

My contract is a complex affair that enforces a short break in tenure for December just in case I—or one of my fellow allotmenteers—get any bright ideas about squatters' rights. It's also probably the reason they won't let us build our own sheds. Eleven months breaks the cycle so that each lease starts anew and therefore negates property rights.

Don't laugh. In Berlin there are still people living permanently in the city centre, in sheds on city-centre allotments that were started right after the Second World War, which are now occupied full time thanks to squatters' rights. When it comes to land grabbing, the city farmer can be the most skilful, the most devious and the most cunning of them all.

When the subject of growing your own food is brought up, it's perhaps strange that it's always the city slicker who perks up, gets enthusiastic and wants to learn more. Across the Western World, it's the urban farmer who is at the forefront of the food-growing movements. In contrast, those from true farming backgrounds wrinkle their noses and snort derisively:

—"What's the point in growing potatoes, onions, cabbages, or whatever, when you can get them at the supermarket so cheaply?"

The Irish dairy farmer with all his acres, and all his problems, these days buys his spuds at Tesco.

While those from rural backgrounds will no doubt remember younger years spent breaking their backs picking spuds or turnips for days on end, these days our farmers tend to satisfy all their fruit and veg needs down at the local supermarket. At the same time, they can leave considerable acres either entirely unused, almost unused or devoted to a form of farming, such as dairying, that has been so tightly squeezed in modern times that it's almost unprofitable.

Today's supermarket pricing tactics and the strongarm buying power of the food companies have squeezed farmers all over Europe by paying them less and less for their produce, then creaming off the profits by hitting the purchaser with prices that outstrip what the farmer gets paid, sometimes by 200 per cent. The middleman wins, and the farmer at one end and the purchaser at the other, lose.

While I can empathise with farmers, and much more so since I started this allotment project, sometimes I truly don't understand them.

First, I'm perplexed that so many will doggedly continue in types of farming—dairying stands out—that prove clearly unprofitable. I can't understand why they don't change to something that might be profitable, be it bison, chinchilla or rabbit farming. If people stop buying the newspaper I work for, I lose my job and I won't expect the EU to subsidise me and my colleagues in producing papers that don't sell or make a profit.

I'm also perplexed by the number of farmers who seem to believe it's their divine right to do what they want with their land, no matter what the impact on the environment, on others, or on future generations in particular. As a fisherman, I'm fed up with diseased streams and poisoned lakes and fish kills caused by farm chemicals and slurry sprayed illegally or carelessly which then gets into the water and makes the fish sick.

As an allotmenteer I get particularly annoyed about the surplus land they're not using, because this land, particularly when it borders city areas, is vitally needed for allotments that the local authorities, despite their best efforts, cannot provide. Why are they being paid to ensure it's not used?

With waiting lists for allotments now as long as three years in some council areas, it's been conclusively proven that people are ready and willing to take on small strips of land such as mine and pay for their use. It's no effort at all for a farmer living within five miles of a population centre to divide an acre into twenty allotments at initial cost of deer/rabbit fencing, a communal water service, insurance, and a secure, communal storage facility.

If an allotment holder pays three hundred quid per year, which is conceivable, that's six grand a year for the farmer per acre. That's a good income in anybody's book.

It is wrong to say that farming is no longer profitable here, where the soil and weather conditions are among the most perfect in the world for growing. Farming is unprofitable if you must slot into the production system painstakingly created over years by the food companies and the supermarkets. But growing on land for your own use, or leasing your land for the same, is much more profitable than anything else. Some farmers have realised the potential.

Karl Hennessy, a dairy farmer in County Meath, charges €280 for allotments on his land, and in Blessington, County

Wicklow, the renowned gardener, plantsman and designer Jimi Blake, formerly of Airfield House and Gardens, in Dublin, has started leasing allotments at Hunting Brook Garden near his former family home. The plots are also rented out at €280 per year and growers benefit from the courses on offer at Hunting Brook, with lessors receiving 20 per cent reductions.

Meanwhile, Zwena McCullough lets eighteen allotments in her half-acre walled garden near Blarney for €125 per allotment. A newspaper item recently reported her profit rate to be €2,000 per acre after costs were deducted. Where is there no profit in farming?

Fingal County Council has just opened new allotments and still has a waiting list of 500 names. With market growers going out of business in Balbriggan, Swords et al, would it not be profitable for the growers to rent their land out for allotments?

Let's cut out the food companies and the supermarkets who have been screwing both the farmer and the consumer. Let's get the farmer talking to the consumer; get the land sublet, and let's get our farms back to producing proper nutritious food via profitable allotment complexes.

In the Cloughjordan Eco Village, a plan to develop a whole sustainable community of like-minded people in County Tipperary, the participants employ their own farmer to grow all their vegetables and to produce their own meat for the table. He gets a good wage, they get the best of food. What's wrong with that?

Meantime we're celebrating the close of a year in which we have become more confident about our growing. We have learned more and feel somehow more comfortable in our shoes. More connected to the real world instead of the one financiers want us to see. The weather is hard work. But in even one of the worst growing seasons ever, we probably met 60 per cent of our fresh produce needs from our own holding for around five months. Money saved? Probably a grand after costs. But had it been an average growing year, we could have done at least double that. And I'm looking forward to attempting that goal in the year ahead.

Chapter Twelve

Was It All Worth It?

It's impossible for me to avoid a certain fact—that, through about 250 consecutive full-page columns in a Sunday newspaper, and now, through a similar number of pages here in this book—I have, by and large, proffered one enormous long-running moan about having an allotment.

The pests, the problems, the predicaments, the flies in my ear, the lost time, the physical effort, the weekends sacrificed, the worry, the mistakes, the crops lost, the hassle and the aches. But in fact, all that's happened is that I've turned into a farmer. Got rain? The crops are suffering. Got sun? The crops are suffering. Nuclear War? The crops are still suffering. Won the Euromillions? What about the crops?

Of course we farmers aren't as miserable as we put ourselves across—it's just that when it comes to growing, the problems always tend to be at the forefront of our minds. And if I was a full-time farmer, who relied on growing food for a living, rather than a city boy trying out an experiment, then I'd really and truly wreck your head.

So when I'm asked about Plot 34, I don't tend to tell you that yesterday I ate the best peas I ever tasted—so much so that I chased the last one all around the plate to get it. Or I'm not telling that the potato plants, of which I'm so proud, have just added another foot to their lush green growth, or even that someone had told me my onions were a revelation in flavour. I want to talk about vine weevils, because that's what's at the forefront of my mind.

221

Plot 34

But if you ask me whether Plot 34 has been worth it all, the answer is quite simply: Absolutely yes. Because if Plot 34 vaporised tomorrow and I couldn't grow my own food anymore, I'd become truly miserable for a number of reasons.

First there are the practical gains. The whole idea of taking on an allotment in the first place was to produce better food for the table. I've since been transformed from someone who viewed vegetables as an accompaniment for meat to a diner who looks forward to the vegetables most of all. From someone whose dinner time vegetables meant mashed potato and mashed swede, to someone who (while still loving his mash) prefers to lay out a selection of homegrown roots on a tray, sprinkle them in homegrown herbs, lash them with honey and roast them to preserve their own flavours.

My own personal favourites are the root crops. And while they're actually quite cheap to buy in the shops, the homegrown versions still surpass them for their unbelievably rich taste. The carrots, the swedes and the celeriac in particular.

Because everything from a homegrown garden, like that first cherry tomato, tastes absolutely supreme, partly because we eat it straight from the plant or the ground, when that food is still alive and hasn't perished on the route from Kenya or Spain, and partly because the varieties and the methods of growing we use are conducive to far better mineral and nutrient absorption and thus nutrition.

For lighter foods, the eating of peas straight from the pod or a tomato from the vine (I now grow about four varieties a year) is akin to the sort of taste pleasure you get from fine chocolates.

But probably more important again, we have eaten far more vegetables and fruits than we normally would have, simply because we've grown them ourselves and they're there to eat. Thus in an effort to use up food we have grown, the old meat and two veg dish has usually become meat and three veg, and sometimes even meat and four veg. All in all we're probably eating 50 per cent more vegetables than we did before having the allotment.

Of course thanks to my research to improve my food-growing skills, I have also learned just how much better that food is for you than shop-bought produce—I have learned how much nutrition and minerals commercially grown foods have lost and why. The improved taste of homegrown food means I'm also eating more varieties of produce.

Salads, which I never would have touched as tasteless plates of leaves, are now a big part of my summer diet. Berries are now a regular staple in our household from mid summer when they start to ripen, right through until new year when we finish the last of our frozen stocks.

And with a combination of eating fresh, and then eating surplus stocks which have been frozen and are almost as good, we have been able to live off our own produce through most of the year. On average, we get four to six months when, apart from tropical fruit, our fresh food bill is almost zero.

We have all our own onions from September to March, our own potatoes from September to Christmas, our own carrots from September to March, our own cabbage from August to March, celeriac from November to March, rhubarb from May to July, tomatoes from June to March (the last three months' are cherry varieties frozen), our own peas from July until November, our own swedes from Christmas to April, sprouts from November to new year, broccoli/calabrese from July to September, our own courgettes from July until October, our own chillies all year round, our own chives and fresh herbs pretty much all year round, leeks and chard from September to well into the new year.

Another unexpected result is that we've become more interested in food as a result of growing our own and our cooking has become far better. Through growing celeriac, for example, which we'd never heard of before growing it (because the corporations can't make machines to process it), we've been forced to find out how to cook it and in what dishes.

Trying to figure out what to do with the only two squashes we grew in Year One led me into learning how to make pumpkin soup.

How to boil potatoes properly? It's not just about boiling them until they go soft. There is a science to it which we are newly appreciating. Thus we soon discovered all the wrong ways in which we always cooked our food—in many cases removing much or most of the nutrition from them in the process. I have always over-boiled broccoli, not realising that I was killing almost all of the nutrition. In that way, when I believed I was eating well in the past, it emerged that I'd been killing it all thanks to many of my bad cooking techniques.

We're only now starting to venture into learning about the chemistry of cooking and also more about the science of nutrition—minerals and microelements and how the body absorbs them.

But it does get to the point for us when we have excellent food in such large amounts, that we start taking it for granted. Until that is, the stocks run out as they do gradually from November to March. That's when I find myself thoroughly disgusted to have to return to the shops to spend money once again on food which seems even more inferior than before, especially after many months spent eating the best of the best.

That's the point in each year when I really realise how well we've been eating. When I look at the above list of what we've grown, and especially when I'm sitting down to eat it, I can't help but be impressed. We didn't need talent to do it, we don't have green fingers and anyone else can do the same.

Another surprise for me was the sheer quantity of what we produced from very small amounts of ground, despite losing large amounts to setbacks, crop failures and pest and disease attacks. What we grew came from an allotment the size of the back garden attached to an average terraced house, and then add to that a few small beds in our existing back garden, a few warm windowsills indoors and a few spots on the floor.

Our potato crop, which fed the family for three months, was grown in a patch exactly the same size as our king-sized bed. The carrots, which lasted us most of the year, came from a plot twice that size, the onions from the same. What it means is that those of us who don't have an allotment, but do have an average city back garden, can achieve similar results in their own back yard once you plant in an area with six hours of sunshine a day—and remember that blackcurrants, the superpower of vitamin C, can grow in the shade.

Indeed even though Plot 34 was a far smaller allotment than the one I'd originally put my name down for, in the two years I worked the ground, it was never actually full. I'd say around 60 per cent of the space was actually utilised at any given time because we just didn't have the time to prepare it. It's also worthwhile pointing out that we would have had a great deal more

success again had it not been for the weather, which was unusually poor for growing throughout the two years.

But perhaps it was a good thing that I'd been unlucky enough
to kick off my experiment in a period which included two of the
worst consecutive summers in living memory—alongside two
unusually mild winters. This made for poor growing conditions,
with the relentless rain often preventing work, maintenance and
digging because the soil was too wet to work.

The conditions brought widespread blights, mould and rot.
The mild winters kept pests alive and increased their populations
and frequency of attacks while the wet brought snails and slugs
in their thousands. Two scorching Easters brought artificial spurts
in our plants which were then ambushed by gales in May.

We couldn't have had it worse. In more average years, I am
convinced we would have grown twice as much. I know that I
got far higher yields of tomatoes and salads—both grown at
home—in the season before taking on Plot 34. The second year,
despite being as wet, we fared better because as time goes on
your expertise and experience does improve.

Once you acquire the basics that you need for growing, as
well as more experience, you can grow more food and you buy
less. In Year Three, not covered in this book, I ceased buying
plants at the garden centre altogether and started growing everything from seed. Of course I couldn't have done that without the
greenhouse and a greater level of experience to give me confi-
dence enough to trust my seed-growing abilities. But that's the
point; as time goes on you get better and wiser and more adept.

It gets better and better until you can no longer dig and they
put you in a box and then you fertilise the plants too.

We also saved a good deal of money—probably grew close
to two grand worth of eating in both years, minus a thousand for
costs. And we expect to save more as the fruit trees become more
established, as the children get older and we can commit more
time to the project, and as we simply get better at it.

But what about the cost of your time? This was, perhaps, the
key sacrifice in my experiment. What is the opportunity cost of a
working day a week through the summer season worth to you?
What is a weekend lost which could have otherwise been spent
at the zoo with the family or lazing about relaxing? How much
would you charge your employer to work that day in the office

and what could you buy for it? If your children or spouse aren't working alongside you, how much quality time with them are you losing?

The allotment brought a pressure on my life which at times became a real millstone around my neck. Because, for certain times of year, come rain or shine, I still had to get up there and work even when it was the last thing I wanted to do. Growing food means that if you're not there, putting in the work when everything needs attention, then you lose the whole lot. This doesn't always sit well with family members who want to use a sunny day to go to the beach, or for extended family members who have missed out on an expected visit because you suspect the calabrese are about to bolt. These are the sacrifices you will make.

In April and May, when most plants have to be settled in dug beds, that pressure became almost unbearable because I couldn't fit the work into that one day a week I had set aside. In both years I ended up falling behind significantly. While my plants caught up eventually with those of my neighbours, I could have had perhaps a month more produce had I managed to get them planted earlier in the year.

At one point I had to ask my editor and boss if it was okay to take a regular working day at the allotment for a few weeks to help me get on top of it. I argued that technically (because I wrote the Plot 34 column for the paper) the work on the allotment was part of my full-time job for the newspaper. He agreed and I got the extra days I needed to get on top of things. The time factor has also meant that Plot 34 sometimes appears borderline fallow and not nearly as impressive looking as its neighbours, who either have more time on their hands, more people involved or considerably more energy. For a time I fretted about this, but I eventually realised that each person does their best and that's as much as they can do.

What I'm underlining here is that an allotment is a serious commitment and not a nice hobby or pastime. Start to dig a small vegetable plot and you'll soon see what I mean—you'll find that progress is about ten times slower than you expect, while the work is physically far more difficult than you might have countenanced, particularly because we all come from the chicken battery generation.

Was It All Worth It?

To know how low you can go when you become bogged down with an allotment, here's a particularly down-heartened entry from my allotment diary of May 2009 (Year Three) which pretty much describes that mental slump:

It's a blisteringly beautiful Sunday and I'm dying with a hangover courtesy of a reunion meal accompanied by three hours of reminiscences and bad red wine. After trying to cure it up here with a gallon of sun-warmed Sprite, I've now got heartburn and a queasy stomach to boot.

The rays are blazing down on this holiday weekend and everyone, except me—and Plot 34's seven-year-old, self-appointed Head of Secret Tunnels (HST)—is off relaxing somewhere, throwing frisbees, walking dogs, eating ice creams or just lying around in the parks.

Not us. Me and HST.

Despite the baking sunshine, it was raining earlier in the week and the sods I'm trying to break are soaked through. Busting them is like beating glue with a wiffle bat. Every time I lift the fork, they're still clinging to it like tree-bound bonobos in a bushfire. And no matter how much I beat them up, they're just refusing to come apart. It doesn't help that every now and again I have to rip off the gardening gloves to free up a digit so I can escort another fly from my ear canal. I'm feeling the pressure because I need to plant a bed of carrots before I leave so I'm working against the clock. Three hours in and just 30 per cent is done.

Since our daughter was born, Her Outdoors has pretty much relinquished her role at our allotment. Her main concern is that it's dangerous for a toddler—which it is. Indeed I feel guilty that I'm not at home helping. And the fact that I still haven't learned to drive and need to be driven up here, mountains of manky implements in tow, doesn't help.

So today I'm also feeling extremely sorry for myself, and indeed for HST who keeps asking "Are we done yet?" as he listlessly slaps a stubborn upended grass rug with his trowel. In the long tradition of dads dragging their sons off for monotonous character-building exercises, I give him the old: "Sometimes we have to do stuff we don't want to do" speech.

So today I'm the bad guy all round.

I learned that to succeed with an allotment of a serious size, you have to be ready for these bad patches—they tend to happen at the same time each year—muddle through them and just keep at it. Indeed in the first year at our new complex, as much as one third of all the other new allotments were returned to the council by the end of the year either because the owners found they just didn't have the time or the willingness to put in the necessary work.

That level of commitment to an allotment can also put strain on family life. You won't end up taking no holidays at all—like a typical full-time farmer—but do be prepared to lose some. If you decide to take an allotment on with family or friends, bear in mind that those helpers and committed persons you start with can experience a change in circumstances or heart and quit altogether, leaving you with a much higher workload.

Her Outdoors who was keen to be involved in the project from the start, latterly saw her interest and her ability to become involved vaporise by the birth of our little girl, Evie Margaret. In Year One, her help was considerable. I'd dig the ground, she'd break the sods up and turn out the weeds. Through the year we weeded and watered together. But in the second year, she became pregnant and as that pregnancy progressed, she was understandably less able to help.

This was even more true after our baby was born in October in Year Two. And despite what some people say, we both feel an allotment is not a place for a very young child, especially on a bad day. Children who aren't old enough to understand can fall or hurt themselves. Even older children have to be watched as I've already related about the weedkiller in the mineral bottle.

Aside from giving me a lift to and from the allotment one day a week, Her Outdoors is now off the scene at Plot 34. Because I haven't learned to drive, this added even more pressure and caused a few rows. My plans to get a car in the short term (I still haven't) should ease things.

Evie Margaret's arrival (her second name after my grandmother) and my lack of driving skills also ruled out summer evenings on workdays because the baby had to be in bed by just after 7pm. And leaving to spend a day on an allotment can seem damned selfish when it's time to take your share of parenting a brand new baby.

Was It All Worth It?

After Her Outdoors went back to work following the expiry of her maternity leave, the pressure on our lives increased even further and the allotment contributed even more to that tension. Slowly, in her view, "Our Allotment" became "The Allotment" then "His Allotment" and eventually,"That ******* Allotment".

When I asked Her Outdoors what she thought of the whole experiment with the benefit of hindsight, she said this:

—"If we didn't have the allotment, I'd really miss the fresh food because I don't think I could do without it now. But I wouldn't miss the hassle of having to drop you off and pick you up all the time, and the arguments that have resulted over that. And I wouldn't miss the fact that the kitchen ends up being mucked up for much of the year."

And then there's the view of HST, my son from my previous relationship, who comes over twice weekly and stays on alternate weekends—as is the case with many modern fragmented families. An inquisitive and kind-hearted lad, he was enthusiastic early on as well. More recently I've lost his help to a handheld Nintendo.

Given that we only have one full day on each weekend to spend together, I have felt guilty that he's found himself up on the allotment when maybe we should have been doing other, less labour-oriented things together for the limited time we have had. His reaction was:

—"I'm glad we have the allotment because no one else has one. I like it when the weather's good but I don't like it when I can't see Mathew and when I get bossed around."

All of which reminded me of my own less enthusiastic "forced labour" days at his age when my own dad had us footing turf all day when we wanted to play football, or when grand-dad press-ganged us into some other mind-numbingly boring, long task like sorting spring bulbs. HST has been going up to the allotment from the age of four to the age of seven. And it has to be said that children this age aren't always keen to spend six hours at the same location watching their dads dig holes. And as he points out, sharp words can be passed when he stands on onions, or starts climbing over the perimeter fence, doing the stuff that bored little boys always do.

Having said this, I do think children should know that life isn't all Spongebob and Playstation. Much as I hate to say it, the enforced 'character building' side of our experiment has done him good, especially when he gets to take home the fruits of his labours. He's very picky about what he eats but he does like his fresh carrots, potatoes and peas, especially when he sees them progressing and then harvested at the allotment.

And there have been some other advantages for my Head of Secret Tunnels. In school where there is now a big emphasis on green projects I think he's proud to know far more than his fellow classmates on the subject of food growing. We've enjoyed building the greenhouse together—he still talks about it. He might remember these projects for the rest of his life, like I do, with belated fondness. Not fun at the time, but so glad they happened.

Fast forward, and our little girl, nearly two, is fascinated by the plants and likes nothing more than wandering around with her own little watering can dispensing a dribble here and a dribble there. It's sometimes as if little children know what's natural and we adults are the ones who have forgotten.

An allotment has also made me a bit fitter than I used to be, particularly in the heavy-duty dig and sow times from March through to mid summer. It hasn't all been good, however, and my inherited bad back has plagued me more than is usual. But as I push towards forty, perhaps that's just nature running its course with me. I come home tired, but pleasantly content and relaxed. You can enjoy your business life, but that content feeling seems to be missing more and more without something like this.

So, running an allotment has given me far more than I expected. Apart from good food and fitness, it's given me a renewed sense of purpose about parts of my life. It's helped me learn a bit of patience and in many ways has increased my determination all round by showing me how prolonged effort pays off through the storms.

I've also become considerably more of an environmentalist and more hardline in my attitudes about the state of the world and how we're destroying it; not least, how we're destroying ourselves by eating from the trough filled for us by huge corporations who are more concerned with the profits they make than the nutrition we and our children get from our food.

Subsequently in growing my own food I have also unearthed a sort of primeval pride in my new ability to be able to provide for our table, and also a pride in being able to wrest some control from the international money-making machine which today dictates what most families in the Western World will eat on any given day. Honey-roasted celeriac anyone? Ha. Yes, I know you can't buy it.

I think my new-found environmentalism comes from a deeper sort of understanding about how nature truly works, not how many middle-class greenies seem to think it does, and this has derived quite simply from working the ground. Farmers, if they think about it, will know what I'm talking about, but my fellow city dwellers will not.

And so, through developing a greater understanding of the minutiae beneath my feet, I have gleaned for myself a bigger and more concise picture of how the world works and breathes and a greater appreciation of how man is stifling it.

So did taking on Plot 34 achieve what I'd hoped for? Could a city dweller in a two-income family with two children, a busy working life, the usual family commitments and a social life, find it all worthwhile?

Absolutely yes. And more besides.

Anyone else can do the same. If you're not sure that you can manage a full-sized allotment, start slowly by preparing one plot at a time in your back garden. Start off as I did with a single Gardener's Delight cherry tomato plant. When the first one ripens to a deep red globe, take a bite out of it. And when you taste it, just see if you can stop yourself...

WHAT WE LEARNED ABOUT VEGETABLES —THE PLOT 34 VIEW

Beans

Whether broad, French, runner, dwarf or otherwise, you don't do beans any favours by planting them too early. We learned this the hard way in our first year when the beans were absolutely shredded and battered to nothing in the winds of May, leaving nothing but a bare bamboo teepee. In their early state especially they're vulnerable to frosts and winds.

Beans don't like recently manured soil so plant them where you had potatoes, swedes, broccoli or other hungry crops which have taken it from the soil the previous year. They have the added advantage, like peas, of catching nitrogen from the air and locking it into little nodules in their root system. This makes them ideal for fixing nitrogen in the soil after heavy feeders have sucked it all out. In our second year we were more successful when we left planting (the seeds go directly into the ground) right until the end of May. You just push the little beans about two inches into the ground and cover them over. Another caveat is that beans do need plenty of watering and, in the early stages, plenty of weeding. Although when they do get going, they'll smother and strangle most plants around them. Train them up a bean teepee or make a wire fence or a pyramid of stout sticks. You'll need 8ft sticks or bamboos to let them grow to a decent height and not overcrowd.

Make sure to stick your teepee well into the ground and bind it well with wire or twine because the weight of the beans, combined with the wind against a teepee in full foliage, can easily sweep it away in a good gust. There's nothing more beautiful in a vegetable garden than the sight of a bean teepee lit up with its beautiful scarlet flowers, or in the case of the Painted Lady variety, red and white blooms. And they grow rapidly. Harvest generally through July, or if it's been a bad year, perhaps a bit later. Beans can be frozen and also dried for storage and they're decent croppers. We filled about eight freezer bags of runner beans in our second year. We didn't eat them because I hate the sight of them and when Her Outdoors said she wanted beans, she meant mange tout rather than tough as boots runner bean pods. When you've finished with them, be sure to leave the roots in the ground if you want that valuable nitrogen stored to be dug-in the following year.

Beetroot

There's been a big resurgence in the growing of beetroot in recent years because people who grew up on the bottled and pickled variety are only just discovering how it tastes so completely different when boiled fresh. Not only does it seem to be a fairly reliable root crop, but with its purple-pink roots and lush veined leaves, it helps make your vegetable garden look the part. Like carrots, they like a fine soil and make sure it's deep—the thin tendril off the tip of the root delves down as much as three feet in search of its nutrients. Another thing about beetroot is that it can do well enough in shadier spots. Don't let the soil dry out and don't fertilise them too heavily or you'll end up with big tops and root in your beet. Harvest them at no more than 3in in diameter or they'll lose flavour and get tough. Plant them in mid March.

Broccoli and Calabrese

Generally speaking vegetable growers bring on purple-headed broccoli, while the green heads we buy at the supermarket—and also call broccoli—are actually calabrese. We had calabrese in the first year, which we bought as juvenile plants, and these did extremely well for us. In Year Two, however, we moved to the purple-sprouting, which didn't produce nearly as much. Broccoli is considered a 'superfood', a fact confirmed by scientific research which showed it to be high in cancer-fighting sulphoraphane and antioxidants.

The ground needs to be rich in organic matter for these very hungry crops and they like a sunny site. They also take up quite a bit of room and can easily overshadow plants which are too close to them, so give careful consideration if you have a small space. In the year before I had an allotment, I tried them in the back garden and they overshadowed a range of plants so I had to pull them out. Thin the seedlings as they come up. Give them plenty of water. Cut the calabrese and new, albeit smaller, heads will spring from the plant's stalks. Some people like to fertilise it further as it grows. Catch the heads when they're firm and keep an eye that they don't go to seed. We lost some of ours this way in Year One. It doesn't store well so be sure you have some freezer space if you're growing a large crop. Blanch it (parboil then plunge it into ice cold water) and freeze it in bags. It's a good choice for any vegetable garden because it tends to be among the more expensive vegetables. You get about 700g per plant and therefore you save loads of cash. On the downside, watch out for caterpillars. And if it fails, you've wasted heaps of growing space.

Cabbages

Cabbages broke our hearts on Plot 34 with both years' crops taken out, first by the cabbage fly and then, in Year Two, by the birds and caterpillars. With such a rush from all species, they're obviously a bit special. Luckily in Year Two we got smaller heads growing again from the ones which were massacred in the summer. The real trouble is that every sort of critter, be it bird, caterpillar or fly, seems to have a taste for it. This means it really needs to be protected in all directions.

In Year Two we used a ground-cover sheet to sow them into, to protect them from the cabbage root fly. This lays its eggs on the soil at the base of the cabbage. It hatches out and burrows down to the roots, which it eats. The next thing you'll need is to cover the whole lot with a fine plastic mesh in order to keep the cabbage white butterflies away.

Their caterpillars eat so fast you can see the leaves actually disappearing if you look closely. Finally, a good-sized flock of birds (which we also suffered from) will turn your cabbages into coleslaw in one day. Sow them in the greenhouse in early to mid spring (depending how early or late they crop) or buy them as we did, as juvenile plants in March or April. There are many varieties of cabbage in all colours and textures and for different times of the year. Cabbages, like all brassicas, are heavy feeders and need plenty of water in the dry months. They're susceptible to bolting if they dry out or get otherwise stressed. Early cabbage should be cut as needed but late cabbage can store well if you pull up the root as well. No easy task though. With early cabbage, cutting a cross shape into the top of the remaining stalk can help encourage the growth of new, albeit smaller, heads.

Carrots
We've got huge crops of carrots from very little space at Plot 34. We've been lucky though not to get an attack of the carrot fly which can wipe them out and ruin your efforts entirely.

Carrots need deep-dug and dry soil of an extra-fine consistency, a reason why some people like to mix agricultural sand into the ground when planting them. Leave too many stones or solids in the ground or fail to till it fine enough and the roots either stop dead when they meet an obstacle or work their way around it in a range of diverse directions. Hence those deranged and suggestively shaped roots once so beloved of the man with the loud dickie bow on Esther Rantzen's *That's Life* programme in the 1980s.

The beds need to be deep and well-drained because a carrot's roots don't just run the length and width of the carrot itself. Finer fronds need to shoot out about four inches all around and below the main root to about the length of the carrot again. So at least 1ft to 18in of finely dug ground is needed. Plant the seeds in the dry, warm conditions that have come to typify our Easter period. Bad weather decimates the early growth.

Plant carrots shallowly and try and work out how many rows you're going to sow before starting, otherwise you'll use up all the seeds before you've planted your plot. Try and sprinkle them in an even but tight-knit trail. Don't do it with wet hands or on a windy day because you get hundreds of tiny carrot seeds in a packet.

In Year One we did well with Nantes Early so we stuck with it for Year Two. It produces an even, thick and rounded root. The smell of the crushed carrot top foliage, often caused by harvesting, is said to draw the carrot fly. We're told that onions in proximity helps deter the little git. The best way to protect them in fact is to grow some onions through them which we plan on doing this year. They need plenty of water early on and drying out will kill them off easily in the early days of sprouting.

Thin them out to avoid overcrowding—the benefit being that the baby carrots are particularly delicious when eaten raw. Carrots need to be eaten straight away if they're not going to be frozen or stored in the dark in damp sand because those types commonly available are not selected for longevity like shop-bought versions so they don't last half as long. Washing them reduces their storage time dramatically.

Cauliflowers
Because neither of us are that fond of cauliflowers, we haven't grown any on Plot 34. Also, among vegetables it's known as one of the trickiest customers for growers with a tendency to bolt easily when stressed. It might be one to try, however, because commercial growers are abandoning it in droves, saying the supermarkets no longer pay them enough to produce it. Plant them by seed in the greenhouse or indoors in January or early February. Put them outside into the ground in April around 20cm apart. Ideally they should go into a soil with plenty of organic matter worked into it from the previous autumn—they are very heavy feeders. Harvest them in November. They freeze well when chopped into small sprigs, blanched and then frozen in family-dinner sized portions.

Celeriac
Celeriac is the most godawful-looking vegetable you can get. You could use them to frighten children. They look like a pale yellow brain with tendrils. Washing them is a bugger because those tendrils gather mud, slugs and bugs so your kitchen sink looks like a swamp afterwards.

Then you have to peel them. Use a knife to cut off a huge head of greenery that resembles thin celery. Then you have to trim the tendrils. It takes a bit of time and this is why you can't often buy celeriac at your greengrocers or your supermarket. They can't make machines to deal with the cleaning and skinning.

The good news is you should grow them in your garden or allotment because they're not too difficult to grow, they look good above ground, they don't get bothered by too many pests (maybe they scare them) and best of all, they taste divine, especially when laced with some olive oil and roasted. They're also good mashed like spuds, they can be chipped and in the Orient they like to shave them raw into slivers and douse them with a bit of lemon.

This year we grew twelve of them in the back garden and we've started eating them. Once you get used to the preparation routine, they're fantastic. They taste like a nutty cross between a parsnip and a celery.

Unlike other root veg, they're extremely low in starch and high in other nutrients so they're ideal for those on diets. We bought them as seedlings/juvenile plants. They went into a shady area in the garden and they did really well. Next year I'm planting twice as many. One of my favourite vegetables to eat and I only discovered they existed at all because I started growing food.

Chard

A pleasant surprise for us was our Swiss chard which we've grown at intervals in the back garden flower bed for two years. That said, we've tended to forget about it and haven't eaten half as much as we should. Chard looks not unlike a shinier dock plant crossed with a rhubarb and with more leaves.

It's easy to grow and its only problems seem to be the slugs. Sow outside after the last frost and leave to its own devices. There are a good many advantages to chard. You can eat the leaves fresh as a salad, boil them like spinach and you can eat the stalks as well. They stir fry as well as they stew. They actually look great in a flower bed and if you left a tray of them unlabelled in the floral section of a garden centre, you can bet people would buy them purely for display value.

One variety, Bright Lights, also known in some quarters as Rainbow, includes yellow, pink, green and red stalks in its spectrum. The other advantage of chard is that it grows continuously. Stagger its planting by sowing a new batch every so often and you might be lucky enough to have it all year round. Swiss chard is a vastly underestimated crop which everyone should avail of.

Chillies and Sweet Peppers

If you're from a temperate climate, chillies are great fun to grow. However, because they're from hot countries, they need to be started off indoors so you're going to have to seal the sown seeds in a plastic or Clingfilm-covered tray of damp compost and pop them in the hot press/airing cupboard for a few days, or maybe even a few weeks, to get them to germinate.

The great thing about chillies is that they're so richly colourful and there are so many to choose from in different shapes, colours and heat strengths. Some are mild and some will leave you fanning yourself for the rest of the day. The good news is that it's possible to grow really hot chillies in a temperate climate. In Year One we grew ours in window boxes in the bathroom for the entire year. The following year we started them indoors in the plastic greenhouse but the plants that did the best actually went outside and we were still picking chillies off them in November.

Unlike other plants, chillies seem to like touching off one another—so there's not too much danger of overcrowding them. Indoors you have to pollinate the flowers yourself with a paintbrush or a feather. Just stick it into the open flower and twist, then to the next one. Try to get the flowers before they close and fall off or you mightn't have a chilli. In both years we found that our plants started going a bit screwy mid-way along, the leaves twisting and developing holes. This straightened itself out after a bit and in both years, production levels were good. We found the jalapeño best for steady reliable production. Cayennes also did the business. We also tried Thai versions. Do try at least four varieties in case one or two don't make it. We also planted sweet peppers which tended to produce a handful of small peppers per plant.

Pinching out the top shoots can help bush the plant out and stop it going tall and stringy. If it does get a bit floppy, simply support it with bamboo. Chillies do really well in containers but, we found, not so well in the ground which might be because the soil is considerably colder and damper in a temperate climate than they're used to back in the sunnier parts of the world they hail from.

But once they get going in planters and pots they're amazingly pest-resistant. It does make sense, however, to put them in the sunniest spot possible. Generally speaking the chilli fruits go from green to yellow to orange to fire-engine-red. But some also go from green to purple to red. Different varieties form different shapes. Combined with the lush foliage and the sweet flowers to boot, these are without a doubt the most colourful characters you can grow.

Chillies are also very good for you and their heat stimulates serotonin, so some growers claim it's possible to get 'high' on them. They store easily and are most handily dried and stored in sealed bags or jars. They can be chopped up and popped into grinders or popped whole into stews to give them that extra kick. They also freeze well. Don't, whatever you do, stick your finger in your eye, up your nose, or go to the bathroom if you've been handling cut chillies and haven't washed your hands thoroughly at least twice—or you'll soon discover why cops in some countries use pepper spray to disable rioters or criminals.

But for the beginner there's no better fun than chillies.

Crop Rotation and Companion Planting

Crop rotation can be a daunting and confusing but vital consideration. This is the long-practised process whereby plants contained within three to four different families are moved strategically in a predetermined order on an annual basis.

Plants from family A move to where plants from family B were; while B moves to C and so on. This exercise is undertaken for two reasons.

Firstly to reduce pests and disease. Diseases like potato blight, for example, can stay in the soil and contaminate a new crop of spuds the following year. Growing peas in the same spot allows the blight to die off and reduces the risk to your potatoes. Some pests can also stay in the ground or the vicinity of the old crop expecting to infest again.

The second reason for crop rotation is to avoid exhausting the soil, which is effectively the food plant's own larder of nutrients. Different families of plants tend to take different nutrients from the soils. Root crops, like swedes and potatoes for example, are heavy feeders and will leech out nitrogen faster than most.

Grow them in the same place for more than one year at a time and the soil will soon be devoid of nitrogen and the crop will fail. However, legumes like peas and beans actually take nitrogen from the air and store it in their roots which can then be dug back into the ground. So planting legumes in the potato patch the following year returns the depleted nitrogen to the soil.

Some crops like heavily manured soils and others don't. So you can move a manured crop on and put the latter type in its place after the former has removed most of it. Also to be considered is overshadowing—you can't have a 7ft load of pea teepees shielding the sun from the ray-loving onions, nor can you have 4ft broccolis shading the shorter, but equally sun-addicted, carrots. Meantime keeping some plants near others also helps discourage pests. Onions near carrots discourage carrot fly for example. Meantime it's a bad idea to put some plants in proximity—tomatoes are a member of the potato family and so shouldn't ever replace them in the rotation.

Herbs

In Year One we tried growing our herbs all together in the same raised bed along with the salads. This created a number of problems, not least because the family of plants we commonly know as 'herbs' don't all come from the same part of the world and they need myriad different soil and watering conditions. In Year Two we did much better by putting most of the herbs into separate pots to provide them with their own particular conditions. Avoid those stupid window box mixes you get in the shops. They don't work because firstly these plants like different conditions and secondly they crowd each other. Some herbs are also prone to transplant shock so it might take a while for them to come right when you move them.

Basil: Basil is easy to sprout from seeds and it likes plenty of water but it also likes plenty of sunshine. Temperate conditions outdoors in the ground draw slugs and promote disease so before long our basil was gone. Even indoors on a windowsill they can get mould, black tips, screwy leaves or simply stretch skywards until they bend over and break. Basil is a bonus really, grow lots of it, keep the plants well separated and grow them in pots, ideally on the indoors side of a sunny windowsill. Pick out the tops to stop it stretching, especially if you see it's about to go to seed. Grow lots of it and don't expect it to last. Pick off the leaves, tear them up and throw them on pasta. Mmm!

Rosemary: For two years we've had our own rosemary every time we eat lamb and it's been a vital component for stuffing. Pungent, sensual and oily, rosemary likes pretty dry conditions. It grows about three foot high and in the new year many of its limbs die off completely. Keep more than one plant going for fear of one dying suddenly. Does well in well-drained sunny positions.

Thyme: We couldn't get this one to grow at all in the first year. The plant we put in the salad bed died. Somewhere through the year I stuck a sprig in the very top of a ceramic planter in which I had a Japanese maple. It thrived and in Year One, that's where we got our thyme. In Year Two we added two flower pots of it to the patio. It seems to like dry conditions. Ideal again for stuffing. Cut it back each year for good results.

Parsley: Again, one that died in the raised bed in Year One but thrived in Year Two in two patio flowerpots. Pick handfuls and come back again. Likes a damp soil and dries out easily in the sun.

Sage: Another dry weather fanatic. I'm guessing it doesn't like its soil too rich in nutrients because any we tried to grow in rich compost in Year One died straight away. It's doing well now in a part of the raised salad bed which hasn't been fertilised for some time. In our experience, the most difficult of the herbs to keep growing both indoors and outdoors. Keep trying.

Fennel and Dill: A doddle to grow anywhere. Great for fish and these look really good in summer, attracting plenty of bees. Be warned though, it does grow high—in the case of fennel up to 4ft or 5ft. It needs a good sunny spot. The seeds, which taste of aniseed, can also be harvested, dried and stored. Cut back hard at the end of every year. And try and keep it controlled or corral it in. Otherwise you'll find yourself picking bits of fennel out of everywhere for years to come. It produces thousands of seeds and spreads them well.

Mint: We've grown both regular mint and lemon mint. We've made our own mint sauce and ice cream. Crush a handful and bring it to your nostrils … mmmm! Be warned though—and do take this very seriously—this plant is a thug which will take over your whole garden. Never, but never, plant it freely in the ground. Put it, not only in a planter on a patio, but also if you can, in a planter with no drainage holes. This plant has to be seen to be believed. It sends out runners under the ground and pops up everywhere. It will even send them through the holes in the bottom of your planter. Let it loose and you'll be sorry for the rest of your days.

Marjoram: This aromatic herb is relatively easy to grow and will come on in most soil types.

Chives: Easy to grow in little clumps, cut it and come back to it again and again. The flowers are also edible apparently.

Leeks

We planted leeks for our second year. You should sow them in March in trays and transplant them outside when they've grown. Trim the roots back to 2in or so with a scissors to make planting more manageable and stick them in about 6in apart. Some growers pile up soil against their base as they mature, saying that it improves the flavour of the plants. Leeks grow in most soils but they do take their time and have a long growing season which can in fact be turned to your advantage in winter when little else is growing. They should be ready from summer, but ours remained noticeably thin despite being almost a year old. We now suspect that they're a lesser available and thinner variety than the more usually available ones with their thick ovoid stems. Leeks over-winter well and can be kept in the ground until needed. They're high in vitamin A and far easier to digest than their more pungent family members, the onions. Don't over-fertilise or you'll make the leaves too tough. Good for stews and soups, the white bulb as well as the stalks are edible. Don't plant them in the same spots over and over or you'll encourage pests.

Onions

Don't bother planting onion seeds unless you've the patience of Job. The spindly little gits are tricky to keep alive and if they die in uneven numbers, you end up with large gaps in your onion plot. Better to buy onion 'sets', the name given to one-year-old bulbs which are ready to go as soon as you get them into the ground.

I'm particularly fond of onions because once they get going they tend to be resilient and survive almost anything. I plant them in raised furrows because they don't like wet soil and this helps keep them well drained although it makes weeding a pain. They tend to do quite well in dry weather. So don't overwater them. Plant the sets into the ground with their tops poking out. Leave a good 6in–8in space between them because the roots do tend to shoot out and about.

Do tie a few strings with paper tapers to blow in the wind around your onion patch in the early days to keep the birds off. They seem to love picking the sets out of the soil. If you see them pulled out, just pop them back in again and more than likely they'll start right on growing where they left off. Plant them in March and just before it's time to harvest them in September, bend the tops right over in proximity to the bulb. This stops them channelling any further energy into the tops and keeps it in the bulb.

Onions provide great value for money given the numbers in which they crop and the weight they put on. The effort comes with harvest and storage. Ideally they should be harvested in dry weather to stop rot in the storage months. They should be pulled up with their tops and let hang on a fence or a washing line, or even dried in the sun on a plastic sheet.

When they're dry, work them into strings and hang them in a dry place. If rot starts to set in, peel off the outer layers and dry them again. This could save your crop. Pick them as you need them and remove any rotting or perished ones to prevent a spread to the rest. Ours last into February when they start to expire.

Parsnips

While we both love parsnips, we haven't yet managed to grow them on Plot 34 because we keep forgetting to sow them in March when we're usually preoccupied with lots of other things. Parsnips need to be sown in soil which has been manured the previous season. Too fresh and it splits their roots. Thin them out as they come up and forget about them until the following spring. They taste best when they've been through a hard frost or two. They store well in the ground and should be eaten sliced into thick chunks and roasted or sliced thin and sautéed in butter.

Peas

The first thing you need to know about peas is that yes they are divine when eaten freshly picked and raw from the pod. The second thing you need to know is that they can give up very little food for the amount of space and effort they demand. We found this out to our detriment in our first year at Plot

34 when an eventually healthy pea bed with a regimented and long running bamboo teepee frame to support it, yielded up the equivalent of two cereal bowls full of peas over the entire season. They also take quite a bit of effort.

First off, peas must be kept well-watered if the weather is dry when they first sprout. Secondly, in their early weeks they require plenty of weeding to ensure they're not overshadowed and blocked out as they flail along the ground. Peas do best with support. So you have to build some. We use a series of 16ft bamboo teepees linked together in a line by other bamboos fixed across the top.

Some people corral them within surrounding frames. Don't put them against a wall because they dry out too easily. Neither do they like being exposed to wind which can leave them in tatters.

When you get them home, you'll need to shell them. You sit down with your sack of pea pods, pop them open one at a time, pick out the peas by squeezing along with your thumb, a pod at a time.

Despite the effort, almost all allotmenteers still adore them, partly because they taste so absolutely incredible, partly for their gorgeous white blooms and partly because ... well you can't have an allotment without peas can you?

Peas are planted directly into the ground. They generally don't do well planted in pots and then transferred, although some people report success with planting them in a line of plastic guttering and then sliding the whole lot out into a trench in the ground. Plant peas from March to June and harvest from June to September—depending on the varieties. They don't like too much heat and stop producing altogether if it gets too warm. The advantage here is that they can do well in more shaded areas though not without some amount of sunlight.

Employing a number of different varieties which plant and crop over different periods allows you to extend your harvest season. Don't plough too much manure into the ground because peas, unlike a lot of vegetables, extract nitrogen from the air and lock it into their roots. By leaving the roots in the ground you can add valuable free nitrogen to the soil. Hiking up the nitrogen levels by throwing in too much manure will cause the plants to bush up and get leafy at the cost of pod production. Peas freeze well after a mild blanching. But nothing beats eating them direct from the pod on the plant.

Potatoes
We grew potatoes for the first time in our second year. With spuds in a temperate climate and with global warming producing many damp, warm summers, you're always taking a gamble. Through summer you need to watch them like hawks because blight can be almost inevitable. Travelling by wind-borne and water-borne spores, which can remain in the soil over a year, blight starts by producing raised button shapes on the leaves, which quickly turn ashen grey/black. Within a few days the foliage shrivels and collapses and the blight works its way into the tubers (the growing potatoes)

under the ground. If you're growing potatoes be sure to have a good supply of blight treatment available because once the scourge hits, it generally sweeps everyone's crops and the cures are quickly cleared off the shelves at the local garden centre.

It's no use them ordering it for you—your spuds will have long turned to smelly mush. If you catch the blight in time you can also cut the plants back to the ground, which in our case saved our crop and allowed us to dig potatoes for many months after we got the infestation. Potatoes are heavy feeders and like a soil with plenty of nutrients.

Many of those who are opening up virgin ground for an allotment grow potatoes only in the first year because they believe it 'breaks up the ground' and makes it more suitable for growing other crops in the years that follow. Their tall lush foliage also kills off weeds by smothering them out completely. Do bear this in mind if you have a small garden because spuds take up a lot of space.

They should be grown in different spots each year to discourage blight, which stays in the soil for over a year, and don't grow them where their relatives, the tomatoes, have been, because they behave the same way when it comes to blight. Potatoes need light and don't do well in the shade.

There is, of course, an upside to growing spuds or people wouldn't bother in the first place. The rewards are rich because pound for pound, the potato probably produces more food than any other plant per square foot of ground. The potato is also one of the most nutritious and complete foods you can eat—containing almost everything you need to remain healthy. For those reasons, most of the Irish population was historically able to live on almost only potatoes for many generations before the tragic potato famine of 1847. If your area is susceptible to blight, cut the risks by selecting blight-resistant varieties.

We grew King Edwards and ended up with enough for two dinners for our family from each plant. From a space the size of a large double bed we grew enough spuds for three entire months. Potatoes also store well, although they should always be kept in the dark and out of daylight. Once they turn green (a mechanism used to protect the tuber when it comes to the surface) they become poisonous and eating enough green potatoes could actually kill you.

People like to give their potatoes a head start before planting them so they 'chit' the seed potatoes. Now this basically means leaving them in a light cool place until they produce sprouts. Because ours were lying around for so long before planting, they actually did this themselves in the bag. Spud varieties are divided into first earlies, second earlies and main crop potatoes. Earlies are planted in March to April and crop from June to July, while main crop potatoes are taken up from July to October. 'Earthing up' is the process of piling up soil onto the sprout to cover it over in the earlier months of the year. Potatoes are prone to frost and this protects them from it. As soon as the sprout pokes through again, cover it over again. Watering is vital through the year to keep them going. Choose your variety of potato depending on whether you need them to be blight-resistant and then whether you want them for mashing or boiling, to be floury or waxy or to store well over time. Potatoes store well if they're kept dry and in the dark. Don't let the light at them.

Rhubarb

This is certainly a mystery plant. Variously termed a fruit and a vegetable, it's actually neither. It's a perennial herb with its closest relations being the dock plant or sorrel.

Because it's one of the first plants of the year to produce food, a learned colleague of mine mentioned that a Gaelic term for rhubarb used in some parts of the country translates as 'monk's curse', or 'monk's purgative'. Normally well-fed friars apparently cursed the time of year when eating naught but rhubarb brought on the flatulent waves of a purgatory far more tangible than the pre-heaven sin bin prescribed in their studies.

While the Chinese have used it for more than 3,000 years as a laxative, we've only started ingesting the stalks as a food relatively recently, pretty much since sugar became widely available in the 17th century.

The fleshy petioles (the sticks) are of course edible when cooked and usually mixed with sugar to sweeten them, but the thick green leaves are highly poisonous. Science still hasn't figured out exactly what it is that makes the leaves so toxic.

The stuff that we grow in our gardens originated in Russia on the banks of the Volga, whose ancient name was Rhu or Rha. There are suggestions that the 'barb' is from from barbarum, meaning barbarian—an ancient slight on the rustic Rhu siders of old. Others say the name comes from 'rheu', Greek for 'to flow', another allusion to the herb's purgative qualities.

Today there's a huge drift towards bright-red-coloured varieties both for display and because of an unfounded belief that they are sweeter. In fact, the common green-stalked ones (with reddish tinges) are more productive and equally as sweet.

Perhaps the most common is Victoria, a tender green, upright, heavy-cropping variety.

There are more than sixty types of the plant, with common ones including the productive hybrid *Rheum x cultorum*, Hawkes Champagne, an old and reliable early variety suitable for 'forcing', and MacDonald Crimson, big and red-stalked, as the name suggests. 'Forcing' rhubarb means producing it out of season by placing a bucket over the crown to block the light and fool it into growing.

Rhubarb is high in vitamin C, and has calcium, potassium and fibre. It's good in tarts, wines and jams, and goes well with hot custard and ice cream. There's the ubiquitous rhubarb fool and more recently, it's been incorporated into chutneys, sauces and even bread.

Salads

Salad is one of the best value foods there is to grow simply because it's relatively expensive in the shops compared to what you'll grow at home and nothing grows faster from seed. There's nothing nicer than a big bowl full of mixed salads laced with bacon bits, crumbled feta, pine nuts and a shower of virgin olive oil. It takes about six weeks to grow.

We found that a raised bed, bounded by rough-cut, half-logs bought on a roll, was best for salads, because it is the salads that slugs and snails really want to get stuck into. In our temperate climate, it's almost impossible to keep them off. The good news is that salads grow quite quickly, so you could grow additional salads to keep the slugs happy. However, salad can also get whacked by weevils. In Year Two we got an attack of sawfly larvae, which ate them from the roots up.

Salad leaves can grow well for a time indoors but they don't tend to last long as they like fresh air flow. We did grow them successfully in window boxes outside.

For the best results grow them in relays. Plant a line of seeds one week and another line of the same seeds two weeks later. In this way there's always fresh salad coming on. Plant it in lines ruled out by two pencils and a piece of string or use the handle of a garden rake or a brush to keep them in order. Sprinkle the hundreds of tiny seeds as evenly as you can to avoid overcrowding and when they do grow a few inches prick out the smaller seedlings to give the others space.

Among the lettuces there are icebergs, butterheads and lollo rossas, all of which we've grown. But get yourself into the fancy leaves like the spices, mixed-leaves packs widely available which include mustard leaves. Rocket is a big favourite but stretches high and goes to seed or bolts quickly. Salads are prone to bolt due to changes in weather conditions. When this happens be ruthless and pull them out. Instead of cutting an entire lettuce head, cut off a few leaves at a time to keep them all going and producing more food.

Salads need plenty of watering and soil with good nutrients. Do keep the seed packets because when the leaves start to grow, and inevitably the weeds in between, you will need the pictures on the packets to identify what's edible and to stop yourself eating weeds. After all, how will you know what's what? On the upside, dandelions are also edible along with a wide range of common weeds.

Cress and mustard can be grown on windowsills even on wet newspaper or tissue and are edible within a few days.

Spinach

As anyone who's watched Popeye knows, spinach gives you strength. It's got more iron than almost any edible plant, but what you probably don't know is that the iron doesn't ingest well into the human body unless you take in enough vitamin C at the same time.

Spinach, which was most likely first farmed in Nepal, is also full of calcium, antioxidants and folic acid. It's easy to grow, it's frost tolerant and it's one of the first crops to be ready for harvest. That's why it's one of the first to go into the ground in the new allotment year. On the downside, for the space it takes up, spinach doesn't give you a lot of yield. The leaves are picked and when steamed or boiled they shrink hugely. So you might need a proper sack of the stuff just to get enough to serve one family dinner.

As with the salads, you should stagger the crop, planting relays of seeds a week or so apart to keep new plants maturing as the older ones are used. Also, rather than pull up whole plants, pick leaves off here and there until the plant goes to seed or bolts. Then pick off the good leaves and pull the rest up. It needs well-fertilised soil or the leaves go pale green. Too much and it develops an unpleasant flavour. For storing, some people blanch it. To stop it sticking together frozen in one big lump, make it into portion-sized globes and flash-freeze it—that is freeze the globes on a tray so they aren't touching. Then put the whole lot into an airtight bag and they shouldn't stick together.

Sprouts

For both years on Plot 34 the sprouts have been reliable. Once they get established, they're rugged and steady and don't need too much attention. Because we don't tend to go up in December and January, we're pleased to see them in droves on upright stalks when we do return, usually in February.

They tend to look blackened and holey but once the outer skins are removed they're perfectly green and edible. Plant them in March or else buy them as small plants, as we do, and pop them into the ground. Plant them so they harvest in winter when there's very little else on the go. Pick them from the bottom up from the stem and cook or freeze them quickly because they don't tend to store very well.

Squash

Other than courgettes, or zucchini as they're also called, squashes include pumpkins, gourds, butternuts and so forth and any member of the Mexican or South American-originated curcurbita family. Up on Plot 34 we didn't have a good experience with the pumpkins, butternuts and gourds (courgettes are dealt with separately) so maybe we're biased.

We lost patience with the brittle slug-attracting seedlings with a propensity to wrap around one another and which departed this life one at a time in rapid succession at the slam of a door or the drop of a hat; we lost our rag with the sprawling monsters among the huge survivors that began crawling across our allotment ground in all directions and needed to be ushered this way and that to keep them in check; we hated the failure of the flowers to stay on long enough to get fertilised. The propensity of the young fruits to drop off the plant without putting on weight had us pulling our hair out. The few undersized pumpkins and butternuts we ended up with were good for soup and pumpkin pie.

And finally, there was the one that eluded us and stayed hidden in the grass until I stubbed my toe on what could only be described as a giant artillery shell.

But if you are keen (and many do have success with them), plant the seeds separately into good-sized pots in March and take care of the resulting plants which break and damage quite easily. Plant them in a rich soil because they're greedy buggers and hoover up lots of soil nutrients, and then give them plenty of room (2ft apart) because when they do get going, they're complete animals and bully anything else, including each other, into oblivion.

Plant another round of them indoors a few weeks after the first batch to plug the holes that will inevitably result when half of the outdoors ones die. Harvest in October—if you've got any with grown fruit on them. When you're finished get a hair transplant because you'll have pulled yours out. Marrows are big courgettes, by the way.

Swedes

Why are they called swedes? Well, they're called all sorts of things depending on where you live. In America they're called rutabaga—Swedish for 'root ram'. More confusing still, in Sweden they're not called rutabaga; real Swedes call them 'kalrot', which translates roughly as cabbage root. This is apt, because they're supposed to be a cross between the cabbage and the turnip proper.

In the north of England swedes are called 'snaggers', in Scotland they're known as 'neeps' and in Ireland we mostly call them turnips—even though they're not really turnips at all.

So, let's clear this up. A turnip proper is a little, white, round guy that is a summer crop and seldom grown in Ireland. Proper turnips, or 'white' turnips (to distinguish them from yellow-and-purple swedes), are thus harvested in the warm months while swedes are harvested from late autumn right through winter.

Oddly enough, they break a couple of rules. First off, frost doesn't tend to damage them—apparently it improves their taste greatly, sweetening them up. With most of our frosts occurring in late winter and early spring, it's best to leave them in the ground until after that before harvesting them.

They also like the soil to be slightly alkaline. If it is too acidic, they will be prone to a disease called club root. Experts advise shuffling a bit of lime around in the soil for them. The other problem is that they're heavy feeders, so for the best result they like a well-manured soil.

From the point of view of the person who's going to be eating them, that soil should be manured for at least a year before the neeps go into them. Apparently they tend to soak up fresh manure and, if that's used, they end up tasting...er...crap.

Tomatoes

There is no comparison between the flavour of a tomato off the supermarket shelf and a homegrown fruit from your own vine. The shining red skin is caused by quantities of lycopene—a hardworking antioxidant. Tomatoes are also high in vitamins A and C and in fibre. Best of all, lycopene absorption is increased by cooking. So fried, stewed or sauced, tomatoes are hugely beneficial. A packet of tomato seeds is also the best-value deal you'll ever make. In a good year a single packet of seeds costing about three quid should produce fifty plants, which in turn should give you forty fruits per plant. That's 2,000 organic tomatoes.

Traditionally tomato-growers in these islands have stuck with greenhouses, which tend to produce earlier and better crops. Tomatoes aren't really at home in northern Europe, and being from the Med they like warmth and sunshine.

Because I'm growing outside, I've picked varieties that are resistant to cold. Ailsa Craig is a sturdy, disease-resistant and rampant plant that produces sweet, mid-sized tomatoes in large numbers. It can scale 3ft of trellis in a month, which means there are more fruits in late summer. Tigerella is another sturdy, pest-resistant, medium-small variety with buckets of taste and a pleasing distinctive yellow stripe from which it gets its name. My favourite though is Gardener's Delight, a high-yielding sweet cherry tomato that produces between six and twelve fruits per truss. Always watch out for yields; I got seeds for the heirloom Marmande variety and while it tasted beautiful, it only yielded a small bag full for all my efforts.

There are actually hundreds of varieties of tomatoes and they don't just come in red. Some fruit in green, yellow, orange, pink, cream or purple. They also come in a range of shapes including plum, sausage, and lemon.

In choosing varieties, you generally decide whether you want to sacrifice numbers for flavour, or numbers for levels of disease resistance. Moneymaker is a hugely popular variety in the British Isles because it's a super-heavy cropper. The downside is that the fruit tastes bland. Blandness also affects beef tomatoes. To avoid it try the zinging Brandywine.

Personally I don't like growing hybrids—genetically modified varieties that crop heavily—because the seeds are useless. The plants are almost infertile and their offspring produce few and sometimes mutated fruits. Also there's the bigger picture—what will happen if you support the industries that have made some 80 per cent of some of the world's food varieties irreproducible in the wild. And at the expense of self-seeding and pollinating varieties.

It's recommended that you plant tomatoes 1ft–2ft apart to allow them to spread and absorb the light. In tight spaces I've gotten away with 6in although I probably would have got more fruit if I'd stuck with the rules. Tomatoes like lots of manure or compost under them and if you're planting in containers, they should be more than a foot deep. Ideally two.

The secret is plenty of watering, the use of a good, mature manure and a granulated or liquid tomato feed once a week.

Tomatoes also need support. Last year I tied mine to the shed. Every time they grew 1ft, I tied a band of wire across them. This year they're on strings—twine hung from frames. Every time the stems grow up a bit more, I twist them around the string.

Some grow cherry tomatoes in hanging baskets where they don't need support or in grow bags attached to the wall. Tomatoes do need the sun and should always be in the sunniest part of your garden. In a temperate climate with lots of rain, watch out for blight, which manifests itself as little raised grey-ash-coloured buttons on the leaves.

Treat it quickly as it can kill the plant in days and infect the others. Use a copper-based blight spray commonly available in garden centres. For higher yields and tidiness, some growers pinch out the trusses that grow between the joints. Most pinch out the tops early on when the plants are smaller to encourage them to strengthen before transplanting. I plant mine in trays in March or early April and plant them outside when the last frosts and heavy winds have passed. Sometimes it's easy to get this wrong and I've had to start again from seed in May. They crop a month later but the results are still good.

DECIDING WHAT TO GROW AND HOW MUCH OF IT

Some time back, we had four little monsters living outside in our raised bed. They spent their time devouring compost and water, and firing fruit at us. They started off indoors as cute and cuddly seedlings, but the minute they were moved outside, they turned rowdy.

Perhaps it was the high content of homemade compost in the soil, but suddenly these baby plants—survivors from a batch of courgette seedlings—began expanding in all directions. Their lily-like leaves bulked up, the stems thickened and the plants sprouted vicious little spines all over. For a time, they resembled smaller versions of the man-eating plant from *Little Shop of Horrors*.

Soon the four had linked up into one big spiky hedgerow, 2ft high and 8ft long. Then it rained, and they flowered and began firing out barrages of fully formed courgettes at the rate of about six or seven a day. They didn't stop all summer.

Anybody who has grown courgettes will know what I'm talking about. In ideal growing conditions, they form fruit in the blink of an eye. Initially I was delighted. We put the courgettes in pastas, we grilled them, and they went into stews. But after a few weeks, the fridge seemed to be filling up with them and our taste for courgettes was waning fast.

I began giving away bags of courgettes to my friends and family and they were heartily welcomed. Soon I was going round with second and third batches, and, for a time, I risked becoming known as the 'courgette guy' as I started dumping them on people I didn't really know. Last year I learnt my lesson. Two courgette plants, put in late, provided just enough for our needs.

But the opposite can also happen. Last year I didn't sow enough peas. We got the equivalent of two or three packets from a supermarket freezer once they were picked and podded.

You should give some thought to what you're going to grow, how much of it you want, how you're going to do it and how you're going to store it. It may sound obvious, but there's no point in growing stuff you'll never eat. Largely because they were so cheap, I invested in a load of blackcurrant bushes. Raw blackcurrants aren't particularly tasty. They're nice in jam, but I don't plan to make any. I used the excuse that, planted on the windward extreme of the allotment, they make good windbreaks.

A good place to start is with your shopping list. What do you buy most of? What do you use most of? Next, after bulk usage, you should aim to try to get value for money. Because they are expensive, we grew large quantities of salads, broccoli, herbs and chillies.

Then consider the difference in quality. Although they're cheap, we grow a lot of peas because they taste so much better than the frozen versions. We'll also grow carrots because the homegrown versions blow away all shop-bought produce in the taste department. Bear in mind the expertise required for certain produce. We have not tried asparagus because we didn't know enough about them. I've had problems growing garlic before, so that's off our allotment menu for now. We didn't grow celery because it's just difficult. We did try to cultivate sweetcorn and squashes, but we won't be repeating the exercise. All our corn died—and so did our squashes. They're too vulnerable in an Irish climate to be reliable.

Think how much you want to grow of everything (we certainly didn't need two bags of courgettes each week) and then, where are you going to store it? We were forced to buy a chest freezer because we didn't have enough space in our fridge-freezer. Now we grow half as many carrots and leave half of them in the ground for storage. We didn't even have room in the chest freezer for the 1,200 strong crop. But while carrots can be cropped over a number of months, plants such as onions and broccoli generally need to be harvested all at once. We had a panic with the broccoli because it was showing signs of going to seed. So four sacks of it had to be harvested in one go. Two sacks had to be given away because we didn't have the freezing capacity for the rest.

You must also realistically consider the space you have available for gardening. Those with small patches of ground or a patio of planters should go for a small number of heavily producing plants, preferably ones that grow upwards. Tomatoes, herbs, some salads, trained courgettes, peas and beans would be good. Smaller patches just aren't suited to some more expensive crops like broccoli, cauliflower or Savoy cabbage.

THE GROWING YEAR

January
Plant rhubarb crowns and top with manure. Plant currants. Start cauliflowers indoors. Chit early potatoes. Plant lettuce, leeks, rocket in the greenhouse or indoors. Harvest sprouts from the bottom of the plant up. Harvest purple broccoli. Harvest celeriac. Harvest kale, parsnips, Swiss chard.

February
Sow parsnips, early carrots, broad beans, leeks, summer cabbage. Prune last year's raspberries, currants and outdoor vines. Plant raspberries. Harvest winter cabbage, celeriac, parsnips, spinach and Swiss chard.

March
Plant onion sets, potatoes, raspberries, currants, parsnips, strawberry runners. Chit later potatoes. Sow tomatoes and sweetcorn indoors.

April
Plant cabbages and cauliflowers out from the greenhouse. Sow chillies, courgettes, peas, squashes indoors.

May
Earth up potatoes. Plant later potatoes. Sow French beans, kale, lettuce, parsnips, peas, rocket, spinach, carrots, cauliflower, broccoli.

June
Plant tomatoes that are not staying in the greenhouse outdoors. Sow lettuce and salads. Harvest raspberries, currants, radishes, early potatoes, peas, spinach, rhubarb, gooseberries, strawberries, beetroot.

July
Sow lettuce, beetroot, peas, Swiss chard. Harvest currants, beans, garlic, cabbage, gooseberries, lettuce, strawberries, potatoes, rhubarb, radishes, raspberries, courgettes, spinach.

August
Sow spring onions, radishes. Harvest onions, garlic, peas, radishes, spinach, sweetcorn, tomatoes, chillies, peppers, beetroot and cabbage.

September
Harvest carrots. Plant spring cabbage, onions, chillies, tomatoes, sweetcorn, radishes, rocket, courgettes, leeks, potatoes, peppers, celeriac and beetroot. Plant spinach and Swiss chard.

October
Plant spring cabbage, broccoli and cabbage plants from seed. Harvest squashes, tomatoes, courgettes, cauliflowers, celeriac, chillies, lettuce, parsnips, peppers, potatoes, cabbage, carrots and marrows.

November
Harvest cauliflowers, leeks, parsnips, cabbages, celeriac, potatoes, Swiss chard, sprouts and carrots.

December
Plant currants, raspberries and garlic. Harvest celeriac, sprouts, cauliflowers, carrots, spinach, leeks, swedes, parsnips, cabbages and radishes.

TERMS YOU MIGHT NEED TO UNDERSTAND

Annual: A plant which grows from seed to expiry within a period of one year.

Biennial: A plant whose life cycle spans over two seasons, usually cropping in the second.

Blanching: A process of treating fresh food so that it lasts longer in the freezing process. It involves parboiling (usually for a period of between thirty seconds and one minute) and then dousing in ice-cold water before freezing.

Bolting: The term used to describe the stage of plant growth which involves it going to seed. This usually involves stretching, flowering and seeding. With annuals this marks the end of the plant's usefulness. It can sometimes happen early in dry spells. It can be delayed for a time in some plants by breaking off the flower buds or the stems containing the flowers.

Chitting: The process of encouraging seed potatoes to sprout a little (generally by two or three inches) before planting them in the ground, thus giving them a head start.

Clay: A soil type which becomes sodden and waxy in wet weather and becomes rock hard and lumpy in drought.

Companion planting: Growing certain crops together for mutual benefit. For example planting onions, which repel carrot fly, near or among your carrots.

Compost: Rotted and broken-down organic matter which improves soil quality and content for plants.

Crop rotation: The process of moving certain families of plants around from year to year to different spots, usually following a rotary order. This is done firstly to prevent disease and pests which occur when plants are put in the same place over and over, but also because different families of plants take and replenish different minerals and nutrients from the soil. Moving them around in a determined and organised order allows one family to replace the minerals taken out by the previous occupants. For example peas, which produce nitrogen, should follow potatoes, which devour it.

Crown: The part of the plant (say in rhubarb) where the stems meet the root.

Cultivar: A plant variety developed by growers for certain characteristics (in much the same way we have developed dog breeds) through selective breeding and cross-fertilisation.

Cut-and-Come: A term used to describe food plants which can be harvested a bit at a time by taking off some fruits or leaves rather than cutting or pulling the whole lot up in one go. Some people say 'cut-and-come-again'. The end result is that the plant survives to produce new leaves/fruits.

Cutting: A slip or portion of a plant cut off for the purpose of planting and producing a new plant other than the parent.

Earlies: A term given to 'new' potatoes or the type which are harvested earlier than 'main crop' potatoes, usually from June.

Earthing Up: The process of heaping earth up over potato shoots as they poke through the ground. Done continuously in the early part of their season to protect them from frost and light.

Humus: The organic matter in the soil created by the rotting process or by earthworms and other organisms or insects. Essentially food for plants.

Loam: A fine textured and good quality soil for growing food which contains an ideal mix of sand, clay, silt and nutrients.

Manure/Muck: The dung of generally herbivorous farm animals, usually rotted and dried for use on plants for its nutritional value. In the case of horse manure, usually mixed with straw bedding material.

Mulch: Material used to place on the soil to keep weeds down and lock moisture in. The most common type is bark chips but sheeting, straw and even newspaper can be used.

Nematodes: Tiny organic parasitic nasties deliberately placed in the soil by gardeners to kill off pests such as slugs or snails.

Overwintered: A plant which has lived through winter and usually produces a spring harvest.

Perennial: A plant which survives for more than one or two years such as soft fruits like blackcurrants.

Pricking/Pricking Out: The process of taking seedlings from a tray and transplanting them into a pot.

Propagation: The process of reproducing plants either through planting seeds, taking cuttings, splitting or taking out offsets.

Pruning: Cutting branches or limbs from a plant to control its growth and/or to encourage better overall growth and food production.

Raised bed: A raised area for planting, usually surrounded and consolidated by a frame of wood, stone or brick.

Seed potatoes: The small potatoes saved and sold for growing new potatoes.

Staggering/Succession/Relay planting: The process of planting seeds and then more again after a period in order to produce plants at different stages of maturity and thus prevent crops maturing all at once.

THE BOOKS OF MANCHÁN MAGAN

Angels and Rabies: A Journey Through the Americas

'[W]hile exposing the chaotic workings of his own soul, Magan reveals the underbelly of the colourful cultural and sociological jigsaw of these two great continents.' *Sunday Telegraph*

'Frightening, funny and lovable.' *The Sunday Times*

'His writing is intimate and immediate, perceptive and humorous.' *Books Ireland*

ISBN 9780863223495

Manchán's Travels: A Journey Through India

'While the local colour is entertaining, it is the writer's personal journey that makes this book so compelling. It's a funny and occasionally sad, but ultimately satisfying read.' *Sunday Telegraph*

'Magan has a keen eye for the hypocrisies of elite urban India and artfully evokes the "fevered serenity" of the Himalayas.' *Times Literary Supplement*

'Mad, brilliant and often hilarious.' *The Irish Times*

ISBN 9780863223686

Truck Fever: A Journey Through Africa

'Like *Lord of the Flies* meets *Lost* meets *The Amazing Race*, *Truck Fever* is an insightful soap opera that does Africa, its radiant and impenetrable muse, justice.' *Metro Life*

'An excellent writer, has a wonderful talent for transporting the reader into the heart of every experience. He is an intelligent observer of people and places, and his writing is sensitive and engaging. *Truck Fever* is a great read.' *Sunday Tribune*

ISBN 9780863223891

www.brandonbooks.com